STUDY GUIDE TO ACCOMPANY

MANAGERIAL ACCOUNTING
SECOND EDITION

JOHN G. HELMKAMP
Indiana University

Prepared by

Gordon L. Nielsen
University of Tulsa

WILEY

JOHN WILEY & SONS
NEW YORK CHICHESTER BRISBANE TORONTO SINGAPORE

ISBN 0 471 51427-6
Printed in the United States of America

10 9 8 7 6 5 4 3 2 1

TO THE STUDENT

Managerial accounting is a study of how managers use accounting-related information for making better decisions. Whether your goal is to become an accountant or to become a manager, this Study Guide will help you master the subject. It should be used on a chapter-by-chapter basis as you study Professor John Helmkamp's *Managerial Accounting* text. To accompany each chapter, this Study Guide will become a Learning Guide as you peruse the

Learning Objectives
Learning Tips
Review of Chapter Learning Objectives
Matching Attributes and Answers
Multiple Choice Questions and Answers
Illustrative Problems and Answers

This Study Guide is designed to help you gain a better understanding of managerial accounting and to prepare for classroom quizzes and examinations. Often instructors will choose questions directly from this Guide. Keep up-to-date and be prepared.

I am always looking for new ways to help students understand managerial accounting. If you have ideas for the next edition, tear out this sheet, with your comments on the back or below, and mail it to me at the University of Tulsa, 600 South College Avenue, Tulsa, OK 74014.

Have a great term!

Gordon L. Nielsen

ACKNOWLEDGMENTS

Every published work results from the efforts of many people. Let every reader know that this material would not be on the book shelves in its present state without the diligent effort of former graduate student Sherri Stiver and undergraduate student Terri Rowland. Also, thanks to University of Tulsa professor Dennis Hudson who provided much of the Chapter 17 material. Melba Nantz helped immeasurably with the manuscript typing and printing. With all this help, if there are any errors found, blame the computer. Nothing human-made is perfect!

Gordon L. Nielsen
University of Tulsa
August, 1989

CONTENTS

CHAPTER 1

MANAGERIAL ACCOUNTING: AN OVERVIEW

This is the ice-breaker chapter. Get your feet wet in understanding this new topic by careful study of the chapter; then ask yourself, "Do I understand the following Learning Objectives?"

LEARNING OBJECTIVES

1. Realize how important it is for managers to obtain and use their organizations' resources in the best possible way.
2. Describe the similarities and differences between managerial and financial accounting.
3. Identify the most significant characteristics of managerial accounting information.
4. Explain the importance of organizational considerations for management.
5. Justify why a major goal of every organization is to achieve satisfactory financial results by being efficient and effective.
6. Describe how the management process with a decision-making focus is used for planning, organizing, directing and controlling.
7. Trace the basic concepts of management and managerial accounting through a case study.
8. Define the work of a controller in an organization.
9. Evaluate how the combination of a microcomputer and an electronic spreadsheet is used in managerial accounting.
10. Recognize why managerial accounting constantly changes in a dynamic business world.

LEARNING TIPS

1. Managerial accounting is similar to financial accounting in many ways, but there are some significant differences. In this chapter, see how the two differ.
2. Make an effort to understand how accounting provides information for management decision making. Put yourself in the manager's position and ask yourself the question,"What kind of information do I need in order to decide this important issue?"
3. Management must be goal-oriented. How does accounting provide information for goal-setting? For goal-attainment?

REVIEW

Let's review the main points of Chapter 1. Using the number key, see how this discussion relates back to the learning objectives listed above.

1. **Realize how important it is for managers to obtain and use their organizations' resources the best possible way.**

    Managers are continually involved with decision making, which requires information—both historical and future-oriented. No one should make a decision in a vacuum.

    Managers—and all of us—make better decisions, and are better able to accomplish their goals, by having the right information at the right time. Putting the firm's resources to work requires knowing a great deal about those resources and the environment in which the firm operates.

2. **Describe the similarities and differences between managerial and financial accounting.**

    Financial accounting and managerial accounting both relate to accountability of managers to stockholders, creditors, employees and others about the use and performance of the firm's resources. Both are rooted in the same accounting information system that encompasses the whole company.

    The differences between financial and managerial accounting are several, including:

    a. Managerial accounting supplies mainly *internal* users (managers) of information.
    b. Managerial accounting is not restricted by accounting rules (GAAP), such as those developed by FASB, SEC, AICPA, IRS.
    c. Managerial accounting is future-oriented instead of historically oriented.
    d. Managerial accounting mainly relates to segments of the firm rather than the entire enterprise.
    e. Managerial accounting supplies information as needed rather than on a strict reporting schedule.
    f. Managerial accounting tends to be more subjective—management-oriented—rather than purely objective as financial accountants are.
    g. Managerial accounting often uses other disciplines in the accomplishment of its work, such as math, science, statistics and behavioral science.

    Test your understanding of the attributes of financial and managerial accounting by playing the matching game in the next section.

3. **Identify the most significant characteristics of managerial accounting information.**

    Characteristics of managerial accounting information are: relevance, accuracy, timeliness, understandability, and cost-effectiveness. Without these qualities, accounting information would lose much of its usefulness. Accounting must, above all else, be useful.

4. **Explain the importance of organizational considerations for management.**

    An organization must have a common purpose, systematic division of labor, integration of its parts through a decision-based information system, and continuity of existence. An organization must be "well-organized" in order to accomplish its objectives. Managerial accounting helps to make the organization operate more efficiently and effectively by supplying information well-fitted to the organization's structure.

5. **Justify why a major goal of every organization is to achieve satisfactory financial results by being efficient and effective.**

The ability to effectively compete, even to survive, depends heavily upon the organization's profitability, which in turn depends upon its efficiency and effectiveness of operations.

Turning a profit is essential to provide adequate funds to continue in operation, i.e., to pay wages and salaries to employees; to purchase additional inventories; and to pay normal operating expenses such as utilities, rent, insurance and supplies.

6. **Describe how the management process with a decision-making focus is used for planning, organizing, directing and controlling.**

Managers plan, organize, direct and control. These functions, which are essential in order to achieve an organization's objectives, are accomplished through competent decision making. Without competent managers, employees would not have proper training and direction in their work; work would not be done on time; the overall direction of the firm would be obscured by the busyness of each day's operations.

7. **Trace the basic concepts of management and managerial accounting through a case study.**

See the case study analysis section of this chapter after you have read the Johnson Automotive Inc. case in the text.

8. **Define the role of a controller in an organization.**

The controller, as chief accounting officer, provides valuable and essential information for management decision making as well as participating in the decision process at the highest levels within the organization. The controller is in charge of general accounting, budget development, taxation, financial planning and analysis, and sometimes inventory control and credit management, although these latter functions are often under the treasurer. These functions are accomplished through a staff of competent assistants.

9. **Evaluate how the combination of a microcomputer and an electronic spreadsheet is used in managerial accounting.**

The microcomputer, the managerial accountant's constant companion, helps perform financial analysis of historical and future-oriented data. Through such software packages as Lotus 1-2-3, SuperCalc and MultiPlan, the accountant can spend more of his or her time thinking, analyzing and planning, and less time pencil-pushing. Managerial accounting is the ideal application of microcomputers because of the power of electronic spreadsheets. Try it; you'll probably like it.

10. **Recognize why managerial accounting constantly changes in a dynamic business world.**

As new products and services appear on the market, new production techniques also appear. These often require new cost relationships and new managerial accounting methods. For example, increasing uses of robots in the manufacturing process results in less labor, more overhead costs. New just in time inventory systems change direct material and overhead costs of products. Services do not have a direct material cost component at all. These kinds of changes result in management accounting taking on new faces.

MATCHING ATTRIBUTES

Below are listed attributes that may be identified with managerial accounting, (M); financial accounting, (F); or both, (B). Indicate, by use of the appropriate letter (M, F, or B), which attribute best matches which category of accounting.

_____ 1. Accounting produces record-keeping type information.

_____ 2. Accounting produces mandatory (required) reports for external users.

_____ 3. Accounting is based on wholly objective reporting of information.

_____ 4. Accounting is founded on the principle of stewardship.

_____ 5. Accounting reports on segments of a firm's operations.

_____ 6. Accounting reports must conform to generally accepted accounting principles.

_____ 7. Accounting is part of a single general (overall) system.

_____ 8. Accounting provides information for decision-making purposes.

_____ 9. Accounting reports principally historical information.

_____ 10. Accounting information extensively uses techniques of other disciplines, such as economics, management, finance, and mathematics.

_____ 11. Accounting reports follow a well-defined schedule and are periodic in nature.

_____ 12. Accounting involves performance evaluation.

_____ 13. Accountants have virtually complete freedom in developing reports.

_____ 14. Accounting reports are designed chiefly for internal use.

_____ 15. Contents and frequency of accounting reports are decided internally.

_____ 16. Accounting is a continually changing discipline.

MULTIPLE CHOICE

For each of the following items choose the most appropriate completion phrase.

1. Among the functions of managers are:

    a. Planning, organizing, and controlling.
    b. Planning, hiring, supervising, and controlling.
    c. Planning, staffing, supervising, reporting and deciding.
    d. Planning, organizing, directing and controlling.

2. The job of company controller is:

    a. To run the company and control operations.
    b. To provide accounting information and participate in high-level decisions.
    c. To control corporate assets, pay the bills, deposit the cash.
    d. To serve as chief accounting officer and microcomputer director.

3. The main point you should have learned about the managerial decision process is that:

   a. Alfred P. Sloan, Jr. ran General Motors with a loose management style—thus he was successful.

   b. Henry Ford was more concerned with producing a lot of cars than with good management practices.

   c. Participative management in a large, diversified corporation requires a sophisticated managerial accounting system.

   d. Automotive manufacturing in this country has gone downhill since the Japanese entered the marketplace.

4. The CMA designation has, since 1972, been a symbol of:

   a. A company that has a high-level *Cost/Managerial Accounting* system.

   b. A person who has passed a rigorous examination in various areas of management accounting, decision analysis, economics and other business-related areas.

   c. High attainment by an individual who has through experience and education been awarded the title, *Chartered Management Analyst.*

   d. A person who hasn't made it in accounting and has been so labeled because he or she *Can't Measure Anything.*

5. The electronic worksheet is a microcomputer development that relates to accounting because:

   a. The worksheet can perform many of the analyses and techniques of managerial accounting, at an accountant's direction.

   b. If present trends continue, the electronic worksheets will substantially reduce employment for managerial accountants.

   c. The thinking portion of managerial accounting performance is being reduced, making the accountant's task less demanding.

   d. Software is available to produce financial statements automatically, allowing the accountant more time for managerial analysis, tax work and other nonfinancial chores.

6. Controlling, as it relates to management responsibility, is best described as:

   a. Closely monitoring operations so nothing (and no one) deviates from the plan.

   b. Doing it yourself if you want it done right, because you just can't get good help these days.

   c. Monitoring deviations from the plan and taking corrective action (or modifying the plan) when there are significant deviations (variations).

   d. Using the management by exception principle to get rid of (by transfer or discharge) those individuals who cause the deviations from the plan.

7. One of the most difficult tasks of management is planning. Its principal difficulty lies in the fact that:

   a. Planning is done once a year and the whole next year's operations have to be planned at one time, before anyone has any idea what the economy will look like for the period.

   b. Planning requires goal-setting, which is part of the concept of management by objective; but managers, by their nature, are very subjective; they find it hard to be objective.

   c. You just can't plan when all the uncertainties of today's world keep everything in a state of chaos—the world unrest, the topsy-turvy political situation, the mixed-up economy, and, worst of all, the Japanese competition.

   d. Planning, by definition, involves anticipating the future—5 years or more for strategic planning—and continually updating plans as conditions change. These plans must be realistic in order to attain the organization's goals.

8. A company organization chart

   a. Indicates the structure of the company's activities and their relationship with each other.

   b. Shows when the company was organized, for what purpose, and by whom.

   c. Is an accounting tool for showing which expenses get charged to which department.

   d. Is generally meaningless, because most people do what they want anyway, regardless of what the chart shows.

9. Within the controller's department are many jobs, which include:

   a. IRS accounting, FASB accounting, SEC accounting, and internal accounting.

   b. Financial reporting, strategic planning, managerial accounting, taxation, financial statement analysis, and internal accounting.

   c. Cash receipts, cash disbursements, general accounting, taxation, financial statement analysis, and internal auditing.

   d. Financial accounting, managerial accounting, cost accounting, inventory accounting, payroll accounting, tax accounting and sales forecasting.

10. There are twenty items of managerial accounting information needs listed in Chapter 1. How might one best summarize these needs?

    a. Management needs to know everything that goes on in the company.

    b. The Johnson Company is completely unrealistic in its expectations of the accounting department.

    c. Accounting information needs by management relate to revenue, cost, and profitability of all phases of company activity.

    d. Managerial accounting information needs extend beyond the capabilities of most accountants to satisfy the needs; outside help may be needed.

11. Service organizations, as different from manufacturing companies, are characterized by:

    a. Having large materials inventories.

    b. Having the same costs as manfacturing companies.

    c. Using just in time inventory systems.

    d. Having no direct materials inventories.

CASE ANALYSIS: JOHNSON AUTOMOTIVE, INC.

Many companies do not realize that their managerial accounting information is inadequate until they observe the symptoms of declining profits, rising costs and unsatisfactory performance. Unfortunately for some of these firms, they realize the inadequacy only after the company's decline is irreversible and its financial condition is on the verge of collapse.

Fortunately for Johnson Automotive, Mr. Johnson was an astute observer of what was happening in his company: sales were declining, costs were increasing and profits were going down, both in the absolute sense and as a percent of sales. More important than merely observing the unfavorable changes in the company's results of operations, Mr. Johnson's observations were turned into action. This action resulted in a meeting of company managers, the bookkeeper and the CPA.

The CPA pointed out their need for management goals, followed by a strategic- and operational-planning process. Looking into the future via the goal-setting and planning processes must be accompanied by the development of current and historical revenue, cost and profitability information for use in analysis of past and current performance in relation to the goals and plans established by management. Performance measurement permits evaluations of progress toward accomplishment of the goals. This performance evaluation permits management to take corrective action and to make more realistic plans for the future. Thus, management is able to perform its functions of planning, organizing, directing and controlling.

Fulfilling the managerial functions described in the chapter is not possible without adequate information. The twenty items of managerial accounting information described by the president and managers of Johnson Automotive, Inc. indicate in some detail the inadequacy of the present accounting system and the needs for the future in order to satisfactorily plan, organize, direct and control the company.

With only one accounting personnel as a full-time member of the Johnson organization, it is apparent that neither the time nor the expertise is available to satisfy the managerial accounting needs from within the firm. Hence, it was wise of Mr. Johnson to call upon the outside CPA for assistance in establishing a system to meet the needs of management.

Questions About The Case

1. Name specific tasks (activities) of management that relate to each of the management functions of:

    a.   Planning,
    b.   Organizing,
    c.   Directing,
    d.   Controlling.

2. Where would the bookkeeper fit into the organization chart of Johnson Automotive? The CPA?

3. What specific items of accounting information do you see missing from the abbreviated income statements of Johnson Automotive (Fig. 1-4)?

ILLUSTRATIVE PROBLEM

1. The Buchanan Company of Owasso, Oklahoma manufactures hoses, belts, and gaskets as replacement parts for the U.S. car and truck industry. During the year just ended its abbreviated income statement, compared to the previous year was as follows:

	a.	Last Year	b.	Previous Year	c.
Sales		$ 6,540,000		$ 5,900,000	
Cost of goods sold		5,035,800		4,307,365	
Gross profit		1,504,200		1,592,635	
Operating expense		1,635,000		1,239,105	
Net income (loss)		$ (130,800)		$ 353,530	

Requested:

a. The company management was stunned by the loss last year following a healthy net income in the previous year. You are asked, as a management accounting student (and offspring of the senior vice-president) to analyze the year's operations and comment thereon. Suggestion: In column a. show percentage changes of last year from previous year; in columns b. and c. show all figures as a percentage of that same year's sales.

b. Provide a few words of explanation to accompany the percentage analysis you have provided in part a.

VOCABULARY

There are a lot of new words and phrases that must be learned as we study a new discipline. Management accounting is no exception. The vocabulary introduced in Chapter 1, with appropriate definitions, follow. Review them carefully, and try to understand the meaning of each.

BUDGET. A detailed plan that shows how resources are expected to be obtained and used in a future period, expressed in financial terms.

CERTIFICATE OF MANAGEMENT ACCOUNTING (CMA). A designation awarded to a person who has demonstrated a specified amount of competence in managerial accounting.

CONTROLLER. The chief accountant responsible for an organization's entire accounting function with the dual responsibilities of providing information and participating in the management process.

CONTROLLING. The management function concerned with making sure the actual results agree with those planned.

DECENTRALIZATION. Dividing an organization into specialized units so decision-making authority and responsibility are spread throughout the operation.

DECISION MAKING. Making a choice among alternative courses of action.

DIRECTING. The management function that provides the leadership and motivation needed to carry out an organization's plans.

EFFECTIVENESS. A measure of how well a firm attains its goals.

EFFICIENCY. Maintaining a satisfactory relationship between a firm's resource inputs and its outputs of products and services.

ELECTRONIC SPREADSHEET. A versatile problem-solving computer program used to electronically manipulate data and predict the impact of future actions.

FINANCIAL ACCOUNTING. A branch of accounting that provides information for external decision makers such as creditors, stockholders and governmental agencies.

LINE AUTHORITY. Right to give orders and direct the activities representing the organization's main missions such as production and marketing in a manufacturing firm whose primary goal is to make quality products and sell them at fair prices.

MANAGEMENT. The persons within an organization with the authority and responsibility to perform planning, organizing, directing and controlling functions.

MANAGEMENT BY EXCEPTION. The concentration on performance results that deviate significantly from those expected.

MANAGEMENT BY OBJECTIVE. The process by which management goals are established and performance is evaluated to determine if the goals are achieved.

MANAGERIAL ACCOUNTING. A branch of accounting that provides information needed by managers to perform the various management functions.

MICROCOMPUTER. A small but fully operational computer that uses a microprocessor contained on a single silicon chip as its central processing unit.

OPERATIONAL (SHORT-TERM) PLANNING. The process used by management to implement the goals established during strategic planning.

ORGANIZATION. A group of people who share common goals with a well-defined division of labor, integrated by an information based decision-making system, and having continuity over time.

ORGANIZATIONAL CHART. A graphic display of the structure within which an organization's activities are performed and managed.

ORGANIZING. The management function used to provide the structure or capacity needed by a firm to operate and achieve organizational goals.

PLANNING. The management function used to decide what action the organization should take in the future and how it should be accomplished.

STAFF AUTHORITY. Right to support line managers with advice and assistance in some specialized area such as accounting.

STRATEGIC (LONG-TERM) PLANNING. The process used by top management to identify a firm's strengths, weaknesses, opportunities, and threats for a lengthy future period such as the next five to ten years.

THE ANSWERS

MATCHING ATTRIBUTES

1.	B	5.	M	9.	F	13.	M
2.	F	6.	F	10.	M	14.	M
3.	F	7.	B	11.	F	15.	M
4.	B	8.	B	12.	B	16.	B

MULTIPLE CHOICE

1. d.
2. b.
3. c.
4. b.
5. a.
6. c.
7. d.
8. a.
9. b.
10. c.
11. d.

CASE ANALYSIS QUESTIONS

1. Examples are:

   a. Planning—setting specific goals on both a long-range and short-range basis; such as market share; profit, in dollars and percent of sales; rate of return percentage (this is income earned relative to total investment in the firm).

   b. Organizing includes establishing responsibilities for reaching goals and accomplishing plans. Those assigned these responsibilities must be granted commensurate authority to make decisions and commit resources to meet these ends.

c. Directing involves the carrying out of the authority mentioned above. Managers get their work done through other people. Therefore, the managers must be allowed to assign tasks and activities to the people who work for them in order to accomplish the necessary work to fulfill the plans. These are essentially the sales, repair and other operating personnel of the company.

d. Controlling involves measurement and evaluation of the performance of the operating personnel against the goals and plans established previously. When there are significant deviations from the plans, it is important for management to take corrective action. Usually this includes instructing and supervising operating personnel in the improved performance of their tasks.

2. Since there is no controller or financial manager of Johnson Automotive, Inc., the bookkeeper would report directly to the president, but would occupy a lower position than the two managers. It is suggested that a vertical line from the president to the bookkeeper occupying a rectangle on the same level as the various department boxes would be appropriate. The CPA is not an employee of the company and so does not fit into the organization chart. However, to indicate the existence of such outside consulting personnel, it is permissible to show a horizontal dotted (or broken) line from immediately below the president to a box on the side just above one of the managers, labeled CPA.

3. Lots. We will be getting into a number of these items later in this text. For now, let's suggest a few such missing items:

a. Budget figures that were developed in the planning process should be shown for each item on the income statement. These would be objectives against which actual performance would be measured.

b. Besides the budget data, there should be a measurement of differences, of deviations, from budget. This measurement could be in absolute dollar differences or percentages.

For example, the following format could be used:

	Current Year	Budget	Deviation
Sales	$8,328,352	$8,800,000	$(471,648) -5.4%

c. An additional or alternative comparison that would be useful would be to show the change from the prior year. Such an analysis tells management whether growth is occuring, and to what degree. For example:

	Current Year	Previous Year	% Change
Sales	$8,328,352	$8,568,540	-2.8%

d. A third, but not necessarily final, possible addition to the income statement would be a percentage analysis of the various items relative to sales. Such percentages, when compared with goal percentages, indicate whether performance on an item-by-item basis is up to standard. An example of this is:

		% of Sales
Sales	$ 8,328,352	100.0
Cost of goods sold	7,909,614	95.0
Gross profit	418,738	5.0
Operating expense	348,572	4.2
Net income	70,166	0.8

ILLUSTRATIVE PROBLEM

a.

	a.	b.	c.
Sales	+ 10.8%	100.0%	100.0%
Cost of goods sold	+ 16.9	77.0	73.0
Gross profit	- 05.6	23.0	27.0
Operating expenses	+ 32.0	25.0	21.0
Net income (loss)	-136.9	-(02.0)	6.0

b.   While sales increased 10.8% over the prior year, cost of goods sold increased by 16.9%, resulting in a decrease in gross profit of 5.6% Also, operating expense increased 32% over the prior year. This combination of factors caused net income to drop 136.9% from the prior year.

CHAPTER 2

COST CLASSIFICATIONS, CONCEPTS, AND USES

Professor Helmkamp has established certain objectives to be learned from the study of Chapter 2. Since this chapter relates heavily to the understanding of terminology, the reader can expect that the learning objectives of the chapter will be vocabulary-oriented. Read these objectives with care, then proceed to the Learning Tips and Review to check your understanding of these points.

LEARNING OBJECTIVES

1. Explain why cost information is so important to managers.
2. Recognize why there are different costs for different purposes.
3. Identify the major differences between service organizations, merchandising businesses, and manufacturing firms.
4. Determine how costs are classified by business function.
5. Distinguish between product and period costs and give examples of each type.
6. Explain the difference between direct and indirect costs and provide examples of each type.
7. Compare the differences in inventories for merchandising and manufacturing firms.
8. Describe the three manufacturing cost elements and give examples of each one.
9. Identify the three inventory accounts maintained by a manufacturing firm and explain how each is used in the balance sheet and income statement.
10. Prepare a manufacturing firm's income statement and related cost of goods manufactured statement in proper form.
11. Discuss why just in time (JIT) inventory systems have become so popular and how they are used in repetitive manufacturing.
12. Classify costs based on their behavior, controllability, and relevancy.

LEARNING TIPS

1. Try to imagine yourself in a place that makes something that you are very familiar with. How about furniture, tennis rackets, or even candy bars (low cal, of course)? Think of the ingredients or materials that would be necessary to make that item. What kind of talent from various workers would be required to do all the things necessary to produce that item? What kind of factory facilities would be required to make them? Now, suppose you were in the business of making those items—hundreds or even tens of thousands of them—for the purpose of making a lot of money. Shall we think about the costs and requirements for producing your product?

2. As the person in charge of production, what kinds of materials do you need to have on hand to produce your product? How much of each? Where will you store your "raw materials"?

3. Will you hire the workers to make your product? How will you account for their time? If you decide to make several different products, how will you keep track of which employees are working on which product and for how long? Remember, we have to figure out the cost of each product.

4. The materials and labor costs are direct. Think of all the nondirect costs necessary to produce your product, such as lights, rent, insurance, payroll taxes, employee benefits and depreciation on the equipment. How will you figure how much of each cost goes into each product?

5. Finally, suppose you need some help from your friendly banker to pay for the materials, wages and other costs before you are able to collect for selling the products. She may want an income statement, or a projected income statement, to show your business will generate enough profit to repay the loan. How will you go about preparing such a statement?

REVIEW

Now that we are thinking about manufacturing a product, let's review the main points of Chapter 2. Refer to the learning objectives above by number as we establish how those objectives fit into the manufacturing process and the textbook discussion.

1. **Explain why cost information is so important to managers.**

   Managers must be certain that revenues of a period exceed the costs of earning that revenue in order to accomplish one of the firm's goals of obtaining a fair profit. "Cost," then, is important in the calculation of profit. In manufacturing your product, how are you going to be sure of your costs of production?

2. **Recognize why there are different costs for different purposes.**

   This chapter defines many different costs. "Cost," by itself is not as meaningful as "cost" with an appropriate modifier in front of it, e.g., direct cost, fixed cost, or controllable cost. These modifications of the general term "cost" are explored more fully in the Matching Attributes section of this chapter. Clearly, one must understand that "cost" is not the same as "expense". The latter term is an expired or used-up cost. The cost of supplies used is an expense, while the cost of materials that will go into your product is a cost, called an asset.

3. **Identify the major differences between service organizations, merchandising businesses, and manufacturing firms.**

   Service organizations do not produce or sell a product, but are in business to sell a service. When you go to the barber shop or beauty salon, you don't carry home a tangible product; you receive a service. The same is true if you go to the bank for a car loan, if you have your will prepared by an attorney, or if you get investment advice.

Merchandising businessses, such as retail stores, sell products, but do not manufacture those products. When you go to a department, grocery or clothing store, you are interested in the products that store carries in stock and has available for sale.

Manufacturers produce the products that merchandising firms sell. Manufacturers buy raw materials from which they produce finished goods, for sale to retailers and wholesalers.

4. **Determine how costs are classified by business function.**

It is important to have standard account classifications for costs in any organization. These costs should be classified (coded) the same each time they occur for the sake of uniformity, comparability and useful financial statement results.

Telephone cost should always go into the same account, as should wages, salaries, repairs, utilities, and so forth. However, this isn't enough. We normally have broad categories of costs such as production, administration and selling. Each broad category will have numerous sub-accounts, e.g.:

Production	**Administration**	**Selling**
Supervisory salaries	Salaries	Salaries
Telephone	Telephone	Telephone
Travel	Travel	Travel
Depreciation	Depreciation	Depreciation
Insurance	Insurance	Insurance

5. **Distinguish between product and period costs and give examples of each one.**

Product costs are the costs that are part of the manufacture of a product of the firm. For example, wood costs, labor costs, and manufacturing overhead are all product costs in the manufacture of wooden furniture. What would be the product costs for the manufacture of candy bars? Of tennis rackets?

Period costs are costs that cannot be easily identified with the product and do not relate to the volume of production. Examples of period costs are executive salaries, office rent, and expired insurance for the salespersons' cars.

6. **Explain the difference between direct and indirect costs and provide examples of each type.**

Direct costs are those costs that can be traced to a specific cost objective because the cost is incurred for the purpose of attaining that cost objective. By contrast, indirect costs cannot be traced to a single cost objective. Usually indirect costs relate to multiple cost objectives. Direct labor and direct materials are direct costs, whereas building depreciation is indirect because it applies to various cost objectives— multiple products manufactured in the building and often multiple activities occurring in the building, such as production, administration and marketing.

7. **Compare the differences in inventories for merchandising and manufacturing firms.**

The primary distinction between manufacturing and merchandising firms is that the manufacturing firms produce products. That is, they convert raw materials to finished (saleable) products through a manufacturing process. Merchandising firms are engaged in the sale of a product produced by someone else. The accounting differences are that manufacturing firms:

a. Have separate inventory accounts for raw materials, work in process and finished goods, and

b. Accumulate production costs in an asset account, work in process, until the product is complete, in order to determine the final product costs. These costs include raw materials, direct labor and manufacturing overhead.

8. **Describe the three manufacturing cost elements and give examples of each one.**

   Direct materials includes purchased parts, steel, plastic and glass in the manufacture of automobiles. What direct material costs relate to tennis rackets?

   Direct labor includes the wages of those workers who are part of the manufacturing and assembly process for the cars. They include welders, painters, and assemblers, among others, but do not include floor sweepers, timekeepers, and maintenance personnel.

   Manufacturing overhead includes all of the other production costs, which are allocated to the various products being manufactured. Examples are machine depreciation, supervisory salaries, heat and light.

9. **Identify the three inventory accounts maintained by a manufacturing firm and explain how each is used in the balance sheet and income statement.**

   The three inventory accounts are:

   a. Raw materials, the cost of purchased materials and parts to be processed into finished products.

   b. Work in process, the accumulated costs of raw materials, direct labor and manufacturing overhead that are in various stages of production, but not yet finished products.

   c. Finished goods, the accumulated costs of completed manufactured products.

   All three of the above inventory accounts are classified as current assets on the manufacturing company's balance sheet. Only the finished goods inventory appears on the firm's income statement— in the same way merchandise inventory appears on the merchandising firm's income statement—in calculating cost of goods sold. However, raw materials inventories are shown on the cost of goods manufactured statement in calculating cost of raw materials used, and work in process inventories are shown on the same statement in calculating cost of goods manufactured. In each of the above three cases, beginning inventory is added and ending (of the period) inventory is subtracted on the applicable statement.

10. **Prepare a manufacturing firm's income statement and related cost of goods manufactured statement in proper form.**

    An income statment and a cost of goods sold statement for an imagined company appear on the following pages. Review them carefully for format and terminology.

UTAH MANUFACTURED PRODUCTS, INC.
Income Statement
For the Year Ended June 30, 1991

Sales			$ 1,300,000
Cost of goods sold:			
Finished goods inventory, July 1, 1990	$ 210,000		
Cost of goods manufactured	865,000		
Goods available	1,075,000		
Finished goods inventory, June 30, 1991	175,000		
Cost of goods sold			900,000
Gross profit			400,000
Operating expenses:			
Selling expenses	110,000		
Administrative expenses	125,000		
Total operating expenses			235,000
Net income before taxes			165,000
Income taxes			49,500
Net income			$ 115,500

UTAH MANUFACTURED PRODUCTS, INC.
Cost of Goods Manufactured Statement
For the Year Ended June 30, 1991

Direct materials:				
Beginning raw materials	$	98,500		
Purchases (net)		560,500		
Raw materials available		659,000		
Ending raw materials		124,000		
Direct materials used			$	535,000
Direct labor				103,000
Manufacturing overhead:				
Indirect labor		41,000		
Supplies		500		
Utilities		10,350		
Rent		60,000		
Insurance		1,250		
Payroll taxes		8,110		
Depreciation		87,770		
Total manufacturing overhead				208,980
Manufacturing costs for the period				846,980
Beginning work in progress				88,020
Total work in progress				935,000
Ending work in progress				70,000
Cost of goods manufactured			$	865,000

11. **Discuss why just in time (JIT) inventory systems have become so popular and how they are used in repetitive manufacturing.**

    Just in time inventory systems were developed in order to reduce the amount of inventory maintained on hand. This substantially reduces inventory investment, including the storage, insurance and tax costs of carrying that inventory.

12. **Classify costs based on their behavior, contollability and relevancy.**

    Fixed costs are those costs that remain constant in total amount per period, regardless of the volume of production. An example is supervisory salaries.

    Variable costs are those costs that vary, in total, in direct proportion to production volume. An example is direct materials.

    Additional examples of the above two costs are as follows:

Volume of Production	Direct Material Cost		Supervisor's Salary	
	Per Unit	Total	Total	Per Unit
100 units	$0.87	$87.00	$2,000.00	$20.00
1,000 units	0.87	870.00	2,000.00	2.00

Another way of looking at costs is in what period of time are the costs controllable, and by whom. For example, building depreciation and property taxes are not controllable by each (or any) production supervisor in the various departments that occupy that building. Probably they are not controllable by any company personnel in the current year because the building cost decisions were made years ago at the vice president (or maybe at the board of directors) level.

Controllable costs are those costs that a given manager can regulate or influence during a particular time period. For example, repair cost is controllable, to some extent, by the supervisor in a manufacturing department by monitoring the way in which machinists work—the care they take of the machines and the preventive maintenance that occurs.

Relevant costs are future expected costs that will differ according to a managerial decision in a particular situation. For example, if management decides to chrome plate a product rather than paint it the cost of plating is a relevant cost as is the cost of the paint.

An irrelevant cost is one that does not change as the result of a particular decision. In the above example, a cost not relevant to the plating versus painting decision is the direct material cost of the product being coated, assuming it will remain constant regardless of the decision.

MATCHING ATTRIBUTES

Below in Group A are listed attributes that may be identified with the cost terms in Group B. Indicate, by use of the identifying letter of the appropriate Group B item, which attribute best matches which Group B cost.

Group A

_____ 1. Production costs other than direct materials and direct labor.

_____ 2. Future expected cost that changes as the result of a particular managerial decision.

_____ 3. Cost identified with a specific cost objective.

_____ 4. A combination of direct material and direct labor costs.

_____ 5. Cost associated with manufactured units; these costs are inventoried, then charged to cost of goods sold when the units are sold.

_____ 6. Costs of direct materials and purchased parts.

_____ 7. Wages of person directly involved with the production process.

_____ 8. A cost that stays constant per unit but varies in total in direct proportion to changes in production volume.

_____ 9. Cost not specifically related to a given cost objective.

_____ 10. An economic sacrifice made in exchange for a product or service.

_____ 11. Cost that is regulated or influenced by a particular level of management in a specified time period.

_____ 12. Accumulated direct labor, direct materials and manufacturing overhead costs for products started but not completed in the manufacturing process.

_____ 13. A cost that has expired or has been used up.

_____ 14. Cost stays the same in total amount for the period regardless of manufacturing volume.

_____ 15. Direct labor and manufacturing overhead costs required to turn raw materials into finished products.

_____ 16. A cost that cannot be regulated or influenced by a particular level of management during a specified time period.

_____ 17. System for minimizing inventories on hand.

Group B

A.	Controllable costs	J.	Manufacturing overhead
B.	Conversion costs	K.	Prime costs
C.	Cost	L.	Product costs
D.	Direct cost	M.	Raw materials inventory costs
E.	Direct labor cost	N.	Relevant cost
F.	Expense	O.	Uncontrollable costs
G.	Fixed cost	P.	Variable cost
H.	Indirect cost	Q.	Work in process inventory costs
I.	Just in time system		

MULTIPLE CHOICE

For each of the following items, choose the most appropriate completion phrase.

1. In the manufacture of jeans or other wearing apparel,

    a. Cutting and Sewing are likely to be service department functions.

    b. Quality Control, Cutting and Sewing would all be production departments.

    c. Service departments are not a part of a production firm; they relate only to service-oriented businesses.

    d. Cutting and Sewing are production departments, while Quality Control would be a service department.

    e. Quality Control is an administrative department, like Purchasing, and so is not classified as either production or service.

2. The difference in cost flows in a manufacturing firm and a merchandising firm is:

    a. In a manufacturing firm all production costs accumulate throughout the manufacturing process and get inventoried as an asset until the products are sold; whereas, in a merchandising firm only the purchased goods' costs are accumulated in the inventory account.

    b. In a manufacturing firm all costs of the period are charged to the inventory of work in process and finished goods; then, when the goods are sold, cost of goods sold goes on the income statement the same as with a merchandising firm.

    c. In a manufacturing firm only direct costs of production become a part of inventory costs, because indirect costs are considered period costs; whereas in a merchandising firm only purchased product costs go into inventory, and all others are period costs.

    d. There is essentially no difference.

    e. Costs don't flow in the merchandising firm, because all costs, except product costs, are fixed.

3. A manufacturing firm, according to your text author, is the most complete type of economic enterprise because it involves all three business functions: production, selling and administration. According to this definition, which of the following *is not* a manufacturing firm?

   a. Printing establishment.
   b. Dairy.
   c. Meat processing plant.
   d. Flour mill.
   e. Day care nursery.

4. The product cost flows in a manufacturing firm, in order, are:

   a. Raw materials inventory, finished goods, work in process.
   b. Raw materials inventory, work in process, finished goods, cost of goods sold.
   c. Merchandise inventory, finished goods, cost of goods sold.
   d. Supplies inventory, work in process, finished goods.
   e. Raw materials, finished goods, cost of goods sold.

5. Manufacturing overhead consists of indirect manufacturing costs such as:

   a. Indirect materials, labor, raw materials and supplies.
   b. Depreciation, utilities, repairs, indirect labor, rent and taxes.
   c. Materials, labor and burden.
   d. Taxes, executive salaries, sales commissions, and insurance.
   e. Direct materials, direct labor and direct expenses.

6. Absorption costing is a manufacturing costing technique

   a. Designed for tax purposes, to minimize inventory taxes.
   b. That is also called variable costing, and includes only variable costs of goods manufactured.
   c. That absorbs the administrative and selling expenses into the total product costs on the theory that without these expenses the product could not result in a profit for the firm.
   d. That treats all manufacturing costs as product costs and includes these in inventory until the product is sold.
   e. That is especially useful for depreciation of factory machinery and equipment, so that such costs do not get mixed up with inventory costs.

7. The variable costing technique

   a. Is used extensively for financial statement purposes, since it is required by GAAP.
   b. Is facilitated by the extensive segregation in separate ledgers of all costs according to whether they are fixed or variable.
   c. Sometimes called direct costing, recognizes as product costs only those manufacturing costs that change as production volume changes.
   d. Includes in product costs the administrative costs as an overhead component.
   e. Is involved with cost behavior and misbehavior, thus introducing a pyschological aspect to cost accounting.

8. The Imdieke Production Company has certain costs applicable to the monthly production of one of its principal products as shown below:

Quantity of Golf Putters Produced	Component A		Cost B	
	Unit Cost	Total Cost	Unit Cost	Total Cost
100	$1.15	$115	$25.00	$2,500
1,000	1.15	1,150	2.50	2,500
5,000	1.15	5,750	0.50	2,500

a. Component A is considered a variable cost and Cost B is a fixed cost in this situation.
b. Both A and B are variable costs, although A varies in total amount and B varies on a per unit basis.
c. Both A and B are fixed costs, although A is fixed per unit while B is fixed in total amount.
d. Neither is fixed or variable, but they are mixed costs, since the total product cost obviously contains both fixed and variable components.
e. Component A is a fixed cost while Cost B is a variable cost of production, based on the per unit cost behavior of each.

9. In preparation of an absorption costing, functional income statement for a manufacturing firm,

a. All inventory balances, including finished goods, work in process and raw materials are shown in the computation of cost of goods sold.
b. Variable product costs are segregated into a separate portion of the statement from the fixed, or period, costs.
c. Many similarities exist when comparing the format with a merchandising firm income statement.
d. It is general practice to not show any inventory costs, but rather to place the three types of inventory on the separate cost of goods manufactured statement.
e. All costs are listed in one category so that the costs are subtracted from sales in one step to arrive at net income.

10. A manufacturing firm's cost of goods manufactured statement

a. Includes the costs of direct materials and direct labor used plus the applicable manufacturing overhead for the period in calculating cost of goods manufactured.
b. Is useful in order to avoid cluttering the firm's balance sheet with a lot of inventory and cost items, thus making the balance sheet more readable.
c. Is shown as of the last day of the fiscal period, whereas the income statement is for the whole period (such as year) ended on that date.
d. Adds the beginning inventory balances of raw materials, work in process and finished goods, and subtracts the end of the period balances of these inventories to calculate cost of goods manufactured.
e. Same as d. above except ending inventory balances are added and beginning balances are subtracted.

ILLUSTRATIVE PROBLEMS

1. Helmsmith, Inc. is a manufacturer of bowling and other recreational equipment. Below are listed selected general ledger account balances as of September 30, 1991, the end of its fiscal year.

Finished goods inventory (beginning of year)	$69,500
Sales	542,100
Cost of goods manufactured	291,700
Interest expense	2,400
Selling expenses	63,100
Administrative expenses	80,800

In addition, you learn that the applicable income tax rate is 25%, and the ending finished goods inventory is $71,300. Prepare, in good form, an income statement using the absorption costing approach, as illustrated in Chapter 2 of your text.

2. Huizingh Motors is a Denver manufacturer of recreational vehicles. At the close of its most recent fiscal year, the following general ledger account balances appear.

Direct labor	260,500
Indirect labor	62,100
Supplies	4,950
Utilities	42,800
Insurance	18,400
Payroll taxes	32,600
Depreciation	42,700
Miscellaneous	5,300
Purchases (raw materials)	280,600

In addition, the various inventory balances were:

	Beginning of Year	End of Year
Raw materials	36,500	32,300
Work in process	41,250	39,750
Finished goods	29,800	24,900

Requested:

You are asked to prepare a cost of goods manufactured statement for the year ended December 31, 1992.

3. The following cost totals apply to the Tempe Tool Co. for June and October, 198x.

	June	October
Supplies	360	960
Utilities	750	2,000
Rent	3,600	3,600
Depreciation	3,200	3,200
Indirect labor	1,200	1,700

During June, Tempe Tool Co. produced 3000 units of its product; during October, 8,000 units.

Requested:

a. Compute the per unit cost of each cost item each month. Establish a column in the schedule above for this purpose.

b. Identify whether each cost item is fixed or variable. Label each appropriately.

4. Refer to the cost of goods manufactured statement below:

Fitchburg Manufacturing Company
Cost of Goods Manufactured Statement
Year Ending December 31, 1992

Direct materials:		
Beginning materials	$ 57,600	
Purchases (net)	169,200	
Raw materials available for production	226,800	
Ending raw materials	56,400	
Direct materials used		$ 170,400
Direct labor		426,000
Manufacturing overhead:		
Indirect labor	67,200	
Supplies	6,000	
Utilities	50,400	
Rent	27,120	
Insurance	21,600	
Payroll taxes	34,080	
Depreciation	38,400	
Miscellaneous	4,800	
Total manufacturing overhead		249,600
Manufacturing costs for the period		846,000
Beginning work in process		42,000
Total work in process		888,000
Ending work in process		36,000
Cost of goods manufactured		$ 852,000

Requested:

Provide the journal entries at December 31, 1992 to record in summary form for the year:
- a.   The cost of raw materials purchases.
- b.   The cost of direct labor used.
- c.   The cost of actual manufacturing overhead.
- d.   The cost of goods manufactured.
- e.   The cost of goods sold.

	Debit	**Credit**
a.		
b.		
c.		
d.		
e.		

VOCABULARY

Here are the new terms introduced in Chapter 2. Carefully read the words and their meanings, and then relate their usage back to the context of Chapter 2.

COMMON COST. A cost incurred for the benefit of more than one cost objective.

CONTROLLABLE COST. A cost that can be regulated or influenced at a particular level of management during a specified time period.

CONVERSION COSTS. The total of the direct labor cost and manufacturing overhead required to produce products.

COST. An economic sacrifice made in exchange for a product or service.

COST BEHAVIOR. The measure of how a cost will react to changes in the level of business activity. Examples are variable costs and fixed costs.

COST OBJECTIVE. An activity for which separate cost measurement is performed. Examples are a department, a product, or an office.

COST OF GOODS MANUFACTURED STATEMENT. A detailed accounting of the manufacturing cost performance reported on the income statement of a manufacturing firm.

DIRECT COST. A cost that can be traced to a specific cost objective.

DIRECT LABOR. Represents the wages paid to employees whose time and effort can be traced to finished goods.

DIRECT MATERIALS. The raw materials that can be identified as an integral part of finished products.

EXPENSE. A cost that has expired and is charged to the income statement because it no longer has future benefit.

FINISHED GOODS. The cost of the products that have been manufactured completely and are ready for sale.

FIXED COST. A cost that will remain constant in total amount over a wide range of business activity.

INDIRECT COST. A cost incurred for the common benefit of multiple cost objectives.

IRRELEVANT COST. A cost that will be the same in a decision-making situation regardless of the alternative selected.

JUST IN TIME (JIT) INVENTORY SYSTEM. A system in which the goal is to maintain zero inventory balances. Instead, inventories are available just in time to be sold or used in the production operation.

MANUFACTURING FIRM. A business that converts raw materials into finished goods.

MANUFACTURING OVERHEAD. All manufacturing costs except direct materials and direct labor required in the production process.

PERIOD (NONINVENTORIABLE) COSTS. Costs charged to the income statement of the time period in which they are incurred rather than being inventoried as product costs.

PRIME COSTS. The total of the direct materials and the direct labor needed to produce products.

PRODUCT (INVENTORIABLE) COSTS. Costs inventoried as assets and charged to the income statement when the related products are sold.

RAW MATERIALS. Represent the cost of the basic materials and parts that have been purchased by a manufacturing firm and are available for conversion into salable products.

RELEVANT COST. An expected future cost that will differ between alternatives in a decision-making situation.

UNCONTROLLABLE COST. A cost that cannot be regulated or influenced at a particular level of management during a specified time period.

VARIABLE COST. A cost that will vary in total amount proportionately with some measure of business activity.

WORK IN PROCESS. The inventory that has been partially converted into finished products.

THE ANSWERS

MATCHING ATTRIBUTES

1.	J	5.	L	9.	H	13.	F
2.	N	6.	M	10.	B	14.	G
3.	D	7.	E	11.	C	15.	A
4.	K	8.	P	12.	Q	16.	O
						17.	I

MULTIPLE CHOICE

1. d.
2. a.
3. e.
4. b.
5. b.
6. d.
7. c.
8. a.
9. c.
10. a.

ILLUSTRATIVE PROBLEMS

1.

Helmsmith, Inc.
Income Statement
For the Year Ended September 30, 1991

Sales		$ 542,100
Cost of goods sold:		
Finished goods, beginning	$ 69,500	
Cost of goods manufactured	291,700	
Goods available	361,200	
Finished goods, ending	71,300	
Cost of goods sold		289,900
Gross profit		252,200
Operating expenses:		
Administrative expenses	80,800	
Selling expenses	63,100	
Total operating expenses		143,900
Net income before interest and taxes		108,300
Interest	2,400	
Income taxes	26,475	28,875
Net income		$ 79,425

2.

Huizingh Motors
Cost of Goods Manufactured Statement
Year Ended December 31, 1992

Direct materials:			
Beginning raw materials	$	36,500	
Purchases, net		280,600	
Raw materials available		317,100	
Ending raw materials		32,300	
Direct materials used			$ 284,800
Direct labor			260,500
Manufacturing overhead:			
Indirect labor		62,100	
Supplies		4,950	
Utilities		42,800	
Insurance		18,400	
Payroll taxes		32,600	
Depreciation		42,700	
Miscellaneous		5,300	
Total manufacturing overhead			208,850
Manufacturing costs for the period			754,150
Beginning work in process			41,250
Total work in process			759,400
Ending work in process			39,750
Cost of goods manufactured			$ 755,650

3. a.

	June			October		
Supplies	360/3,000	=	$0.12	960/8,000	=	$0.12
Utilities	750/3,000	=	0.25	2,000/8,000	=	0.25
Rent	3,600/3,000	=	1.20	3,600/8,000	=	0.45
Depreciation	3,200/3,000	=	1.067	3,200/8,000	=	0.40
Indir.labor	1,200/3,000	=	0.40	1,700/8,000	=	0.2125

   b.   Variable costs vary in total in direct response to changes in production volume; fixed costs remain the same in total, regardless of production volume changes. By this definition, supplies and utilities are variable costs in the above example, and rent and depreciation are fixed costs.Indirect labor fits neither definition, and contains both fixed and variable components. We'll study more about this in a later chapter, but if you remember how to work simultaneous equations or the point slope formulas, you can probably figure out the fixed and variable portions of each.

4.

a. Purchases	169,200	
Accounts payable		169,200
b. Direct labor	426,000	
Accrued wages payable		426,000
c. Manufacturing overhead	249,600	
Accrued wages payable		67,200
Supplies inventory		6,000
Accounts payable		82,320
Prepaid insurance		21,600
Accrued payroll taxes		34,080
Accumulated depreciation		38,400
d. Finished goods inventory	852,000	
Work in process inventory		852,000
e. Cost of goods sold	840,000	
Finished goods inventory		840,000

CHAPTER 3

JOB ORDER COSTING SYSTEMS

Chapter 3 deals with a major technique for cost accumulation for products, called job order costing. As the chapter implies, this technique is part of a total costing system that results in definitive and meaningful costs for all products produced by the firm. Below are listed Professor Helmkamp's eleven learning objectives related to job order costing systems for students planning to have a firm understanding of this topic.

LEARNING OBJECTIVES

1. Recognize why product costing is so important to managers of a manufacturing firm.
2. Distinguish between job order costing and process costing as well as identify industries that use each type of system.
3. Trace the flow of transactions through a job order costing system.
4. Identify the role of a job order cost sheet.
5. Explain how direct materials are accounted for in a job order costing system.
6. Explain how labor is accounted for in a job order costing system.
7. Describe the problems associated with accounting for manufacturing overhead and why cost allocation is necessary.
8. Compute a predetermined overhead rate and account for manufacturing overhead in a job order costing system.
9. Explain why manufacturing overhead is often overapplied or underapplied during a given accounting period and what to do with the amount involved.
10. Discuss the concept of a cost driver as it is used in many automated manufacturing operations.
11. Apply the percentage-of-completion method to recognize revenue for long-term jobs.

LEARNING TIPS

Did you ever work for the school newspaper? Suppose that you have been given the assignment to find a new source for getting the school paper printed. As you think about going to various printers to get estimates of the cost for the job, what information do you suppose the printers will need to know in order to give you a bid?

What costs will the printer incur from the time the newspaper staff brings in the copy until the final printed product is produced?

How will the printer know if he or she has made a profit on the job?

Print shops, like certain other types of business described in Chapter 3, use a job order costing system for accumulating the various costs of performing each job. One reason for this is that each job is unique—different from the other jobs the company does. When the printer does your school's newspaper, the work and the costs of that work differ from other jobs done by the shop, such as printing advertising brochures, wedding announcements, instructional materials to accompany equipment sent to customers, and so forth.

As you study Chapter 3, try to think of the labor, such as typesetting, running the presses and physically handling the paper, that are a part of turning out your paper. Then consider the materials—ink, paper and photographic materials—that go into the printing process. By giving thought to such a real product as the school paper, you will better understand the job order system and its function in accounting.

REVIEW

As you consider the school newspaper as a job going through a manufacturing plant, let's now review the Chapter 3 topics, as they relate to the learning objectives.

1. **Recognize why product costing is so important to managers of a manufacturing firm.**

    Product costs are a necessary part of the total cost information system required to manage a manufacturing firm. Many decisions by managers are based on the costing information system. Examples of the information provided are, "Are we making a profit on this job?" "What are the actual costs of the job?" "How do the costs compare with our preliminary estimates?"

2. **Distinguish between job order costing and process costing as well as identify industries that use each type of system.**

    Job order costing systems are used by manufacturing firms that produce separately identifiable units or groups of units. Examples of such units are houses produced by building contractors, furniture produced by furniture factories, accounting services produced by CPA firms, advertising campaigns developed by ad agencies, and books produced by publishers and printers. As you see, not all users of cost accounting systems are manufacturers in the traditional sense. Also, job costing techniques are equally applicable, whether one unique product is being produced, such as a huge hydroelectric dam, or hundreds of similar products grouped together in a lot, such as size 9 designer blouses.

    Process costing is the system used by producers of homogeneous and continuous production. Flour milling, mining, petroleum refining, raw steel production, water purification, and dairy (and beer) processing are examples of industries that commonly use the process costing system. These all consist of a continuous flow of identical or nearly identical product. Some factories may treat metal plating or painting operations as process costing situations while other parts of the factory use a different costing method.

3. **Trace the flow of transactions through a job order costing system.**

    In a job order costing system raw materials costs flow out of the raw materials inventory accounts (as credits) and into the work in process accounts (as debits). Direct labor also flows into the work in process accounts (as debits), with credits in the accrued wages payable account. Manufacturing overhead costs also are debited to work in process, with credits to the overhead applied account.

    Each of the costs referred to above are also recorded on the job order cost sheet for the job to which the costs apply. Therefore, the total of all the costs on the individual job order cost sheets equal the balance in the work in process inventory account in the general ledger.

    When the jobs in process are completed, the total cost of the completed jobs are credited to work in process and debited to finished goods inventory. Finally, when the products are sold, the costs are removed (credited) from finished goods inventory and debited to cost of goods sold.

This cost flow is shown as:

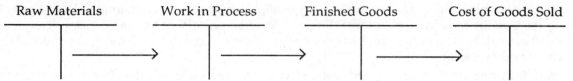

Raw Materials   Work in Process   Finished Goods   Cost of Goods Sold

4. Identify the role of a job order cost sheet.

The job order cost sheet serves the role of a cost accumulator on which are recorded the various cost components as the products, for which it is accumulating costs, are being produced. Once the products are completed and their costs fully recorded on the job cost sheet, the costs are totalled by category, that is, direct materials, direct labor and manufacturing overhead, and the sum of these three categories is computed for the aggregate job cost.

This total is divided by the quantity of products produced to determine a per-unit cost of production. In addition to serving as cost accumulation records, the job order cost sheets in the aggregate are the subsidiary ledger of work in process inventory control account while the jobs are in process, and finished goods inventory after the products are completed and before they are sold.

5. Explain how materials are accounted for in a job order costing system.

The costs of all direct materials are initially accounted for by properly recording costs and quantities of each type of material in perpetual inventory records. In the aggregate, these inventory records constitute the raw materials inventory subsidiary ledger and must be in agreement with the raw materials control account in the general ledger.

As materials are drawn from stock for use in the production process, the materials cost is credited to the raw materials account and debited to work in process, being added to the applicable job cost sheet. The sum of all materials put into production is the sum of direct materials charges to the job cost sheet. The total of all such charges for a period equals the total debit to the work in process control account for material usage that period (and concurrently equals the credit to raw materials for the same purpose).

The document used for recording the withdrawal from stock of direct materials and charging the appropriate costs to the job cost sheet is the materials requisition.

6. Explain how labor is accounted for in a job order costing system.

Direct labor charges originate from the labor time ticket on which each employee records the job number, time worked and other pertinent data as each employee works during the day. These time tickets are summarized each pay period for purposes of computing the employee payroll, and the tickets are also summarized by job number for recording the direct labor costs applicable to each job.

7. Describe the problems associated with accounting for manufacturing overhead in a job order costing system.

Whereas direct materials and direct labor are direct costs of each job, and thus rather easily identifiable with the job, manufacturing overhead is an indirect collection of costs which are not traceable to specific jobs. This is true because of the nature of overhead costs:

a.   Frequently they are common costs, such as property taxes and building depreciation, that apply to all of the firm's functions, i.e., production, selling and administration.

b.   Of those that are only production costs, such as machine depreciation and production supervisory salaries, they normally apply to several jobs that are being produced during the period.

In either case, the overhead costs must be allocated to the applicable production function and eventually the job on a fair basis. The intent in choosing an allocation method is to attempt to charge costs based on the benefits received. To facilitate the cost allocation process, one or more bases of applying the overhead to jobs is employed, such as a percentage of direct labor cost or so much per direct labor hour consumed by the job.

Manufacturing overhead is the third cost component of each job and it, like direct materials and direct labor cost, is recorded on the applicable job cost sheet.

8. **Compute a predetermined overhead rate and account for manufacturing overhead in a job order costing system.**

Because actual overhead cannot be computed until the end of a period of time, and because job costs must be determined whenever the job is completed, overhead is applied to the jobs on a predetermined basis.

Usually once a year a predetermined overhead is computed. This is done by dividing the estimated overhead for the period by some measure of production activity for the year, such as direct labor hours. The Claiborne Company estimates that total manufacturing overhead for 1992 will be $5,400,000. Also the company estimates it will incur 2,000,000 direct labor hours in in 1992. Then its predetermined overhead rate for 1992 will be $2.70 per direct labor hour, as follows

$$\text{Predetermined overhead rate} = \frac{\text{estimated overhead for the year}}{\text{estimated production activity for year}}$$

$$= \frac{\$5,400,000}{2,000,000 \text{ direct labor hours}}$$

$$= \$2.70 \text{ per direct labor hour}$$

This overhead is applied to jobs on the basis of the number of direct labor hours incurred on each job. The Claiborne Company makes clay bells, per customer orders. Job #2929 has the following direct costs.

	Amount
Direct materials	$3,120.00
Direct labor	
125 hours @ $8.50 per hour	1,062.50

In addition, overhead must be applied, as an indirect job cost as follows:

125 direct labor hours x $2.70 predetermined overhead rate
= $337.50

Therefore, the total job #2929 costs are:

Direct materials	$3,120.00
Direct labor	1,062.50
Manufacturing overhead	337.50
Total costs	$4,520.00

9. **Explain why manufacturing overhead is often overapplied or underapplied during a given accounting period and what to do with the amount involved.**

Since overhead is applied to jobs as they are processed and before the total of all overhead for the period is known, there is, at each month end, a difference between the total costs applied to jobs during the period and the sum of overhead charges incurred. If the aggregate applied to jobs exceeds the total of overhead costs incurred, we say we have overapplied overhead; if the reverse is true, the overhead is underapplied.

Because the amount over- and underapplied will fluctuate monthly because of seasonal variances in cost incurrence and in production volumes, it is not normal practice to adjust these monthly variances. However, at the end of the fiscal year, the accumulated over- or underapplied overhead must be disposed of in the accounts. This may be allocated to all production costs of the period pro rata, and thus reflected as adjustments to work in process, finished goods and cost of goods sold accounts. On the other hand, if the balance (over or under) is relatively minor in amount, the total may be closed into the cost of goods sold account.

When a job is completed and all the applicable costs are recorded, the costs must be transferred out of work in process to finished goods inventory. Similarly, when the products are sold, the cost of these products must be transferred from finished goods to cost of goods sold. Also, at the time of sale the sales price must be recorded as revenue.

The following are sample entries to reflect these transactions:

	Debit	Credit
a. Completion of job:		
Finished goods inventory	27,900	
Work in process inventory		27,900
(To record the completion of job #2217 and transfer applicable costs to finished goods.)		
b. Sale of job:		
Accounts receivable	55,800	
Cost of goods sold	27,900	
Sales		55,800
Finished goods		27,900
(To record sale of job #2217 for $55,800 and to remove cost of job from inventory.)		

10. **Discuss the concept of a cost driver as it is used in many automated manufacturing operations.**

A cost driver is a business activity that causes manufacturing overhead costs to be incurred. For example, if much of the overhead is made up of employee benefits and costs, such as vacation pay, payroll taxes, medical and hospital insurance, then a likely cost driver would be direct labor hours or cost.

However, in some situations, direct labor is minimal, because of highly automated techniques. Then, overhead might consist mainly of utilities, taxes, depreciation, heating and air conditioning, and other costs related to space used or investment. In this case, the cost driver might be investment in plant and equipment used for manufacturing.

In this latter situation, we say that it is the investment in manufacturing facilities that causes the overhead to be incurred. Thus, we should apply overhead to the various departments on the basis of the investment in each department or cost center.

11. **Apply the percentage-of-completion method to recognize revenue for long-term jobs.**

Because jobs frequently remain in process for extended periods of time, income could be substantially distorted if recognition were not given for revenue earned on a percentage-of-completion basis.

This is especially true of road-building and large building, bridge or dam construction jobs that sometimes require several years to complete. The percentage-of-completion method requires the reporting of costs, revenues and gross profits based on appropriate percentages of the estimated total costs and revenues. For example, if 40% of the expected total job costs occur in year 1, 40% of the total expected gross profit would be recognized in the accounts during that period.

MATCHING ATTRIBUTES

Below in Group A are attributes that may be identified with terms that have been introduced in Chapter 3. Indicate, by use of the identifying letter of the appropriate Group B item, which attribute in Group A best matches which Group B term.

Group A

_____ 1. System for accumulating costs for manufactured products when production is performed according to customers' specifications and the identity of groups of products is kept separate.

_____ 2. System for accumulating costs for manufactured products when products are manufactured on a continuous or homogeneous basis so that products can not be easily identifiable.

_____ 3. Control document used for cost accumulation for materials, labor and overhead applicable to each separately identifiable batch or group of products.

_____ 4. Document used for identifying specific materials required for production and for charging the costs of those materials to work in process.

_____ 5. Record of the materials received, issued and balance on hand.

_____ 6. Record on which employee's hours worked are recorded for each specific job or overhead assignment.

_____ 7. Journal for detailed listing of employees' payroll for a given period, usually classified by department.

_____ 8. An indirect cost that cannot be traced to specific products.

_____ 9. A method of assigning common costs to departments on a basis of expected benefit received.

_____ 10. Basis for applying indirect costs to production, usually based on a measure of production activity.

_____ 11. Actual overhead incurred exceeds amount applied to production.

_____ 12. Method of including a proportionate amount of gross profit in a period even though a long-term construction project is not complete.

_____ 13. Measure of business activity for applying manufacturing overhead to production on the basis of the activity that caused the overhead costs to occur.

Group B

A. Cost allocation
B. Cost driver
C. Job order costing system
D. Job order cost sheet
E. Labor time ticket
F. Manufacturing overhead
G. Materials ledger card

H. Materials requisition
I. Percentage-of-completion method
J. Predetermined overhead rate
K. Process costing system
L. Payroll register
M. Underapplied overhead

MULTIPLE CHOICE

For each of the following items, choose the most appropriate completion phrase.

1. A job order costing system is best used when

    a. Products are separately identifiable units or groups of units.
    b. Products are produced on a continuous or homogeneous basis.
    c. Products are produced continuously throughout the year without substantial change.
    d. Products are mass-produced, such as textbooks or automobiles.
    e. Products are standard, not according to customer's specifications.

2. The calculation of a predetermined overhead rate for applying indirect costs to production is

    a. $\dfrac{\text{Estimated manufacturing overhead}}{\text{Estimated number of units to be produced}}$

    b. $\dfrac{\text{Estimated manufacturing overhead}}{\text{Estimated production activity level}}$

    c. $\dfrac{\text{Estimated production activity level}}{\text{Estimated manufacturing overhead}}$

    d. Estimated manufacturing overhead x budgeted direct labor hours

    e. $\dfrac{\text{Estimated number of units to be produced}}{\text{Estimated manufacturing overhead}}$

3. When the actual overhead costs for a period exceed the amount of overhead allocated to production during the same period,

    a.   The difference is charged to work in process.
    b.   The difference is called underapplied overhead.
    c.   The difference is called overapplied underhead.
    d.   The difference is called overapplied overhead.
    e.   The difference is credited to cost of goods sold.

4. If overhead is overapplied on interim (monthly and quarterly) financial statements, the amount overapplied is best shown as:

    a.   A period cost on the cost of goods manufactured statement.
    b.   A current asset on the balance sheet.
    c.   A cost of goods sold adjustment in the income statement.
    d.   A current liability on the balance sheet.
    e.   An adjustment to retained earnings on the retained earnings statement.

5. The Mark Russell Fabricating Company manufactures metal furniture in Chicago. During May, job #5906 was completed with the following costs:

Direct materials	$ 7,407
Direct labor	12,323
Manufacturing overhead	8,770
Total cost	$28,500

The correct entry to transfer this completed job is:

    a.   Debit cost of goods sold and credit sales for $28,500.
    b.   Debit finished goods $28,500 and credit raw materials $7,407; direct labor $12,323; and manufacturing overhead $8,770.
    c.   Debit accounts receivable and credit sales $28,500.
    d.   Debit finished goods and credit work in process $28,500.
    e.   Debit finished goods and credit sales $28,500.

6. A debit balance in the manufacturing overhead account at the end of a month means

    a.   Manufacturing overhead was overapplied that month.
    b.   Manufacturing overhead was underapplied that month.
    c.   Manufacturing overhead was underapplied in total year-to-date.
    d.   Manufacturing overhead was overapplied in total year-to-date.
    e.   The predetermined manufacturing overhead rate is wrong.

7. Accounting for long-term construction contracts involves use of the completed contract method or the percentage-of-completion method. When Arizona Bridgebuilders, Inc. were constructing an auto bridge over the Salt River, it involved an 18-month construction period.

   Assuming the completion of the contract would result in a gross profit of $300,000, and that 40% of the contract was completed by the end of the first fiscal year and the remainder was completed in the second year,

   a. The percentage method would result in a smaller reported income the first year than the completed method would.

   b. The percentage method would result in a smaller reported income the second year than the completed method would.

   c. The percentage method would report $120,000 net income the first year and $180,000 the second.

   d. The completed method would report $120,000 net income the first year and $180,000 the second year.

   e. The completed method would result in a larger reported income in the two years combined than would the percentage method.

8. A direct materials requisition form is used in the job order costing system

   a. For the ordering of needed materials from suppliers.

   b. As a form for keeping track of what materials are on hand and on order.

   c. As a cost sheet, to accumulate all job costs while a particular job is in process.

   d. For requesting that the purchasing department order materials from suppliers.

   e. As a document to draw materials from the storeroom for production usage.

9. Bart Repairs, Inc. of San Francisco manufactures repair and replacement parts for rapid transit vehicles. The company distributes service department costs to producing departments and allocates producing department indirect costs, including those distributed from service departments, to products. The best way to distribute Human Resource Department (personnel hiring and training activities) costs to producing departments would be pro rata on the basis of

   a. Square feet of floor area in each department served.

   b. Investment in machinery and equipment in each department.

   c. Dollar value of direct material used in each department.

   d. Number of employees on the payroll for each department.

   e. A weighted average of all of the above.

10. Manufacturing overhead is considered an indirect, but necessary, product cost. Based on this, which of the following is best described as a manufacturing overhead cost?

    a. Wages for workers who work directly on products.

    b. Light, heat, power and machine depreciation.

    c. Sales and executive salaries and applicable payroll taxes.

    d. Materials that become a part of products.

    e. Indirect cost of advertising company's products.

11. Charles Jenkins is looking for a cost driver for the allocation of manufacturing overhead costs for his furniture manufacturing company, Chuck's Comfortable Couch Co. He heard that direct labor cost is commonly used for this purpose. Direct labor cost is generally a good cost driver if

   a. The manufacturing plant is highly automated.

   b. The company is mainly involved in furniture assembly, rather than actual manufacturing.

   c. Much of the production work is performed by employees who work directly on the manufacture of the furniture.

   d. Each process of production is completely different in the way it is produced, some highly roboticized, some through automatic assembly techniques.

ILLUSTRATIVE PROBLEM

1. During March, The Millstone Company of Cranbury, New Jersey incurred the following overhead costs. Their accountant, David Piburn, had developed a predetermined overhead rate for applying overhead to production costs of 75% of direct labor cost. At June 30, 1991, the company's fiscal year-end, the account balances relating to overhead costs showed the following balances:

Manufacturing overhead debits	786,400
Manufacturing overhead credits	777,850

Requested:

   a. Was manufacturing overhead overapplied or underapplied for the year, and by how much?

   b. What methods are available for handling or disposing of the balance of the overhead account at year-end?

   c. Following the "most practical" method suggested for dealing with this rather minor balance (approximately 1% of total overhead costs), show the appropriate journal entry.

	Debit	Credit

2. Referring to problem 2 of Chapter 2, how would the Huizingh Motors financial statement presentation be modified at December 31, 1992, if the following additional data were known?

	Debit	Credit
Manufacturing overhead	208,850	210,550

Be specific as to where changes would be made as a result of this new data.

3. Samuel Edward is the accountant for the Redd Budd Manufacturing Company of Tulsa, Oklahoma. He wishes to instruct his assistant, Sara, in the process of allocating indirect manufacturing costs to final product costs, using a job order costing system. Redd Budd has three service departments: Maintenance, Timekeeping, and Power. There are two producing departments: Cutting and Assembly. Briefly list the procedures he might use to describe

   a. The process of allocating service department costs to producing departments.

   b. The process of developing a rate for charging producing department overhead costs to units produced in each department.

4. Lindbergh Printers, Inc., celebrating its 65th year in business, does custom printing for local businesses in southeastern Wisconsin. Job order costing is used. Estimated manufacturing overhead costs for 1993 are $3,600,000. Estimated production level for the year is 300,000 direct labor hours. Job #2809 is completed on February 26 with accumulated activity as follows:

Direct labor hours:	180	
Direct labor rate:	$15.00	per hour
Direct materials used:	$1,350	

Requested:

   a. Calculate the predetermined manufacturing overhead rate for the year 1993, assuming direct labor hours are considered to be the cost driver.

   b. Calculate the amount of overhead to be included in Job #2809.

   c. Prepare the journal entries to (1) record the cost components in work in process, and (2) to transfer the cost of the completed job out of work in process.

	Debit	Credit

5. The Lindbergh Printers, Inc., in Problem 4, is considering the installation of highly automated printing presses that would result in a substantial decrease in the amount of direct labor hours and a substantial increase in estimated manufacturing overhead costs for 1993. Because of the planned change in production methods, it was decided to use separate cost drivers for each of two departments as follows. (Cost driver is underlined in each department.)

	Printing Department	Cut and Fold Dept.
Estimated machine hours	180,000	80,000
Estimated manufacturing overhead	$3,870,000	$1,980,000
Estimated direct labor hours	60,000	120,000

Requested:

Calculate the predetermined overhead rate for each department for 1993:

	Printing Department	Cut and Fold Dept.
Predetermined overhead rate:	_____	_____

6. The Nitz Construction Company is the prime contractor for construction of an earthen dam across the Joyce River. The expected construction period is approximately 2 years beginning in July 1990.

Costs and gross profits are as follows (in thousands):

		1990	1991	1992
a.	Actual costs incurred (cumulative)	$ 2,100	$ 6,960	$ 10,440
b.	Estimated total costs	10,500	10,800	10,750
c.	% of total costs a/b = c	20%	64%	
d.	Est. total gross profit	1,500	1,200	1,250
e.	Cumulative gross profit (c x d)	300	768	
f.	Less: gross profit recognized previously		-300	
g.	Current year gross profit (e - f)		468	

Requested:

Calculate the gross profit to be reported in 1992 if the contract is accounted for on a percentage-of-completion basis. Show all work.

VOCABULARY

ACTIVITY COSTING. Concepts and procedures used by a firm to accumulate the costs of a nonmanufacturing activity such as a service, program, or project.

COST ALLOCATION. The assignment of a common cost to one or more cost objectives in proportion to some reasonable measure of the anticipated benefits from the cost.

COST DRIVER. A measure of business activity that causes the incurrence of overhead.

JOB. A product or group of products being produced when job order costing is used.

JOB ORDER COSTING. A product costing system with which costs are accumulated for jobs as the work is performed.

JOB ORDER COST SHEET. The control document used with job order costing to provide a detailed listing of the manufacturing costs incurred during the production of a job and a subsidiary ledger accounting.

LABOR TIME TICKET. A record of how much time an employee spends on a job or an overhead assignment.

MATERIALS LEDGER CARD. A form representing a subsidiary ledger for each type of raw material used in the production process that provides a perpetual accounting of the purchases and requisitions of the materials.

MATERIALS REQUISITION FORM. A record of the amount of raw material requisitioned from the storeroom for a job or as indirect materials.

OVERAPPLIED MANUFACTURING OVERHEAD. The excess of the manufacturing overhead applied to work in process with a predetermined overhead rate over the actual manufacturing overhead incurred.

OVERHEAD APPLICATION. The use of a predetermined overhead rate to charge manufacturing overhead to work in process as a job is worked on.

OVERTIME PREMIUM. Amount paid to an employee above his or her regular hourly wage for every hour worked in excess of 40 hours a week.

PAYROLL REGISTER. A detailed listing of a firm's payroll, usually on a departmental basis, for a given period.

PERCENTAGE-OF-COMPLETION METHOD. Recognition of revenue for a long-term project in proportion to the progress made on the project during its life.

PREDETERMINED OVERHEAD RATE. A rate used to apply manufacturing overhead to work in process that is computed by dividing the estimated manufacturing overhead for a period by some measure of production activity.

PROCESS COSTING SYSTEM. A product costing system used with a continuous production process and homogeneous products.

PRODUCT COSTING. A system used to accumulate the manufacturing costs needed to produce products.

TIME CARD. A document used to control the hours worked each day by an employee.

UNDERAPPLIED MANUFACTURING OVERHEAD. The excess of the actual manufacturing overhead incurred during a particular period over the manufacturing overhead applied to work in process.

THE ANSWERS

MATCHING ATTRIBUTES

1. C	4. H	7. L	10. J
2. K	5. G	8. F	11. M
3. D	6. E	9. A	12. I
			13. B

MULTIPLE CHOICE

1. a	4. d	7. b	10. b
2. b	5. d	8. e	11. c
3. b	6. c	9. d	

ILLUSTRATIVE PROBLEMS

1. a. The manufacturing overhead was underapplied by $8,550. The amount applied was $777,850, while the actual manufacturing overhead was $786,400.

    b. Theoretically, the over- or underapplied manufacturing overhead should be allocated among work in process, finished goods and cost of goods sold on a pro rata basis, according to the manufacturing overhead for the period remaining at year-end in each of the respective accounts. The practical difficulty of this method is in making that determination and in getting the correct amount into each of the appropriate subsidiary accounts as well as the general ledger control accounts. A simpler method is described in part c. A third alternative, seldom used, is to leave the over- or underapplied overhead in the appropriate balance sheet account, carrying it forward to the next year.

    c. A common method of disposing of the over- or underapplied overhead, if the balance is relatively minor in relation to the total overhead cost for the year, is to charge or credit the difference entirely to the income statement account, cost of goods sold, as follows:

	Debit	Credit
Cost of goods sold	8,550	
Manufacturing overhead		8,550

2. Cost of goods sold would be reduced by $1,700, the amount of overapplied manufacturing overhead for the year.

3. a. Since service departments, by definition, do not produce products for sale to outsiders (customers of the company), the costs accumulated in those departments must be allocated to the producing departments, so that all production-related costs eventually get charged to the products that are actually produced. These service department costs are charged on the basis of benefit received or service rendered. Maintenance keeps the building clean and the machines in good repair. These costs are frequently charged to producing (and sometimes other service) departments on the basis of square feet of floor area in each department.

For the Maintenance Department, suppose the total cost is $65,520 for the year. The floor area of the departments served might be:

Power	2,400	sq. ft.
Cutting	10,800	sq. ft.
Assembly	12,000	sq. ft.
Total	25,200	sq. ft.

The cost allocated to the Assembly Department is 12,000/25,200 x $65,520 = $31,200. Another way of calculating this amount, is to first compute a per square foot cost: $65,520/25,200 = $2.60 per square foot. Then, multiplying: 12,000 x $2.60 = $31,200 for Assembly, and similarly for other departments.

Timekeeping keeps track of the employee hours worked. Therefore, that department's costs might be charged to the other departments on the basis of the number of employees in each department served. For example, if there are 1,800 employees in the departments served, and the total Timekeeping Department cost is $36,000, the cost allocated to each department would be $20 per employee in that department. [$36,000/1,800 = $20.]

Finally, the Power Department produces (usually electrical) power to be consumed by the producing departments. Sometimes each department has its own electric meter, so that the total kilowatt hours (KWHs) of power consumed will be known for each department. Then, the total power consumed is divided into the total Power Department costs to arrive at a per-KWH cost. The amount charged to each department equals the number of KWHs of power consumed times the derived rate.

b. Charging each producing department's overhead costs (after including the indirect costs allocated from service departments) to the products produced by that department is done on a pre-determined basis. We estimate, in advance, the overhead costs for the period and divide this amount by the expected production activity for the period, say direct labor hours. This gives us a per-hour charge for overhead to be applied to each job as it is worked on in the department. For example, if the expected overhead costs for the Assembly Department for 1992 is $1,080,000 and the expected direct labor hours for the year are expected to be 120,000, the overhead rate would be calculated as $9.00 per direct labor hour. [$1,080,000/120,000 = $9.00.]

4. a. Predetermined overhead rate is:

$$\frac{\$3,600,000}{300,000} = \$12.00 \text{ per direct labor hour}$$

b. 180 x $12.00 = $2,160.

	Debit	Credit
c. (1) Work in process, Job #2809	6,210	
Raw materials		1,350
Wages payable		2,700
Manufacturing overhead		2,160
(2) Finished goods	6,210	
Work in process, Job #2809		6,210

5. The predetermined overhead rate for the Printing Department is:

$$\frac{\text{Estimated manufacturing overhead}}{\text{Estimated machine hours}} = \frac{\$3,870,000}{180,000} = \$21.50 \text{ per machine hour}$$

The predetermined overhead rate for the Cut and Fold Department is:

$$\frac{\text{Estimated manufacturing overhead}}{\text{Estimated direct labor hours}} = \frac{\$1,980,000}{120,000} = \$16.50 \text{ per direct labor hour}$$

6. Apparently the dam is not quite complete at the end of 1992. The cumulative actual costs incurred $10,440, which is 97% of the total expected costs of $10,750. Therefore, 0.97 x $1,250 gross profit, or $1,213, minus the previously recognized gross profit of $773, or $440, should be recognized as gross profit in 1992. Any remaining (unrecognized) gross profit at the end of the contract, in 1993, would be recognized at that time.

CHAPTER 4

PRODUCT COSTING FOR REPETITIVE PRODUCTION

LEARNING OBJECTIVES

1. Describe how process costing is used by manufacturing and nonmanufacturing firms.
2. Identify a processing center.
3. Explain how products and costs flow through a production process and know the accounting procedures needed to accumulate costs perpetually.
4. Calculate unit costs for products produced in a process costing operation.
5. Determine equivalent units of production.
6. Prepare a cost of production report.
7. Recognize how the weighted-average method and the FIFO method are used with a beginning work in process inventory.
8. Compute equivalent units of production with the weighted-average and FIFO methods.
9. Interpret cost of production reports prepared with the weighted-average method and the FIFO method.
10. Evaluate how costs incurred in a preceding department are treated in a cost of production report.
11. Prepare the journal entries needed to record the production costs, the transfer of products and the sale of products with process costing.
12. Compare job order costing with process costing.
13. Identify hybrid product costing systems and explain how they are used in repetitive manufacturing.

LEARNING TIPS

In Chapter 4, we see a different way of accounting for production costs than was used in Chapter 3. In Chapter 3 we used the job order costing system because production was kept track of and accounted for on a lot or job basis. All production belonged on one job or another. All costs were separately compiled for each job. In production, inventory and cost of sales, all units were identified with a particular job.

However, in Chapter 4, the process costing system is introduced to account for continuous production of more-or-less homogeneous units. For example, when processing fresh milk from farms into saleable milk, cream, cottage cheese and ice cream all the milk starts pretty much the same (although there might be some differences for fat content, etc.). When we buy a half-gallon of low fat milk or a pint of ice cream from the supermarket, we can't distinguish whether it came from Farmer Brown's cows near Peoria or from the Gold Medal Dairy Farm of Racine County. All the materials flow continuously, and the continuous processing of relatively homogeneous materials and products permits a somewhat more straightforward cost accounting system.

In process costing, we divide total costs of the process for the month by the number of units processed. The complications in Chapter 4 are more concerned with units than with costs.

Therefore, concentrate your study on equivalent units (both weighted-average and FIFO). We also have to learn one report form, the Cost of Production Report, and some journal entries for the flow of units and flow of costs.

REVIEW

After a careful reading of Chapter 4 and the learning objectives listed above, let's review each of those objectives to see how well you understand process costing systems. Remember that process costing systems are an alternative way to accumulate and determine product costs. (The other way we've studied is job order costing systems—Chapter 3.)

1. **Describe how process costing is used by manufacturing and nonmanufacturing firms.**

   Process costing systems are used whenever production is carried on in a continuous flow of homogeneous products, as opposed to producing smaller lots or producing according to customer specifications. This continuous processing lends itself to accumulating costs by process over a period of time, such as a month, instead of by lot or job, as we learned in Chapter 3. Examples of products often produced by the continuous-flow, homogeneous product system are: flour, gasoline, pharmaceuticals, chemicals and various types of beverages (yes, beer as well as soft drinks).

2. **Identify a processing center.**

   A processing center is a segment of the total production facility that mixes, blends, heats, cools, or in some other way processes the product. A vat in the winery where grapes ferment, a blast furnace in a steel mill, a grinding unit in a flour mill, and a homogenizer in a dairy are all examples of processing centers.

   Sequential processing occurs when products all flow through the same workstations or processing centers in a predetermined sequence, i.e., first station A, then B, and finally C. In a parallel processing system, products may pass through separate work stations initially, then converge, such as a finishing or packaging station. An example of parallel processing is the production of pharmaceutical products such as aspirin and extra-strength pain capsules that are processed separately up to the point of packaging, then they go through the same bottling and packaging process.

3. **Explain how products and costs flow through a production process and know the accounting procedures needed to accumulate costs perpetually.**

   Cost flows follow product flows in the manufacturing process. Costs of materials, labor, and overhead are accumulated by cost center, which is identical with the processing center. Thus the accounting process must identify all production costs as belonging to a particular processing center. Then these total costs for the center, say the Mixing Department, are divided by the number of units, e.g., gallons, of product produced by that center that month.

4. **Calculate unit costs for products produced in a process costing operation.**

If all of the material, labor and overhead costs of a certain milk processing center in a dairy amounted to $176,000 for May, and if the total gallons of milk processed by the department in May were 320,000 gallons, the unit cost would be

$$\frac{\$176,000}{320,000 \text{ gallons}} = \$0.55 \text{ per gallon.}$$

On a separate cost basis (for the major cost categories) assume the following:

	Total Cost	Product Volume	Unit Cost
Direct materials	$ 86,000	320,000 gallons	$ 0.26875
Direct labor	46,400	320,000 gallons	0.14500
Overhead	43,600	320,000 gallons	0.13625
	$ 176,000		$ 0.55000

5. **Determine equivalent units of production.**

Equivalent units are the number of units of product still in process (unfinished) in a department or processing center at the end of a period multiplied by the fraction of work completed. So, if the pill-making department of a pharmaceutical company has 6,000 pills in process 1/3 complete, the calculation would be 6,000 x 1/3 = 2,000 equivalent units.

However, some cost elements are frequently at a different stage of production than others. In the pill example above, all the material may already be in the process, and only labor and overhead are unfinished. If this is the case, the calculation might be:

Cost Element	Number of Units	Stage of Completion	Equivalent Units
Materials	6,000	100%	6,000
Labor	6,000	1/3	2,000
Overhead	6,000	1/3	2,000

6. **Prepare a cost of production report.**

A cost of production report consists of three parts:

a.   A physical flow schedule, which shows the beginning and ending work in process with the stage of completion for each, and the number of units started and completed during the period.

b.   Costs to be accounted for, which lists each cost element, and the equivalent units and unit cost applicable to each element. These costs are input and processing costs.

c.   Costs accounted for are the detail costs of units completed during the period and of the units still on hand at the end of the period (work in process). The total of these costs must equal the total of the input and processing costs above.

A cost of production report for Belle City Dairy follows:

Belle City Dairy
Cost of Production Report (Weighted-Average Method)
Ice Cream Department
July, 1992

Physical flow schedule

Work in process, July 1	200	gallons	(1/2 converted)
Units started	2,200	gallons	
Units completed	2,000	gallons	
Work in process, July 31	400	gallons	(3/4 converted)

Materials are all added at the beginning of the process; labor and overhead are added proportionately throughout the process.

Costs to be accounted for

Cost Elements	Beginning	Current	Total	Equivalent Units*	Unit Cost
Materials	$152	$1,528	$1,680	2,400	$0.70
Direct labor	28	524	552	2,300	0.24
Overhead	37	584	621	2,300	0.27
Total	$217	$2,636	$2,853		$1.21

*Refer to review item #8 below for the equivalent units calculations.

Costs accounted for

Units completed and transferred (2,000 gallons x $1.21)		$2,420
Work in process, July 31:		
Materials (400 gallons x $0.70)	$280	
Direct labor (400 gallons x 3/4 x $0.24)	72	
Overhead (400 gallons x 3/4 x $0.27)	81	433
Total costs accounted for		$2,853

Let us now extend this example to include the FIFO method, using the equivalent units of production computation from part 8 below.

Costs to be accounted for

Cost elements	Amount of cost	Equivalent Units*	Unit Cost
Beginning work in process	$ 217		
Current cost elements:			
Raw materials	1,528	2,200	$ 0.69454
Direct labor	524	2,200	0.23818
Overhead	584	2,200	0.26545
Costs to be accounted for	$ 2,853		$ 1.19817

*See review item 8 below.

Costs accounted for

Complete beginning inventory 200 gallons		
Beginning inventory cost		$ 217.00
Direct labor added 200 gallons x 1/2 x $0.23818		23.82
Overhead added 200 gallons x 1/2 x $0.26545		26.55
Total cost of beginning inventory		$ 267.37
Units started, finished and transferred:		
1,800 gallons @ $1.19817		2,156.72
Ending work in process inventory:		
Raw materials (400 gallons x $0.69454)	$277.82	
Direct labor (400 gallons x 3/4 x $0.23818)	71.45	
Overhead (400 gallons x 3/4 x $0.26545)	79.64	428.91
Total costs accounted for		$ 2,853.00

7. **Recognize how the weighted-average method and the FIFO method are used with a beginning work in process inventory.**

   First-in, first-out, or FIFO, is a cost flow assumption, but does not necessarily correspond with the actual flow of units. It says those costs first incurred are those first consumed. When computing equivalent units, the FIFO method is calculated differently from the weighted-average method.

   The FIFO method involves computation of the number of equivalent units necessary to complete the beginning work in process inventory *plus* the units started and completed during the period *plus* the equivalent units in the ending inventory. The weighted-average method ignores the beginning work in process inventory. These two methods are illustrated in item 8 (next).

8. **Compute equivalent units of production with the weighted-average and FIFO methods.**

Using the preceding example as an illustration, the equivalent units by the *weighted-average method are:*

	Material	Labor	Overhead
Units completed	2,000	2,000	2,000
+ Equivalent units in ending work in process	400	300	300
Totals	2,400	2,300	2,300

For the *FIFO method*, completion of the beginning work in process inventory must be considered:

	Material	Labor	Overhead
Equivalent units needed to complete beginning inventory	0	100	100
+ Units started and completed	1,800	1,800	1,800
+ Equivalent units in ending inv.	400	300	300
= Total equivalent units	2,200	2,200	2,200

9. **Interpret cost of production reports prepared with the weighted-average method and the FIFO method.**

Refer to review item 6 above. The Belle City Dairy Cost of Production Report shows the three parts of the report:

a.   A physical flow schedule,

b.   The costs to be accounted for, and

c.   The costs accounted for

Notice how in this report all units in, consisting of beginning inventory and units started, must equal units completed (and transferred) plus units in the ending inventory. This is also true of the dollar amounts.

Beginning inv. + units started   =   units finished + ending inv.

Units

200 gallons + 2,200 gallons   =   2,000 gallons + 400 gallons

Amounts (weighted-average)

$217 + $2,636   = $2,420 + $433

Amounts (FIFO)

$217 + $2,636   =   ($267.37 + 2156.72) + $428.91

10. Evaluate how costs incurred in a preceding department are treated in a cost of production report.

If two or more processing centers are involved in a manufacturing process, the units finished in and transferred from the earliest process flow to the next process, and then to the next, until the units are completely manufactured. The units finished in the earlier process become inputs to the following process. Also, the costs from the earlier process flow into the later process and the costs of the later process are added to the earlier process costs.

Refer back to review item 6. Assume the Belle City Dairy has a Packaging Department process following the Ice Cream Department. The 2,000 gallons transferred in July and the $2,420 cost of those 2,000 gallons would be inputs into the Packaging Department physical flow and costs to be accounted for in July.

For example:

Belle City Dairy
Cost of Production Report (partial)
Packaging Department
July, 1992

Physical flow schedule

Work in process, July 1	- 0 -
Units transferred in	2,000 gallons
Units completed	2,000 gallons
Work in process, July 31	- 0 -

Costs to be accounted for

Cost Elements	Current	Equivalent Units	Unit Cost
Units transferred in	$2,420	2,000 gallons	$ 1.21
Materials	220	2,000 gallons	0.11
Labor	330	2,000 gallons	0.165
Overhead	440	2,000 gallons	0.22
Total	$3,410		$ 1.705

11. **Prepare the journal entries needed to record the production costs, the transfer of products, and the sale of products with process costing.**

For the required general journal entries, refer once more to review items 6 and 8 above for the Belle City Dairy:

	Debit	Credit
Work in process, Ice Cream Dept.	2,636	
Raw materials		1,528
Payroll payable		524
Overhead		584
(Record production of Ice Cream Dept. for July.)		
Work in process, Packaging Dept.	2,420	
Work in process, Ice Cream Dept.		2,420
(Record costs of 2,000 gallons of ice cream completed and transferred to Packaging Dept. in July.)		
Finished goods inventory	3,410	
Work in process, Packaging Dept.		3,410
(Record production and packaging of 2,000 gallons of ice cream completed and transferred in July.)		
Cost of goods sold	2,557.50	
Accounts receivable	3,450.00	
Finished goods inventory		2,557.50
Sales		3,450.00
(Record sale of 1,500 gallons of ice cream at $2.30 per gallon.)		

12. **Compare job order costing with process costing.**

In comparing the process costing system in this chapter with the job order costing system of Chapter 3, we see the many ways the two differ. The main differences are summarized below:

	Job Order Costing	Process Costing
Product type	Heterogeneous	Homogeneous
Product flow	By job or lot	Continuous
Control document	Job order cost sheet	Cost of production report
Cost accumulation	By job	By department (process center)
Output measure	Jobs completed	Equivalent units completed
Point of focus	Job	Processing center
Records required	Very detailed	Less detailed
Report form	Job order cost sheet	Cost of production report
Report period	Duration of job	Month (usually)

13. **Identify hybrid product costing systems and explain how they are used in repetitive manufacturing.**

A hybrid costing system is a blend of both job order and process costing. In batch processing, operation costing is often used, while in continuous flow manufacturing, JIT costing is frequently applied.

Operation costing is used to cost the production of large batches of homogeneous products. In this system, a work order is used to specify both materials and operations to be performed on the batches. Direct labor is not accounted for separately, but is combined with manufacturing overhead and called conversion cost. (This is a term we learned in Chapter 2.) These conversion costs are accumulated by operation (similar to process) and applied on a predetermined overhead (conversion) rate. This results in less detailed accounting than when job order or process costing is used.

JIT costing results in a lack of detail cost records for continuous (constant) flow production. Often work in process inventory accounting is eliminated, because of the nature of just in time inventory policies. All materials are charged to the raw and in-process (RIP) inventory account when purchased and not removed until the products have been completed. Such simplified accounting requires a system called backflush or postmanufacturing-deduction procedure to account for production costs between goods in inventory and for cost of goods sold.

MATCHING ATTRIBUTES

Below, in Group A, are listed attributes that may be identified with the process costing terms in Group B. Indicate, by use of the identifying letter of the appropriate Group B item, which Group A attribute best matches which Group B term.

Group A

_____ 1. Focal point of process costing—where work is performed.

_____ 2. Costs that are incurred first are consumed first.

_____ 3. Total of beginning inventory costs and costs added during the period.

_____ 4. Quantity computed differently for FIFO and weighted-average methods.

_____ 5. Inventory system that diminishes or negates the need for equivalent unit computations.

_____ 6. Ending inventory cost plus cost of units completed.

_____ 7. Every unit passes through the same processes in order.

_____ 8. Some units go through processes 1 and 3, others through processes in order.

_____ 9. Contains three segments: physical flow and two cost segments.

_____ 10. Costs of product received from previous department.

_____ 11. All units treated identically, cost-wise.

_____ 12. A postproduction procedure to allocate production costs between cost of goods sold and inventories.

_____ 13. A hybrid costing procedure in which direct labor is combined with manufacturing overhead costs, and as combined, called conversion costs.

_____ 14. Product costing system for constant flow manufacturing.

Group B

A.	Backflush costing	H.	JIT inventory system
B.	Cost of production report	I.	Operation costing
C.	Costs accounted for	J.	Parallel product flow
D.	Costs to be accounted for	K.	Processing center
E.	Equivalent units	L.	Sequential product flow
F.	FIFO cost flow	M.	Transferred in costs
G.	JIT costing	N.	Weighted-average cost flow

MULTIPLE CHOICE

For each of the following items, choose the most appropriate completion phrase.

1. Process costing systems are usually used in continuous production flow situations. Which of the following is *not* likely to use a process costing system?

    a.   Refinery that produces gasoline and related products.

    b.   Company that transforms raw grains into a popular brand of cereal.

    c.   Dairy that pasturizes and homogenizes milk into several dairy products.

    d.   Printing company that produces a variety of printed products for different customers.

    e.   Post office sorts mail by zip code on high speed machines.

2. According to the text format for a cost of production report,

    a.   Costs to be accounted for always equal costs accounted for.

    b.   Work in process beginning inventory plus units started always equal ending work in process plus units completed.

    c.   The physical flow schedule is not related to the cost schedule.

    d.   The costs to be accounted for follow a FIFO flow while the costs accounted for use the weighted-average cost method.

    e.   a. and b. above are both correct.

3. In the computation of equivalent units of production in a process costing situation, using the weighted-average method,

    a.   The stage to be completed of beginning inventory is added to units started to get equivalent units.

    b.   The beginning inventory times percent completed is added to units completed.

    c.   The units completed are added to percent completed times ending inventory.

    d.   The units completed are added to percent to be completed times ending inventory.

    e.   The units started are added to the ending inventory times percent completed.

4. When computing equivalent units of production using a FIFO cost flow, the computation involves:

    a.   Beginning inventory, times percentage previously completed, plus units started and completed, plus equivalent units in ending inventory.

    b.   Beginning inventory, times percentage completed this period, plus units started and completed, plus equivalent units in ending inventory.

    c.   Is not concerned with beginning of the period work in process inventory.

    d.   Beginning inventory, times percentage previously completed, plus units started and completed, but excludes ending inventory.

    e.   Beginning inventory, times percentage completed this period, plus units started and completed, but excludes ending inventory.

5. Many products are produced on a continuous basis. At the end of a day, which may be the end of a month, some product may be still in process, i. e. unfinished. Therefore, the costs of the month may have to be allocated over whole (completed) units and partial (unfinished) units. This requires the computation of:

   a. Manufacturing overhead costs
   b. Direct labor costs
   c. Direct material costs
   d. Equivalent units of production
   e. All of the above

6. The journal entry for recording costs incurred by the Bottling Department in a soft drink company is:

   a.   Work in process, Bottling Dept.   xxx
        Work in process, Blending Dept.   xxx

   b.   Finished goods   xxx
        Work in process, Bottling Dept.   xxx

   c.   Cost of goods sold   xxx
        Finished goods   xxx

   d.   Work in process, Bottling Dept.   xxx
        Raw materials   xxx
        Manufacturing payroll   xxx
        Manufacturing overhead   xxx

   e.   Raw materials   xxx
        Manufacturing payroll   xxx
        Manufacturing overhead   xxx
        Work in process, Bottling Dept.   xxx

7. When transferring costs from Sharpening Department to Finishing Department, Sword Steel should journalize as follows:

   a.   Work in process, Sharpening   xxx
        Work in process, Finishing   xxx

   b.   Work in process, Finishing   xxx
        Work in process, Sharpening   xxx

   c.   Finished goods inventory   xxx
        Work in process inventory   xxx

   d.   Work in process, Finishing   xxx
        Raw materials   xxx
        Manufacturing payroll   xxx
        Manufacturing overhead   xxx

   e.   Work in process, Sharpening   xxx
        Raw materials   xxx
        Manufacturing payroll   xxx
        Manufacturing overhead   xxx

8. Simkins Brewing Co., an ale producer in Oregon, has the following physical flow data for the Fermenting Department for October:

Work in process, October 1	6,000 gal., 1/3 complete
Units started	36,000 gal.
Units completed	40,000 gal.
Work in process, October 31	2,000 gal., 1/2 complete

If raw materials are added at the beginning of the process, the equivalent units of production for materials for October, using the weighted-average method, would be:

a.   36,000 gallons
b.   40,000 gallons
c.   42,000 gallons
d.   38,000 gallons
e.   41,000 gallons

9. Referring to Problem 8 above, the overhead is added equally and consistently throughout the fermenting process. Using a weighted-average method, the equivalent units for October for overhead are:

a.   36,000 gallons
b.   38,000 gallons
c.   40,000 gallons
d.   41,000 gallons
e.   42,000 gallons

10. Referring to Problem 8 above, compute the equivalent units of production for raw materials if FIFO flow is assumed.

a.   34,000 gallons
b.   36,000 gallons
c.   38,000 gallons
d.   40,000 gallons
e.   37,000 gallons

Illustrative Problems

1. The Tabor Company of San Mato produces carbonated beverages. In the Blending Department in August the following product flows occurred:

Work in process, August 1	6,000 gal., 1/3 complete
Units started	42,000 gal.
Units completed	44,000 gal.
Work in process, August 31	4,000 gal., 1/2 complete

Requested:

Prepare a computation, in good form, of equivalent units of production for August using:

a.   Weighted-average method.

Beg Inv	–0		44,000
Finished	44,000		
end inv	4,000		2,000
	48,000		46,000

b.   FIFO method.

Beg Inv	(6,000)		(2,000)
Finished	44,000		44,000
end inv	4,000		2,000
	42,000		44,000

2. Referring to the Tabor Company above, the cost records for Blending show:

	Work in Process August 1	August Costs Added
Raw materials	$600	5,040
Direct labor	200	4,400
Overhead	260	6,640
	1060	

Requested:

Prepare the "Costs to be accounted for" and "Costs accounted for" sections of the Cost of Production Report for Blending for August, using:

a.   Weighted-average method.

Raw Materials = 600   5040 = 5640   48,000 = .1175
DL   = 200   4400 = 4600   46000 = .10
MO   = 260   6640 = 6900   46000 = .15
                         17140   .3675

                                        16,170.00

FG 44,000 x .3675
   RM 4,000 x 100% x .1175 =   470–
   DL 4,000 x 50% x .10   200
   mo 4,000 x 50% x .15   300   970.00
                               970   17140.00
                                        1060–

b.   FIFO method.

Beg WIP 1060–
RM   5040   42,000 = .12   DL Added 6,000 x 2/3 x .10   400–0
DL   4400   44,000 = .10   mo   6,000 x 2/3 x .1509 603.60   2063.64
MO   6640   44,000 = .1509
      17140   .3709   4,000 x 100% x .12 =   480.00   981.78
                                  4,000 x 50% x .10 =   200.00   14094.58
                                  4,000 x 50% x .1509 = 301.80   17140.00
                                  38,000 x .3709 =

3. The Harris Mill of Ogden processes grains into a health food cereal sold throughout the country. During July, it had the following physical flow and cost data applicable to its production. (Grain is usually measured in bushels rather than pounds or tons.)

Physical Flow

Work in process, July 1	-0-
Units started	24,000 bushels
Units completed	20,000 bushels
Work in process, July 31	4,000 bushels, 1/4 complete

Costs Incurred

Raw material A	$ 84,000
Raw material B	23,100
Direct labor	57,750
Overhead	69,300
	$ 234,150

Raw material A is added at the beginning of the process. Material B, labor and overhead are all added evenly and continuously throughout the process.

Requested:

Prepare the "Costs to be accounted for" and "Costs accounted for" sections of the Harris Mill Cost of Production Report for July, assuming a weighted-average costing method.

4. The Hudson Buckle Co. of Dennis, Colorado produces western belt buckles out of brass alloy. Two departments are involved: Casting and Finishing.

	Casting	Finishing	
Work in process, November 1	0	1,200	(1/2 comp)
Units started	6,000	5,000	
Units completed	5,000	5,600	
Work in process, November 30	1,000	600	
	(1/2 comp)	(1/3 comp)	
November cost data:			
Raw materials requisitioned	$ 1,872	$ 250	
Direct labor cost	2,750	520	
Manufacturing overhead	1,375	672	

Requested:

a. Complete the costs to be accounted for, Finishing Department, for November, assuming the following November 1 work in process balance. Materials are added at the beginning of each process.

Transferred-in costs	$ 1,200.00
Raw materials	75.50
Direct labor	60.00
Manufacturing overhead	53.00
Total	$ 1,388.50

Use the weighted-average method.

b. Complete the costs accounted for, Finishing Department, for November.

5. Referring to Illustrative Problem 2, prepare general journal entries for the Tabor Company, using the weighted-average method,

   a. To record the production costs incurred in the Blending Department during August, and

   b. To record the costs of goods transferred to the next department (Bottling) in August.

	Debit	**Credit**

6. Referring to Illustrative Problem 4, prepare general journal entries for the Hudson Buckle Co. for November to record:

   a. Production costs incurred for the Finishing Department and costs transferred from the Casting Department;

   b. Transfers of completed goods from Finishing to finished goods inventory; and

   c. Sales of 1,000 buckles produced in November at $4.50 each.

	Debit	**Credit**

   a.

   b.

   c.

7. Ponca City Ceramics has developed a new automated process for manufacturing ceramic chips that are electronic processor components. They are manufactured in a constant flow process, with a JIT inventory system. During March,

    a.   Raw materials costing $145,000 were purchased and put into process;

    b.   Raw materials included in finished units amounted to $141,000;

    c.   Raw materials included in products sold, and transferred to cost of goods sold were $136,000;

    d.   Total recorded conversion costs for March were $89,000; and

    e.   The production manager estimates at month end that conversion costs in the ending inventories were:

Raw and in-process	$3,500
Finished goods	4,700

Requested:

Using the backflush costing approach, show the journal entries that would be required to record the above transactions and the month-end inventories. (Assume there were no beginning-of-the-month inventories.)

VOCABULARY

AVERAGE UNIT COST. The unit cost determined in a process costing system by dividing the costs of a processing center for a specific time period by the center's production output for that period.

BATCH MANUFACTURING. A type of repetitive manufacturing in which identical products are produced in long production runs with intermittent changes to slightly different products.

CONSTANT FLOW MANUFACTURING. A type of retitive manufacturing in which production takes place at a fixed rate established by the assembly of finished units.

COST OF PRODUCTION REPORT. The control document used in a process costing system to account for the production activity and the related costs in a processing center during a specified time period.

EQUIVALENT UNITS OF PRODUCTION. A measure of how many whole units are represented by the units finished plus the units partially completed.

FIFO METHOD. The flow assumption used in process costing that accounts for the beginning work in process inventory separately from the products entered into production during the period.

HYBRID PRODUCT COSTING SYSTEM. A product costing system containing elements of both job order and process costing.

JIT COSTING. A product costing system for constant flow manufacturing.

OPERATION COSTING. A product costing system for batch manufacturing.

PARALLEL PRODUCT FLOW. The arrangement of multiple processing centers in which certain phases of the work are performed concurrently and then are combined for further processing or completion.

PROCESS COSTING SYSTEM. A product costing system used when a firm produces homogeneous units with a continuous production flow.

PROCESSING CENTER. A segment of a manufacturing firm in which homogeneous units are produced and process costing is used to account for the manufacturing costs incurred.

SEQUENTIAL PRODUCT FLOW. A product flow in which production starts in the first processing center and flows through every processing center with each succeeding center being dependent on the preceding work performance.

TOTAL COSTS ACCOUNTED FOR. The allocation of the total costs to be accounted for by a processing center to products completed in that center or left in ending work in process inventory.

TOTAL COSTS TO BE ACCOUNTED FOR. The total costs charged to a particular processing center for a specific time period as beginning work in process inventory or current production costs.

TRANSFERRED IN COSTS (PREVIOUS DEPARTMENT COSTS). The total production costs transferred into a particular processing center that have been required in all preceding centers to produce the related products.

WEIGHTED-AVERAGE METHOD. The flow assumption used in process costing that combines the costs and units in the beginning work in process inventory with those of the current period.

THE ANSWERS

MATCHING ATTRIBUTES

1.	K	5.	H	9.	B	13.	I
2.	F	6.	C	10.	M	14.	G
3.	D	7.	L	11.	N		
4.	E	8.	J	12.	A		

MULTIPLE CHOICE

1.	d	4.	c	7.	b	10.	b
2.	e	5.	d	8.	c		
3.	c	6.	d	9.	d		

ILLUSTRATIVE PROBLEMS

1. a. Equivalent units, Blending Dept., August, weighted-average:

	Raw Materials	Direct Labor	Manuf. Overhead
Units completed	44,000	44,000	44,000
+ Equiv. units in ending inv.	4,000	2,000	2,000
= Total equivalent units	48,000	46,000	46,000

   b. FIFO method:

	Raw Materials	Direct Labor	Manuf. Overhead
Units completed	44,000	44,000	44,000
+ Equiv. units in ending inv.	4,000	2,000	2,000
- Equiv. units in begin. inv.	6,000	2,000	2,000
= Total equivalent units	42,000	44,000	44,000

2. a. *Costs to be accounted for*

Cost Element	Beginning	Current	Total	Equivalent Units	Unit Cost
Raw materials	$ 600	$ 5,040	$ 5,640	48,000	$ 0.1175
Direct labor	200	4,400	4,600	46,000	0.10
Manufact. overhead	260	6,640	6,900	46,000	0.15
	$ 1,060	$ 16,080	$ 17,140		$ 0.3675

Costs accounted for

Units finished and transferred (44,000 x $0.3675)		$ 16,170
Work in process, August 31:		
Raw materials (4,000 x $0.1175)	$ 470	
Direct labor (2,000 x $0.10)	200	
Overhead (2,000 x $0.15)	300	970
Total costs accounted for		$ 17,140
		======

2. b.   (FIFO)

Beginning work in process $ 1,060

Current Cost Elements		Equivalent Units	Unit Cost
Raw materials	5,040	42,000	$ 0.12
Direct labor	4,400	44,000	0.10
Overhead	6,640	44,000	0.1509
Totals	$17,140		$ 0.3709
	======		======

Costs accounted for

Beginning inventory finished (6,000 gallons)

Work in process	$ 1,060.00	
Direct labor added		
(6,000 x 2/3 x $0.10)	400.00	
Overhead added		
(6,000 x 2/3 x $0.15091)	603.64	$ 2,063.64
Started, finished and transferred (38,000 x $0.37091)		14,094.58
Work in process, ending:		
Raw materials (4,000 x $0.12)	480.00	
Direct labor		
(4,000 x 1/2 x $0.10)	200.00	
Overhead (4,000 x 1/2 x $0.15091)	301.78*	981.78
Total costs accounted for		$ 17,140.00
		========

*Adjusted for rounding difference.

3.

The Harris Mill
Cost of Production Report
(Weighted-Average Method)
July

Physical Flow Schedule

Work in process, July 1	0
Units started	24,000 bushels
Units completed	20,000 bushels
Work in process, July 31	4,000 bushels (1/4 converted)

Costs to be accounted for:

Cost Element	Beginning	Current	Total	Equivalent Units	Unit Cost
Raw material A	0	$ 84,000	$ 84,000	24,000	$ 3.50
Raw material B	0	23,100	23,100	21,000	1.10
Direct labor	0	57,750	57,750	21,000	2.75
Overhead	0	69,300	69,300	21,000	3.30
Totals	0	$ 234,150	$234,150		$ 10.65

Costs accounted for

Units finished and transferred (20,000 x $10.65)		$ 213,000
Work in process, July 31:		
Raw material A (4,000 x $3.50)	$ 14,000	
Raw material B (1,000 x $1.10)	1,100	
Direct labor (1,000 x $2.75)	2,750	
Overhead (1,000 x $3.30)	3,300	21,150
Total costs accounted for		$ 234,150

4.

Costs to be accounted for

Cost element	Beginning	Current	Total	Equiv. Units	Unit Cost
Transferred-in cost	$ 1,200.00	$ 5,310 *	$ 6,510.00	6,200	$1.05
Raw materials	75.50	250	325.50	6,200	.0525
Direct labor	60.00	520	580.00	5,800	.10
Manufacturing overhead	53.00	672	725.00	5,800	.125
	$ 1,388.50	$ 6,752	$ 8,140.50		$1.3275

*Transferred in costs this month equal the 5,000 units completed in Casting Dept. at a unit cost of $1.062. This unit cost comes from:

	Cost	Equivalent Units	Unit Cost
Materials	$1,872	6,000	$0.312
Direct labor	2,750	5,500	0.500
Overhead	1,375	5,500	0.250
			$1.062

Equivalent Units Finishing (weighted-average):

	Raw Materials	Direct Labor	Manuf. Overhead
Units completed	5,600	5,600	5,600
+ Equivalent units, ending inventory	600	200	200
= Total equivalent units	6,200	5,800	5,800

Costs accounted for

Units finished and transferred (5,600 x $1.3275)		$ 7,434.00
Work in process, November 30		
Units transferred from Casting Dept.		
(600 x $1.05)	$ 630.00	
Raw materials (600 x $0.0525)	31.50	
Direct labor (600 x 1/3 x $0.10)	20.00	
Overhead (600 x 1/3 x $0.125)	25.00	706.50
Total costs accounted for		$ 8,140.50

5.

	Debit	Credit

a. Work in process, Blending Dept.   16,080
       Raw materials   5,040
       Manufacturing payroll   4,400
       Manufacturing overhead   6,640
     (To record production costs incurred by the Blending Dept. during August.)

b. Work in process, Bottling Dept.   16,170

      Work in process, Blending   16,170

     (To record the total costs of the products transferred to the Bottling Dept. in August.)

6.

a.

    Work in process, Finishing Dept.   6,752
      Raw materials   250
      Direct labor   520
      Manufacturing overhead   672
      Work in process, Casting Dept.   5,310
    (To record production costs incurred in the Finishing Dept.
    in November and the costs transferred from Casting Dept.)

b.

    Finished goods inventory   7,434
      Work in process, Finishing Dept.   7,434
    (To record total costs of goods transferred to Finished goods inventory in November)

c.

    Accounts receivable   4,500
      Sales   4,500
    Cost of goods sold   1,327.50
      Finished goods inventory   1,327.50
    (To record sales of 1,000 buckles @ $4.50 and cost of goods sold of $1.3275 each.)

7. Ponca City Ceramics journal entries at March 31.

a.

    Raw and in-process inventory   145,000
      Accounts payable   145,000
    (To record the purchases of raw materials for March.)

b.

    Finished goods inventory   141,000
      Raw and in-process inventory   141,000
    (To record raw materials costs of units completed in March.)

c.

    Cost of goods sold   136,000
      Finished goods inventory   136,000
    (To record the cost of raw materials for units sold in March.)

d.

Cost of goods sold	89,000	
Conversion costs		89,000
(To record March conversion costs.)		

e.

Raw and in-process inventory	3,500	
Finished goods inventory	4,700	
Cost of goods sold		8,200
(To adjust for conversion costs estimated to be in inventories at March 31.)		

CHAPTER 5

COST BEHAVIOR AND CONTRIBUTION MARGIN REPORTING

We know that behavior is related to people. We all behave differently under different circumstances. Have you considered that costs behave differently, too? We see in Prof. Helmkamp's Chapter 5 that some costs are variable, some fixed, and some partially fixed (or partially variable). This chapter is all about how costs behave and how this behavior affects company profit margins. After studying this chapter, you should be able to:

LEARNING OBJECTIVES

1. Recognize the limitations of a functional income statement for managerial use.
2. Develop an income statement with a contribution margin format.
3. Explain the meaning of a cost function.
4. Identify the cost functions involved with variable costs, fixed costs, and mixed costs.
5. Determine how certain costs that are not completely variable or fixed are treated in managerial accounting applications.
6. Understand how the concept of the relevant range is used with cost behavior.
7. Analyze cost behavior with three methods—visual fit of a scatter diagram, high-low, and linear regression.
8. Recognize how variable costing is used for internal reporting.
9. Reconcile the difference between variable costing net income and absorption costing net income.
10. Discuss the benefits and limitations of variable costing.

LEARNING TIPS

Put yourself in the chair of the company manager of Needham Machine Shop. You must look into the future to plan for the purchase of new equipment, the hiring or retention of employees and the purchase of inventory and supplies. Also, you want to know whether to search out new business and how to figure bids on potential new contracts. All these decisions depend on the expected costs, revenues and income of future periods. (The results of prior periods are meaningless now. We can never do anything about the past.)

In order to make these critical managerial decisions about the future, you must have accurate revenue and cost data. How much will costs and revenues change if you are able to increase sales 20%? If sales go down by 15%? Will costs and revenues change in direct proportion to sales volume changes?

As a managerial accounting student you are able to provide the information you would need if you were the manager. This means you need to have a thorough understanding of cost behavior and the contribution margin concepts. How do costs change as volume changes? What kinds of cost behaviors are you concerned with? How do inventory fluctuations affect net income? Let's review these and other Chapter 5 topics so that you will have a better understanding of these important ideas for managerial decision-making.

REVIEW

1. **Recognize the limitations of a functional income statement for managerial use.**

   Managers, of course, need to be aware of the way the results of operations are reported to stockholders and taxing and regulatory authorities. This means managers are concerned with the conventional or functional income statement.

   However, in this chapter, and throughout most of the remainder of this textbook, our principal concern will be with the variable costing, or contribution margin format income statement. The reason for this is that with such a statement format, the manager can develop a pro forma, or future-oriented income statement so that he or she can forecast the results that will occur based on certain decisions that must be made about the future.

2. **Develop an income statement with a contribution margin format.**

   Remember that a contribution margin format income statement separates fixed and variable costs. Variable costs are subtracted from revenues to arrive at contribution margin. Then fixed costs are subtracted from contribution margin to determine net income. Mixed costs are separated into their fixed and variable components so that they may be included in the appropriate income statement section. Below is an income statement using the contribution margin format developed for the Owasso Company:

Owasso Company
Income Statement
For the Year Ended June 30, 1992

Sales		$ 350,000
Variable cost of goods sold	$ 80,000	
Variable operating expenses	22,000	
Total variable costs		102,000
Contribution margin		248,000
Fixed costs:		
Manufacturing	120,000	
Selling and administrative	87,000	
Total fixed costs		207,000
Net income		$ 41,000

3. **Explain the meaning of a cost function.**

A cost function describes the relationship between the cost and activity, volume or passage of time.

a.   Some cost functions are simply:

$$y = a$$

where y is the amount of the cost, and a is a fixed dollar amount per month.
Example: if y = $13,000, the cost is fixed at $13,000 per month.

b.   Another common cost function is:

$$y = a + bx$$

where y and a are the same as above,

  b is a coefficient for x, and

  x is a measure of activity or volume.

Example: $y = \$3,000 + \$0.26DLH$

This cost is $3,000 per month plus $0.26 per direct labor hour.

c.   Another cost function is:

$$y = a + bx + c^2$$

or

$$y = a + bx + cz$$

As these functions become three-dimensional or curvilinear, they go beyond the scope of this introductory text.

4. **Identify the cost functions involved with variable costs, fixed costs, and mixed costs.**

Variable Costs. Variable costs are those costs that vary directly, in total amount, with some activity of the business, such as units produced. A typical example of a variable cost is the cost of raw materials used in the manufacture of a product such as skis. The more skis that are manufactured, the higher the cost of raw materials that are a part of those skis. If ski production doubles, the cost of raw materials can be expected to double.

Fixed Costs. Fixed costs are those costs that remain constant as the volume of production changes. The building rental agreement for a manufacturing company specifies that the rent is fixed at a constant amount each month regardless of the level of production. Similarly, supervisory salaries, depreciation and insurance costs are fixed (although one can always develop a rationale for why these or any costs might have a different behavior pattern).

Mixed Costs. Mixed costs are those costs that contain some element of both variable and fixed costs. Examples of mixed costs, sometimes called semivariable costs, are:

a.   Rent for retail store space in a shopping center often has a fixed base per month plus a certain percentage of sales. Thus, the rent for Gray's Jewelry store might be $1,200 per month plus 2% of sales.

b.   Sometimes managers' salaries are established as a fixed amount per month plus a certain amount per unit sold or per unit produced, or a percentage of the division's contribution margin.

c.   Another type of mixed cost frequently is maintenance. There is a certain amount of cleaning (which often is included in the maintenance department function) and repair that is fairly constant. In addition, there is an increase in such costs with increased activity. The factory often gets dirtier and machines need more repair work done if the volume of work increases.

Whereas a. and b. items are mixed costs because of contract arrangements, item c. is a mixed cost because of the natural behavior of the maintenance function. The diagrams of each of these cost functions are as follows.

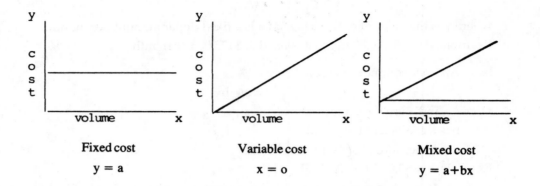

Fixed cost	Variable cost	Mixed cost
$y = a$	$x = o$	$y = a + bx$

Where y = total cost
x = activity level in units
a = fixed cost
b = variable cost per unit

5. **Determine how certain costs that are not completely variable or fixed are treated in managerial accounting applications.**

Some costs are neither completely variable nor completely fixed. Mixed costs contain some element of both variable and fixed costs, as described above. However, still other costs are curvilinear. These costs are clearly shown in economic analysis in very low and very high portions of the cost curve. The economies and diseconomies of scale, as studied by economists, affect the cost function. These curvilinear cost curves will not be dealt with in this introductory discussion.

6. **Understand how the concept of the relevant range is used with cost behavior.**

The relevant range is the range of activity within which a firm expects to operate. Activity levels both above and below the relevant range are irrelevant because the firm will not be conducting operations at those levels.

Often fixed costs are only fixed within some limited range of activity. For example, if a firm's production level increases, it may be necessary to hire another maintenance employee to keep the machines in good repair and adjustment. This increase in cost occurs at a predictable volume level. This type of cost is said to have a step function, i.e., the fixed cost steps up to a higher level at some known point. Often one level of the function or another can be determined to be the relevant range of production activity.

For example, management policy determines a degree of cleanliness for a factory, and this degree determines the number of custodial staff that will be retained to perform the clean-up tasks. Company policy determines the amount of property insurance that will be carried, and that amount determines the fixed insurance expense. The amounts of advertising, training and research are all determined at the discretion of management. Although these are normally considered to be fixed costs, they may be increased to a higher (fixed) level as production increases or reduced to a lower (fixed) level as production decreases. Thus, they are step costs. In order to determine the cost behavior for these types of costs, management policy must be made known to the accountant who schedules the cost.

A committed fixed cost results from the longer-term impact of a prior management decision. For example, a decision to build or buy a building or machinery (or large-scale computer) results in increased depreciation, property taxes and insurance for several years to come.

7. **Analyze cost behavior with three methods—visual fit of a scatter diagram, high-low, and linear regression.**

Three methods of separating mixed costs into their fixed and variable parts are described in Chapter 5. They are the high-low method, scatter diagram and linear regression analysis.

High-low. High low is generally considered the simplest but also the least accurate method. From the manufacturing cost ledger the high point of cost and activity for the year is chosen along with the low point. (If these points are not considered to be representative of the year, the second highest and second lowest points may be selected instead.)

The following formula and technique are employed:

$$\text{variable cost rate} = \frac{\text{high point cost - low point cost}}{\text{high point activity - low point activity}}$$

High point cost - (variable cost rate x high point activity) = fixed cost

Example: Sheri Fabricating Company of LaFayette had $3,600 in cost for lubricants in May, its highest activity month, when 21,500 direct labor hours were employed. During August, its lowest activity month, $2,484 was the lubricant cost for 12,200 direct labor hours. Using the formulas above, the fixed and variable components of the lubricant cost are:

$$\frac{\$3,600 - \$2,484}{21,500 \text{ DLH} - 12,200 \text{ DLH}} = \frac{\$1,116}{9,300 \text{ DLH}} = \$0.12/\text{DLH}$$

$3,600 - ($0.12 x 21,500) = $3,600-$2580 = $1,020 Fixed cost per month

Scatter Diagram. Scatter diagram is a method that employs more pairs of data than the high-low method. This technique involves the plotting of points on a two-dimensional graph for the data set. Then, using the points plotted, a best-fit straight line is drawn through the points with the objective of minimizing the sum of the plus-and minus-differences from the points to the drawn line. Where this line intersects the vertical axis of the graph is representative of the fixed cost component. The slope of the line is representative of the variable cost coefficient.

Referring to Figure 5-1, it appears that the drawn line crosses the verticle (y) axis at point 1,000.

	Direct Labor Hours	Cost
	x	y
JAN	19,900	$3,400
FEB	18,200	3,100
MAR	19,800	3,570
APR	20,700	3,380
MAY	21,500	3,600
JUN	20,250	3,550
JUL	17,700	3,220
AUG	12,200	2,484
SEPT	15,750	3,050
OCT	16,300	2,930
NOV	17,800	3,150
DEC	18,100	3,180

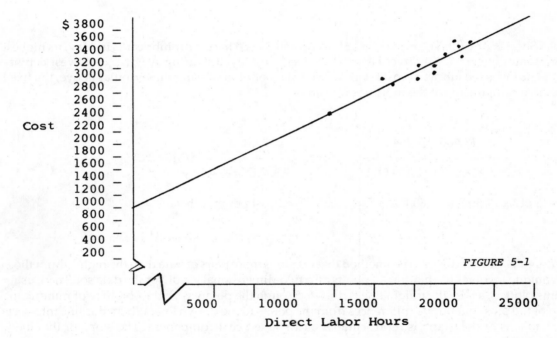

FIGURE 5-1

Regression Analysis. Regression analysis is a mathematical technique for doing what the scatter diagram does. Instead of plotting the points on a visual graph, the regression formulas compute the a and b values of the cost function—with greater accuracy than can be accomplished with free-hand graphics discussed in review items 3 and 4 above:

$$y = a + bx$$

The two equations presented by Prof. Helmkamp and the following table of values result in the a and b values shown below:

```
                   SHERI FABRICATING COMPANY
               REGRESSION ANALYSIS--LUBRICANT COST

                DIRECT
                LABOR   LUBRICANT
                HOURS    COST
      MONTH       X        Y          XY           X SQ
      JAN       19,900   3,400   67,660,000    396,010,000
      FEB       18,200   3,100   56,420,000    331,240,000
      MAR       19,800   3,570   70,686,000    392,040,000
      APR       20,700   3,380   69,966,000    428,490,000
      MAY       21,500   3,600   77,400,000    462,250,000
      JUN       20,250   3,550   71,887,500    410,062,500
      JUL       17,700   3,220   56,994,000    313,290,000
      AUG       12,200   2,484   30,304,800    148,840,000
      SEP       15,750   3,050   48,037,500    248,062,500
      OCT       16,300   2,930   47,759,000    265,690,000
      NOV       17,800   3,150   56,070,000    316,840,000
      DEC       18,100   3,180   57,558,000    327,610,000
      SUM      218,200  38,614  710,742,800  4,040,425,000

      b =     0.118255
      a =     1067.553
```

$$b = \frac{n\Sigma xy - (\Sigma x)(\Sigma y)}{n\Sigma x^2 - (\Sigma x)^2}$$

$$a = \Sigma y/x - b(\Sigma x/n)$$

Compare these results with those obtained in the two previous methods.

8. Recognize how variable costing is used for internal reporting.

Using variable costing, one can develop various internal reports by using the variable costs per unit times the number of units produced or sold, and the fixed costs per period of time. For example, see the income statement in item 2 above. Also, suppose a manager wanted to estimate the operating costs for Division 1, which is a producing division with no sales or selling expenses, for the year ending June 30, 1993. Assume the following facts:

Fixed manufacturing costs, $14,500 per month
Fixed administrative costs, 9,500 per month
Variable manufacturing costs, $2.90 per unit manufactured
Estimated production volume, 320,000 units

Estimated Operating Costs
Year Ending June 30, 1993

Variable cost of good manufactured		
(320,000 x $2.90)	$	928,000
Fixed manufacturing costs		
($14,500 x 12)		174,000
Fixed administrative costs		
($9,500 x 12)		114,000
Total operating costs	$	1,216,000

9. Reconcile the difference between variable costing net income and absorption costing net income.

The following is a variable costing income statement, showing proper format and content:

Haried Manufacturing Company
Variable Costing Income Statement
For the Year Ended December 31, 1991

			% of Sales
Sales[1]	$	1,575,000	100.0%
Cost of goods sold[2]		525,000	33.3
Manufacturing margin		1,050,000	66.7
Variable selling and administrative exp.[3]		105,000	6.7
Contribution margin		945,000	60.0
Fixed costs:			
Manufacturing		560,000	35.6
Selling and administrative		225,000	14.3
Total		785,000	49.8
Net income	$	160,000	10.2%

[1]150,000 units @ 10.50

[2]			
Units produced	160,000	@ 3.50 =	$560,000
Ending inventory	10,000	@ 3.50 =	35,000
Cost of good sold	150,000	@ 3.50 =	$525,000

[3]150,000 units @ $0.70

If the Haried income statement were prepared using the absorption costing technique, it would have the following contents:

Sales	$	1,575,000
Cost of goods sold[1]		1,050,000
Gross profit		525,000
Selling and administrative expenses[2]		330,000
Net income	$	195,000

The difference in net income between the absorption costing method, above ($195,000) and the variable costing method (previous example) ($160,000) is $35,000. This is accounted for as the increased inventory of 10,000 units times the fixed manufacturing cost per unit of $3.50.

[1]Units produced	160,000 @ 7.00 ($3.50 variable + $3.50 fixed) =	$1,120,000
Ending inventory	-10,000 @ 7.00	- 70,000
Cost of good sold	150,000 @ 7.00	$1,050,000

[2]150,000 units @ $2.20

10. **Discuss the benefits and limitations of variable costing.**

The major benefits of variable costing are that it:

a.   Reports net income that is directly related to the volume of sales and is unaffected by inventory fluctuations;

b.   Forces management to consider the behavior of costs;

c.   Provides useful information for cost-volume-profit analysis;

d.   Emphasizes fixed costs by displaying all fixed costs together after contribution margin;

e.   Provides flexible budget data; and

f.   Provides useful management decision-making information.

The major limitations of variable costing are that:

a.   The behavior of some costs is difficult to discern;

b.   This method of accounting is unacceptable for income tax purposes and financial statement reporting;

c.   It results in understated balance sheet costs for inventory, and consequently current assets; and

d.   By ignoring fixed costs in inventory may give an erroneous concept of inventory for pricing purposes.

MATCHING ATTRIBUTES

Below in Group A are listed attributes that may be identified with cost behavior terms listed in Group B. Indicate, by use of the identifying letter of the appropriate Group B item, which description in Group A best matches which Group B term.

Group A

_____ 1. Income statement not acceptable for financial reporting purposes.

_____ 2. Costs change in total amount according to certain patterns.

_____ 3. A future-oriented income statement.

_____ 4. Cost that changes with volume, but also has a fixed element.

_____ 5. Calculated by deducting variable costs from revenues.

_____ 6. Mathematical method of separating the fixed and variable cost elements from a semi-variable cost.

_____ 7. Some variable costs, such as labor, cannot be purchased in small divisible units and have a somewhat different pattern.

_____ 8. Graphic, free hand, technique for separating fixed and variable cost elements from a semi-variable cost.

_____ 9. Measures direction and strength of relationship between two variables such as cost and activity.

_____ 10. Conventional income statement, classifying costs by business purposes.

_____ 11. Inventory fluctuations result in net income fluctuations.

_____ 12. Activity spread in which the firm expects to operate.

_____ 13. Fixed cost that can be changed by management decision.

Group B

A.	Absorption costing	H.	Mixed cost
B.	Contribution margin	I.	Proforma
C.	Correlation coefficient	J.	Relevant range
D.	Cost behavior	K.	Scatter diagram
E.	Discretionary cost	L.	Step function
F.	Functional	M.	Variable costing
G.	High-low		

MULTIPLE CHOICE

For each of the following items choose the most appropriate completion phrase.

1. The income statement of the future

    a. Is usually called a functional statement.

    b. Separates costs according to different behavior categories.

    c. Separates revenues according to different behavior categories.

    d. Is sometimes called a conventional statement.

    e. Subtracts only variable costs from revenue to determine net income.

2. Contribution margin format for an income statement

a. Subtracts only production costs from revenue to compute contribution margin.
b. Subtracts only fixed costs from revenue to compute contribution margin.
c. Subtracts only variable costs from revenue to compute contribution margin.
d. Combines all costs and expenses together.
e. Is used mainly for financial reporting purposes.

3. When determining fixed and variable costs,

a. Fixed costs are primarily administrative in nature.
b. Fixed costs are fixed per unit produced or sold.
c. Fixed and variable costs are separately categorized in most accounting charts of accounts.
d. All costs are either fixed or variable.
e. Some analysis may be necessary to determine whether costs are fixed, variable or mixed.

4. When attempting to determine the behavior of costs,

a. Many costs are curvilinear and cannot be analyzed by conventional means.
b. Many costs are based on the step function, so the least-squares method must be used.
c. If all costs fall within the relevant range, they don't have to be analyzed because they are fixed.
d. Linearity is often assumable within the relevant range.
e. If costs are discretionary, there is no need to analyze them, because they are controlled by management.

5. The step function

a. May apply to both fixed costs and variable costs.
b. Usually has wider steps for variable costs than fixed costs.
c. Is a variable cost concept; true fixed costs don't change.
d. Is a revenue concept, but does not apply to costs.
e. Is another way of expressing a curvilinear cost function.

6. UWR Industries has production levels for its auto bumper business varying from a low of 32,000 direct labor hours (DLH) per month to a high of 45,000 DLH per month. In February, when DLH was 32,000, the cost of indirect manufacturing materials was $8,900. In July, when the high volume was reached, the total indirect materials cost was $11,890. Using the high-low method, what were the fixed and variable components of indirect manufacturing materials cost?

a. No fixed, only variable cost of $0.27 per DLH.
b. It is a fixed cost; there is no variable component.
c. $1,540 fixed, $.23 per DLH, variable.
d. $1,540 fixed, $.26 per DLH, variable.
e. $2,990 fixed, $.27 per DLH, variable.

7. Regarding the three methods for separating mixed costs into variable components described by Professor Helmkamp,

    a.   The advantage of the high-low method is its accuracy and reliability.

    b.   The advantage of the least-squares method is its simplicity and speed of calculation.

    c.   The scatter diagram is the most objective, because it includes more values than the high-low method.

    d.   Many hand-held calculators and many computers permit easy calculation of the least-squares method.

    e.   Only the scatter diagram method permits use of the correlation coefficient for further analysis.

8. The difference in net income between the variable costing income statement presentation and the absorption method

    a.   Is nil if there is no change in the fixed costs in the beginning and ending inventories.

    b.   Is attributable to the variable costs in the inventory.

    c.   Is attributable to the fixed costs in the ending inventory.

    d.   Is attributable to the fixed costs in beginning inventory.

    e.   Is equal to the fixed cost per unit times the number of units sold.

9. Among the limitations of variable costing is:

    a.   Management must evaluate the cost behavior pattern of each cost item.

    b.   Variable costing is mainly an income tax technique.

    c.   Variable costing usually leads to flexible budgeting, an unacceptable concept.

    d.   Variable costing makes management decision making more difficult because fixed costs are set out separately.

    e.   Variable costing understates inventories and current assets.

10. Variable costing offers several benefits. Which of the following is *not* a benefit of variable costing?

    a.   Variable costing may cause lack of concern for full costs in pricing inventories by recording only the variable costs of inventories.

    b.   Variable costing requires management to evaluate cost behavior patterns for each cost item.

    c.   Variable costing provides the basis for flexible budgeting.

    d.   Variable costing assists in management decision-making by providing a separation of fixed and variable costs.

    e.   Cost-volume-profit information is provided directly from the variable costing income statement.

ILLUSTRATIVE PROBLEMS

1. Claudia Wiseley, vice-president of Wiseley Production Co. of Findlay, Ohio, learned at a seminar for executives of the usefulness of variable costing for income statement preparation. Wiseley has always had the conventional (functional) income statement prepared in the past. Following is the latest such statement, without heading:

Sales (100,000 units at $3.60)	$	360,000
Cost of goods sold (100,000 units at $2.40)		240,000
Gross profit		120,000
Operating expenses:		
Selling and administrative		90,000
Net income	$	30,000

Fixed costs included in the above figures are:

Manufacturing overhead	$	100,000
Selling and administrative		60,000

Requested:

Prepare a variable costing income statement for Wiseley Production Co. from the above data. Assume no change in inventories.

Sales   360,000

UC   170,000-

CM   190,000

FC   160,000

NI   30,000

2. Claudia Wiseley would like to analyze the costs of production for Wiseley Production Co. for the year. In order to examine various techniques, she asks you to assist in analyzing the factory maintenance cost using the three methods described in Chapter 5:

a.   High-low

b.   Scatter diagram, and

c.   Least-squares method.

The following data are applicable to this cost. (Hint: Use the column space to the right for development of the additional columns needed for the least-squares method.)

	Direct Labor Hours	Maintenance Cost
October, 1991	21,500	$ 9,900
November	23,200	10,650
December	20,900	9,700
January, 1992	24,200	11,000
February	19,500	9,450
March	21,400	10,200
April	18,700	8,900
May	18,300	9,200
June	18,000	9,200
July	14,600	9,600
August	12,500	8,500
September	18,500	9,400
Totals	231,300	$ 115,700

$$24,200 \qquad 11,000$$
$$\underline{12,500} \qquad \underline{8500}$$
$$11,700 \qquad 2500$$

$$\frac{2500}{11,700} = .21$$

$$11,000 - (24,200 \times .21)$$
$$5082 = 5918.00$$

3. Greensboro Company has the following costs applicable to its Tampa production facility.

	Operating Costs	
	Per Unit	Per Month
Materials	$ 0.77	
Direct labor	0.58	
Manufacturing overhead	1.42	$ 12,500
Administrative	0.21	9,600
Selling expenses	0.46	6,300

Administrative and selling per unit costs are calculated on a unit-sold basis; other per unit costs relate to units produced.

Per-unit costs are fixed in the 80,000-100,000 units per month range.

Requested:

Using two adjacent amount columns prepare income statements for March and April 1992 for Greensboro Company, employing the variable costing approach, assuming the following sales and production data. There were no March 1 inventories on hand. Sales price per unit is $6.25.

	March	April
Units produced	100,000	80,000
Units sold	80,000	100,000

Greensboro Company
Variable Costing Income Statement
Months of March and April, 1992

	March	April
Sales $(6.25 \times 80,000 -)$ $(6.25 \times 100,000)$	500,000	625000 —

4. Referring to the Greensboro Company in Problem 3 above, prepare additional income statements for March and April employing the absorption costing approach. Expected annual production is 1,200,000 units.

Greensboro Company
Absorption Costing Income Statement
Months of March and April, 1992

	March	April

5. Referring to Illustrative Problems 3 and 4 above, reconcile the difference in the net income amounts in March and April resulting from using the two different approaches.

VOCABULARY

ABSORPTION (FULL) COSTING. The inventory valuation method required for a manufacturing firm by generally accepted accounting principles and the tax law in which all manufacturing costs are inventoried, regardless of their cost behavior.

COMMITTED FIXED COSTS. Fixed costs that are required even if the operation has extremely low activity.

CONTRIBUTION MARGIN. Sales revenue less all variable costs (manufacturing, selling, and administrative).

CONTRIBUTION MARGIN RATE. The contribution margin divided by the related sales revenue.

CORRELATION COEFFICIENT. A statistic available with linear regression analysis that measures the strength and direction of the relationship between two variables such as cost and production volume.

COST BEHAVIOR ANALYSIS. The evaluation of how a cost responds to changes in the level of business activity.

COST FUNCTION. The relationship between a cost as a dependent variable and some measure of the level of activity as an independent variable.

CURVILINEAR COSTS. Cost functions with slopes that are not constant over all levels of activity.

DISCRETIONARY FIXED COSTS. Fixed costs that can be reduced or discontinued by management if adequate time is available.

HIGH-LOW METHOD. A cost behavioral analysis technique based on the changes in costs and levels of activity between the highest and lowest levels of activity.

LEAST-SQUARES METHOD. The mathematical technique underlying linear regression analysis.

LINEARITY ASSUMPTION. The assumption used in managerial accounting to reduce nonlinear cost functions to linear cost functions.

LINEAR REGRESSION ANALYSIS. A statistical technique used to mathematically determine the line that best fits a scatter of data points.

MANUFACTURING MARGIN. Sales revenue less the variable cost of goods sold.

MANUFACTURING MARGIN RATE. The manufacturing margin divided by the related sales revenue.

MIXED COST. A cost that has both a variable component and a fixed component (sometimes called a semi-variable cost).

PRO FORMA INCOME STATEMENT. An income statement projected for a future period.

REGRESSION LINE. The line fit to the scatter of data points in such a way that the sum of the squared deviations between the data points and the line is minimized.

RELEVANT RANGE. The range of activity within which a business expects to operate and incur variable costs with constant slopes as well as fixed costs that are constant in total amount.

STEP-FIXED COSTS. Cost functions that change abruptly after remaining constant over a wide range of activity.

STEP-VARIABLE COSTS. Cost functions that change abruptly after remaining constant over a narrow range of activity.

VARIABLE (DIRECT) COSTING. The inventory valuation method used by a manufacturing firm for internal reporting in which only the variable manufacturing costs are treated as product costs.

VISUAL FIT OF SCATTER DIAGRAM METHOD. A cost behavioral estimation technique with which the analyst draws a straight line through the data points so that the line comes as close to as many points as possible.

THE ANSWERS

MATCHING ATTRIBUTES

1. M	5. B	9. C
2. D	6. G	10. F
3. I	7. L	11. A
4. H	8. K	12. J
		13. E

MULTIPLE CHOICE

1. b	5. a	8. a
2. c	6. c	9. e
3. e	7. d	10. a
4. d		

ILLUSTRATIVE PROBLEMS

1.

Wiseley Production Co.
Variable Income Statement

Sales (100,000 units @ $3.60 per unit)		$ 360,000
Cost of goods sold (@ $1.40 per unit)		140,000
Manufacturing margin		220,000
Variable selling and administrative expense		30,000
Contribution margin		190,000
Fixed costs:		
Manufacturing	$ 100,000	
Selling and administrative	60,000	160,000
Net income		$ 30,000

2.a. High-low method shows the variable cost rate =

$$\frac{2500}{11700} \qquad \frac{11,000 - 8,500}{24,200 - 12,500} = 0.213675$$

Monthly fixed costs = 11,000 - (24,200 x .213675) = $5,829.07

Maintenance cost = $5,829.07 + .213675 x DLH

b.

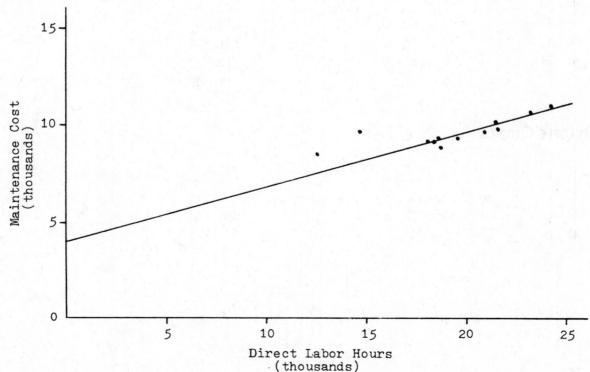

c.

	Direct Labor Hours x	Maintenance Cost y	xy	x^2
October, 1987	21,500	$ 9,900	212,850,000	462,250,000
November	23,200	10,650	247,080,000	538,240,000
December	20,900	9,700	202,730,000	436,810,000
January, 1988	24,200	11,000	266,200,000	585,640,000
February	19,500	9,450	184,275,000	380,250,000
March	21,400	10,200	218,280,000	457,960,000
April	18,700	8,900	166,430,000	349,690,000
May	18,300	9,200	168,360,000	334,890,000
June	18,000	9,200	165,600,000	324,000,000
July	14,600	9,600	140,160,000	213,160,000
August	12,500	8,500	106,250,000	156,250,000
September	18,500	9,400	173,900,000	342,250,000
Totals	231,300	$ 115,700	2,252,115,000	4,581,390,000

$$b = \frac{12(2,252,115,000) - (231,300)(115,700)}{12(4,581,390,000) - (231,300)^2} = 0.178721$$

$$a = \frac{118,100}{12} - 0.178721 x \frac{231,300}{12} = 6396.81$$

Maintenance cost = $6,396.81 + .178721 x DLH.

3.

Greensboro Company
Variable Costing Income Statement
March and April, 1992

		March		April
Sales (@ $6.25 per unit)	$	500,000	$	625,000
Cost of goods sold *		221,600		277,000
Manufacturing margin		278,400		348,000
Variable selling expenses		(36,800)		(46,000)
Variable administrative expenses		(16,800)		(21,000)
Contribution margin		224,800		281,000
Fixed costs:				
Manufacturing		12,500		12,500
Selling		6,300		6,300
Administrative		9,600		9,600
Total fixed costs		28,400		28,400
Net income	$	196,400	$	252,600

*Cost of goods sold:				
Beginning inventory	$	-0-	$	55,400
+ Production costs @$2.77 per unit		277,000		221,600
Inventory available		277,000		277,000
- Ending inventory		55,400		-0-
= Cost of goods sold	$	221,600	$	277,000

4.

Greensboro Company
Absorption Costing Income Statement
March and April, 1992

	March	April
Sales (@ $6.25 per unit)	$ 500,000	$ 625,000
Cost of goods sold*	231,600	292,000
Gross profit	268,400	333,000
Operating expenses:		
Selling**	43,100	52,300
Administrative***	26,400	30,600
Total	69,500	82,900
Net income	$ 198,900	$ 250,100

*Cost of goods sold:

	March	April
Beginning inventory	$ -0-	$ 57,900
+ Production costs:		
100,000 x $2.895	289,500	
80,000 x $2.895		231,600
= Inventory available	289,500	289,500
- Ending inventory	57,900	-0-
+ Underapplied overhead		2,500
= Cost of goods sold	$ 231,600	$ 292,000

**Selling expenses:

	March	April
80,000 x $0.46 + $6,300	$ 43,100	
100,000 x $0.46 + $6,300		$ 52,300

***Administrative expenses:

	March	April
80,000 x $0.21 + $9,600	26,400	
100,000 x $0.21 + $9,600		30,600

5.

	March	April
Variable costing net income	$ 196,400	$ 252,600
Absorption costing net income	198,900	250,100
Difference	$ (2,500)	$ 2,500

The difference of $2,500 is a result of the increased inventory of 20,000 units times the fixed manufacturing cost of $0.125 per unit. This inventory was sold in April, thus offsetting the net income difference that resulted in March.

CHAPTER 6

COST-VOLUME-PROFIT RELATIONSHIPS

In Chapter 6 we will use the tools of Chapter 5 regarding cost behavior and different forms of the income statement to develop some more management decision tools that help plan profit. Isn't that why we are in business?

LEARNING OBJECTIVES

1. Describe the importance of cost-volume-profit (CVP) analysis as a managerial accounting technique.
2. Explain how an income statement with a contribution margin format provides the information needed in CVP analysis.
3. Recognize the limiting assumptions of CVP analysis.
4. Calculate and evaluate a break-even point.
5. Prepare a CVP chart using different formats.
6. Use CVP analysis to plan profits.
7. Realize how managers use the margin of safety as a measure of risk.
8. Evaluate the impact of changes in selling prices, sales volume, sales mix, and costs using "what if" analysis.
9. Perform CVP analysis for a multiproduct firm.
10. Describe the concept of operating leverage as it is used to evaluate the sensitivity of profits to changes in sales volume.

LEARNING TIPS

Workers have complained of the tedium of a particular assembly job in the factory. Because the job is so boring and repetitive, many mistakes are made. Management is considering acquisition of a robot to do the tasks. How would such a decision affect fixed costs? Variable costs? Profit? This chapter is bottom-line oriented, and if you can continually remember how important profit is to management, you'll know why the material in Chapter 6 makes the management accountant so valuable in the organization.

REVIEW

1. **Describe the importance of cost-volume-profit (CVP) analysis as a managerial accounting technique.**

$$\text{Net income (profit)} = \text{revenue} - \text{expenses}$$

is a common, and important, accounting formula. It applies on a firm basis and on a product basis, using variable costing terminology,

$$\text{Margin} = \text{revenue} - \text{variable costs.}$$

Since we're ultimately interested in the bottom line,

$$\text{Net income} = \text{revenue} - \text{fixed costs} - \text{variable costs.}$$

Therefore, the cost of a product, and eventually all costs—product and nonproduct—must be considered to attain one of management's principal goals of a satisfactory income level. Understanding these costs and revenues and how they behave is the essence of cost-volume-profit analysis. These concepts, and the techniques described in this chapter, are crucial to the maximizing of the firm's income.

2. **Explain how an income statement with a contribution margin format provides the information needed in CVP analysis.**

The contribution format income statement consists of the following components:

> Sales
> Variable costs
> Gross margin
> Fixed costs
> Net income

We say that this format emphasizes cost behavior because costs are divided into their two major behavioral categories of the contribution margin income statement are required for a CVP analysis, as seen in the equation

$$\text{Sales} = \text{fixed costs} + \text{variable costs} + \text{net income.}$$

3. **Recognize the limiting assumptions of CVP analysis.**

CVP analysis is based on certain assumptions that constrain the use of the formulas. These assumptions are:

a.   Unit sales prices do not change during the period.
b.   Costs can be separated into the two categories of fixed and variable.
c.   Variable costs vary, in total amount, directly with product volume changes.
d.   Fixed costs do not change in total within the volume range being considered.
e.   Productivity (units of input per unit of output) does not vary during the period.

f. Sales mix remains constant during the period.

g. Variable costing will be used to report the results of operations, *or* product inventories do not change from the beginning to the end of the period.

4. Calculate and evaluate a break-even point.

The Jason Mason Company molds lawn and garden decorative items out of masonry. Their animal line consists of statuary items of approximately the same size, with virtually equal variable and fixed costs and sales price, that is:

Sales price	$	24.95
Variable costs		8.95
Fixed costs per month	$	20,800

We can calculate the break-even point in units per month, as follows:

Sales price	$	24.95
Variable costs		8.95
Contribution	$	16.00

Let S = break-even sales volume:

$$\$24.95S = \$8.95S + \$20,800$$
$$\$16.00S = \$20,800$$
$$S = 1,300 \text{ units or } \$32,435$$

Alternatively,

$$S = .35872S + \$20,800 \left(\text{because } \frac{8.95}{24.95} = .35872 \right)$$
$$.64128S = \$20,800$$
$$S = \$32,435$$

5. Prepare a CVP chart using different formats.

The graphic approach to CVP analysis involves the drawing of a CVP chart. We will use the example of the Jason Mason Company in item 4 above for these charts. Three forms of the CVP chart are presented.

a. The first CVP chart shows dollars (in thousands) on the vertical axis and units (in thousands) on the horizontal axis. Fixed costs are represented by a horizontal line at $20,800, the fixed costs per month. The revenue line begins at zero volume and $0.00 revenue and rises at the rate of $24.95 per unit. Total costs begin at zero volume, but at the dollar level of the fixed costs. That is, variable costs are added on top of fixed costs to represent total costs. Where the revenue line meets the total cost line represents the break-even point.

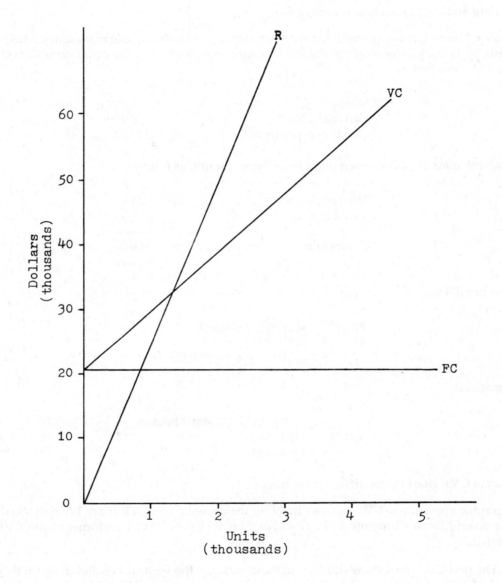

b. An alternative form of the CVP chart has the variable cost line start at zero volume and $0.00 and rising at the rate of $8.95 per unit. Fixed costs are added on top of variable costs, so that the total cost line begins at $20,800 and rises with a line parallel to the variable cost line and equidistance from (above) it. The revenue line again begins at $0.00 and zero units. As in the previous graph, the point where the revenue line crosses the total cost line represents the break-even point.

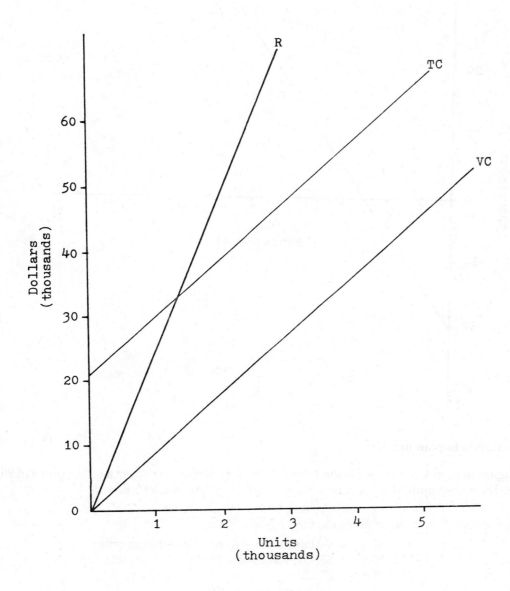

c. The third form of the CVP chart is called the profit-volume chart. On it the focus is on the horizontal line at $0.00 in order to emphasize the point of break-even and to change in profit (loss) on either side of that point. This chart is drawn with a line starting at zero units and dollar loss equal to the fixed costs with that line crossing the zero profit line at the break-even volume, in units. The following drawing represents this form.

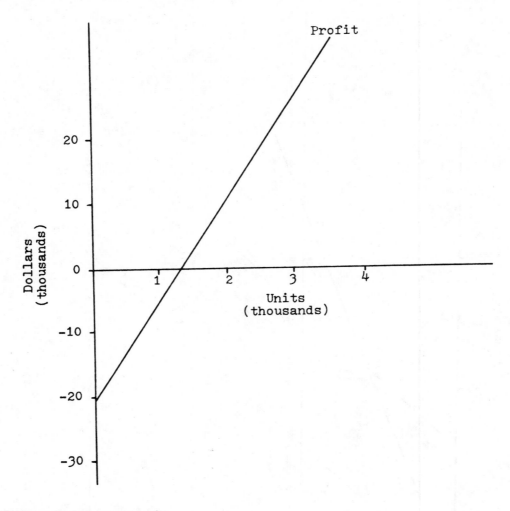

6. Use CVP analysis to plan profits.

Referring again to item 4 above, the Jason Mason Company wishes to project a target profit of $8,000 per month. The sales required to meet this target would be calculated as follows:

Let X = the number of units to produce the target profit. Then,

Sales	= variable costs + fixed costs + target profit
$24.95X	= $8.95X + $20,800 + $8,000
$16.00X	= $28,800
X	= 1,800 units or $44,910

Alternately, let Y = the sales volume required to produce the target profit.

Y	= .35872S + $20,800 + $8,000
.64128Y	= $28,800
Y	= $44,910

CVP formulas may be used to project the required sales for whatever target profit level management may establish.

7. **Realize how managers use the margin of safety as a measure of risk.**

The margin of safety is the gap or difference between the actual (or expected) sales and the break-even sales. In item 4 above, if the Jason Mason Company's actual sales for May 1988 are $37,500 the margin of safety is $37,500 - $32,435 or $5,065. Thus, a sales decline of $5,065 or 13.5% (5,065/37,500) could occur, and the company would still break even. Managers seek a comfortable margin of safety to protect their position.

8. **Evaluate the impact of changes in selling prices, sales volume, sales mix, and costs using "what-if" analysis.**

"What if" analysis answers the question, "What if a certain component of our formula changes; what would be the result?"

Assume the following three products and applicable data for 1989, for the Janowitz Company:

	Per Unit	Phi	Per Unit	Delta	Per Unit	Sigma	Total
Sales (10,000 units)	100	$ 1,000,000	100	$ 1,000,000	100	$ 1,000,000	$ 3,000,000
Variable costs	60	600,000	70	700,000	80	800,000	2,100,000
Fixed costs		250,000		150,000		50,000	450,000
Net income		$ 150,000		$ 150,000		$ 150,000	$ 450,000

a. What if the sales price for each product increases 10% (with no proportional increase in variable costs)?

	Phi	Delta	Sigma
Sales (10,000 units)	$1,100,000	$1,100,000	$1,100,000
Variable costs	600,000	700,000	800,000
Fixed costs	250,000	150,000	50,000
Net income	250,000	250,000	250,000

What if the sales price for each product decreases 10%?

	Phi	Delta	Sigma
Sales (10,000 units)	$900,000	$900,000	$900,000
Variable costs	600,000	700,000	800,000
Fixed costs	250,000	150,000	50,000
Net income	50,000	50,000	50,000

As we can see, equal percentage increases and decreases in selling prices for each product have equal impact on net income, if there is no corresponding change in variable costs, i.e., variable costs remain the same per unit.

b.   The results of 10% sales *volume* increase for each product provide the following results:

	Phi	Delta	Sigma
Sales (11,000 units)	$1,100,000	$1,100,000	$1,100,000
Variable costs	660,000	770,000	880,000
Fixed costs	250,000	150,000	50,000
Net income	190,000	180,000	170,000

The results of 10% sales volume decreases for each product provide the following results:

	Phi	Delta	Sigma
Sales (9,000 units)	$900,000	$900,000	$900,000
Variable costs	540,000	630,000	720,000
Fixed costs	250,000	150,000	50,000
Net income	110,000	120,000	130,000

Whereas, in a. above equal percentage increases and decreases in the sales *price* result in equal dollar impact on net income, in this instance, with equal percentage increases and decreases in sales *volume* the impact on net income is not at all equal. Notice that the ranking of the net incomes for the products reverses between volume increases and volume decreases. (Phi has the highest net income when the volume increases and the lowest net income when volume decreases.)

c.   What if the Janowitz Company's sales mix changes? Suppose the total sales volume of 30,000 units remains the same, but the product volumes are Phi, 13,000; Delta, 12,000; Sigma, 5,000. The following results would occur:

	Phi	Delta	Sigma	Total
Sales units	13,000	12,000	5,000	30,000
Sales	$1,300,000	$1,200,000	$500,000	$3,000,000
Variable costs	780,000	840,000	400,000	2,020,000
Fixed costs	250,000	150,000	50,000	450,000
Net income	270,000	210,000	50,000	530,000

As an alternative, what if the sales mix changed to Phi, 8000; Delta, 9,000; Sigma, 13,000?

	Phi	Delta	Sigma	Total
Sales units	8,000	9,000	13,000	30,000
Sales	$800,000	$900,000	$1,300,000	$3,000,000
Variable costs	480,000	630,000	1,040,000	2,150,000
Fixed costs	250,000	150,000	50,000	450,000
Net income	70,000	120,000	210,000	400,000

Sales mix changes improve total net income if the high contribution margin products' sales increase. The contribution margin, per unit, of each product is as follows:

	Phi	Delta	Sigma
Sales price	$ 100.00	$ 100.00	$ 100.00
Variable costs	60.00	70.00	80.00
Contribution margin	$ 40.00	$ 30.00	$ 20.00

Sales mix changes in favor of Phi and Delta over Sigma will increase overall company profitability. Sales mix changes in favor of Sigma over Phi and Delta reduces overall company profits.

d. What if the fixed costs of the company were allocated to each product evenly? Overall profitability would not change, but the computed profits for each product would change, as follows: (The following data are the original values, except for the even allocation of the $450,000 of fixed costs.)

	Per Unit	Phi	Per Unit	Delta	Per Unit	Sigma	Total
Sales (10,000 units)	100	$ 1,000,000	100	$ 1,000,000	100	$ 1,000,000	$ 3,000,000
Variable costs	60	600,000	70	700,000	80	800,000	2,100,000
Fixed costs		150,000		150,000		150,000	450,000
Net income		$ 250,000		$ 150,000		$ 50,000	$ 450,000

9. Perform CVP analysis for a multiproduct firm.

Muskogee Muskrat Company produces water sports equipment. In its Sands Springs plant two models of a motorized water ski are manufactured. The following data apply:

	Baby Bob	**Big Betty**
Selling price	$600.00	$840.00
Variable costs	240.00	280.00

James Dowgray, general manager, in preparing a forecast for next year, wants to know how many units of each must be sold in order to produce an operating income of $120,000. Fixed costs are expected to be $388,400, and the sales ratio of 3 Baby Bobs to each Big Betty is expected to remain constant for the year.

Solution

1. Calculate contribution margin for each product.

   Contribution margin = selling price - variable costs.
   Baby Bob contribution margin = $600 - $240 = $360
   Big Betty contribution margin = $840 - $280 = $560

2. Compute weighted-average contribution per unit. Since there are three Baby Bobs sold for each Big Betty, the sales ratio is 3:1 or 75% Baby Bobs and 25% Big Bettys. Therefore, the weighted-average contribution margin per unit is:

$$.75\ (\$360) + .25\ (\$560) = \$270 + \$140 = \$410$$

3. Compute target sales volume to cover fixed costs of $388,400 and income of $120,000.

$$S = \text{Sales target}$$

$$S = \frac{\text{Fixed costs + target profit}}{\text{Weighted-average contribution margin}}$$

$$S = \frac{\$388,400 + \$120,000}{\$410}$$

$$S = 1,240 \text{ units}$$

The projected income statement for the budget year is:

	Baby Bob	Big Betty	Total
Sales—units	930	310	1,240
Sales—dollars	$558,000	$260,400	$818,400
Variable costs	223,200	86,800	310,000
Contribution margin	334,800	173,600	508,400
Fixed costs			388,400
Net income			$120,000

10. **Describe the concept of operating leverage as it is used to evaluate the sensitivity of profits to changes in sales volume.**

Operating leverage is a term that describes a firm's sensitivity of profit to changes in sales volume. Here are the Hollis and Altus companies' cost-revenue structures:

	Hollis Company		Altus Company	
	Amount	%	Amount	%
Sales	$200,000	100	$200,000	100
Variable costs	120,000	60	100,000	50
Contribution margin	80,000	40	100,000	50
Fixed costs	50,000	25	70,000	35
Net income	30,000	15	30,000	15

To determine the sensitivity to sales changes for each company, assume (a) a sales increase of $20,000 and (b) a sales decrease of $20,000 for each company.

a. Sales increase of $20,000 for each company:

	Increase in sales	x	Contribution margin	=	Increase in profits
Hollis Company	$20,000	x	.40	=	$8,000
Altus Company	$20,000	x	.50	=	$10,000

Because of Altus Company's higher fixed costs and higher contribution margin, a $20,000 sales increase has a greater impact on net income than does the same dollar increase for Hollis Company.

b. Sales decrease of $20,000 for each company:

	Increase in sales	x	Contribution margin	=	Decrease in profits
Hollis Company	$20,000	x	.40	=	$8,000
Altus Company	$20,000	x	.50	=	$10,000

The break-even sales volume for each company is computed as follows:

		Fixed costs	/	Contribution margin %	=	Break-even sales
Hollis Company	=	$50,000		.40	=	$125,000
Altus Company	=	$70,000		.50	=	$140,000

This example illustrates that the firm with the higher fixed costs and higher contribution margin percentage has a higher break-even sales point than a firm with lower fixed costs and lower contribution margin percentage. The former firm's net income is more sensitive to sales volume changes than is the latter firm.

MATCHING ATTRIBUTES

Below in Group A are listed attributes that may be identified with the cost-volume-profit terms in Group B. Indicate, by use of the identifying letter of the appropriate Group B item, which attribute best matches which Group B term.

Group A

_____ 1. A measure of the extent fixed costs are utilized.

_____ 2. Measure of changes in net income to changes in sales volume.

_____ 3. Sales volume at which no net income exists.

_____ 4. The ratio of sales of a product times that product's contribution margin added to each other product's ratio of sales times its respective contribution margin.

_____ 5. The combination of a company's products constituting its total sales for a period of time.

_____ 6. An operating proposal to achieve a certain income target.

_____ 7. Sales revenues minus variable costs.

_____ 8. A graphical analysis depicting the break-even point and areas of profit, and fixed and variable costs.

_____ 9. Actual (or expected) sales for a period minus break-even sales.

_____ 10. Sales volume that produces the desired net income.

Group B

A. Break-even sales	F. Profit plan
B. Contribution margin	G. Profit sensitivity
C. CVP chart	H. Sales mix
D. Margin of safety	I. Sales target
E. Operating leverage	J. Weighted-average contribution margin

MULTIPLE CHOICE

For each of the following items, choose the most appropriate completion phrase.

1. Professor Helmkamp addresses certain assumptions that are necessary for cost-volume-profit analysis. Which one of the following is *not* a correct CVP assumption?

   a. Unit sales prices remain constant throughout the period.
   b. Fixed costs remain constant (within the relevant activity range).
   c. Efficiency remains constant.
   d. Sales mix remains constant, if more than one product is sold.
   e. Volume of sales remains constant during the period.

2. Cost-volume-profit analysis can help plan a firm's profit performance by looking at alternative sales prices, volume, sales mix and costs. Which one of the following questions would normally not be answered by CVP analysis?

   a. What is the most profitable sales mix?
   b. How will profits change if advertising expenses are increased by $20,000?
   c. How much additional plant capacity should be acquired if a 15% return on investment is required?
   d. How does break-even point change if fixed costs of $150,000 replace variable costs of 20% of sales price?
   e. How does a 10% increase (or decrease) in sales price affect net income?

3. CVP analysis requires that certain data be available,

   a. As filed on the corporate income tax return.
   b. As it appears in the company's contribution margin income statement.
   c. As it appears in the financial statements distributed to stockholders.
   d. As it is found in the personnel records.
   e. As it is found in sales records.

4. The McNamara Company manufacturers women's golf clubs sold only in full sets and named after the famed woman golfer, Nancy Lopez. The Lopez clubs sell for $480 per set. Costs are as follows:

Variable costs:
        Sales and distribution   20% of sales price
        Production   17.5% of sales price
Fixed costs:
        Production $150,000 per year

How many dollars of sales of Lopez clubs must be attained each year for the company to break even?

  a. $ 150,000
  b. $ 400,000
  c. $ 750,000
  d. $ 93,750
  e. $ 240,000

5. Referring to problem 4 above, how many sets of Lopez clubs must be sold to show a profit of $60,000?

  a.   88
  b.   700
  c.   1,167
  d.   200
  e.   625

6. Using the CVP graph below, identify the total fixed costs:

  a.   Line segment OA
  b.   Line segment AC
  c.   Line segment PC
  d.   Line segment OB
  e.   Point P

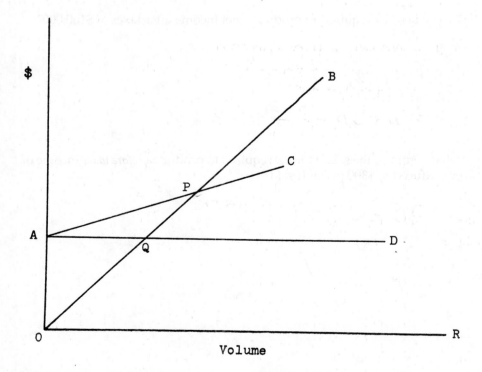

7. Referring to the CVP graph in problem 6 above, identify the loss area.

    a.   Area OADR
    b.   Area PBC
    c.   Area OAQ
    d.   Area OAP
    e.   Area BQD

8. Your company president, Raymond Buchanan, wants you to explain to him the meaning of the CVP term, margin of safety. Margin of safety can best be described as:

    a.   The difference between selling price and variable costs per unit.
    b.   The difference between total sales and total costs at the break-even point.
    c.   The difference between projected sales and break-even sales.
    d.   The difference between total sales and fixed costs for the period.
    e.   The difference between projected sales and projected costs.

9. Sally Delavan of Rock, Michigan makes religious vestments and sells them by mail. Her budgeted income statement for 1993 is:

Sales (1,000 units @360)	$	360,000
Variable costs (1,000 units at $144)		144,000
Contribution margin	$	216,000
Fixed costs		90,000
Net income, before taxes		126,000
Income tax (20%)		25,200
Net income	$	100,800

What sales volume (in dollars) would be required to produce a net income after taxes of $160,000?

    a. $416,667
    b. $483,333
    c. $250,000
    d. $625,000
    e. $419,200

$$.60 = 90,000 + 160,000/.80$$
$$.60 = 90,000 + 200000$$
$$.60 = 290,000$$
$$= 483333.33$$

10. Referring to item 9 above, what would be the sales volume required to produce a *before taxes* income of $100,000 if selling price were reduced to $300 per unit sold?

    a. $190,000
    b. $475,000
    c. $316,667
    d. $300,000
    e. $365,385

$$.60 = 90,000 + 100,000$$
$$.60 = 190,000$$
$$= 316,667.$$

11. Referring to item 9 above, what sales volume would be required to break even if total fixed costs were increased to $120,000?

    a. $242,000

    b. $200,000

    c. $300,000

    d. $350,000

    e. $420,000

$$\frac{120,000}{.60} = 200,000$$

ILLUSTRATIVE PROBLEMS

The Bloomington Barrel Company produces barrels for storage of wines. The current price and cost structure is:

Selling price	$ 100.00
Variable costs	50.00
Fixed costs per year	$ 75,000.00
Corporate income tax rate	30%

Fred Bloomberg, sales vice president, is worried about sales because of competitive containers making larger and larger inroads into the market. He believes the selling price must be reduced to $80 per barrel. Variable costs could be cut to $32 by installing new equipment that would add $66,000 to fixed costs.

1. Compute the current break-even point.

$$\frac{\begin{array}{c}100\\50\end{array}}{50} = 50\%$$

$$\frac{75000.}{50\%} = 150,000$$

2. Compute the break-even point under the new proposal.

$$\frac{\begin{array}{c}80\\32\end{array}}{48} = 60\%$$

$$\begin{array}{r}75,000\\66,000\\\hline 141,000\end{array}$$

$$\frac{141,000}{60\%} = 235,000$$

3. Compute the required sales volume to produce an *after tax* income of $42,000, assuming the proposed changes are made.

$$.60 = 141,000 + 42,000/.7-$$

$$.60 = 141,000 + 60,000$$

$$.60 = 201,000.^{00}$$

$$= 335,000$$

4. Draw CVP charts for situation 2 above, using the three methods described in this study guide.

5. Referring to item 1 above, compute the margin of safety if the sales volume is $180,000.

6. Sherri Stiver is the new accountant hired by Amerada Company which has two divisions, Austin and Ames. Their cost- revenue structures are:

	Austin Co.	Ames Co.
Sales	$ 400,000	$ 400,000
Variable costs	140,000 35%	180,000 .45
Fixed costs	180,000	140,000
Net income	80,000	80,000

The company controller has asked Ms. Stiver to determine each division's sensitivity to changes in sales volume.

Requested

Prepare schedules to show:

a.   The effect on each of the two divisions' net income of an increase of $50,000 in sales, assuming no change in fixed costs and the variable cost percentage remains constant.

b.   The effect on each of the two divisions' net income of a decrease of $50,000 in sales, with the same assumptions as in a.

c. Break-even points for each division.

VOCABULARY

BREAK-EVEN EQUATION. Mathematical expression used to compute a break-even point.

BREAK-EVEN POINT. The sales volume at which revenue and total costs are equal, with no net income or loss.

CONTRIBUTION MARGIN APPROACH TO BREAK-EVEN ANALYSIS. An alternative method used to calculate break-even sales by dividing fixed costs by the contribution margin per unit or percentage.

COST-VOLUME-PROFIT (CVP) ANALYSIS. A managerial accounting technique used to evaluate how costs and profits are affected by changes in the level of business activity.

COST-VOLUME-PROFIT CHART. A graphic display of the break-even point and the net income or loss for a range of activity.

MARGIN OF SAFETY. The amount by which sales can decrease before a loss results.

OPERATING LEVERAGE. A measure of how much profits respond to changes in sales volume.

PROFIT-VOLUME CHART. A graphic display showing how profit changes in relation to volume.

TARGET NET INCOME. A profit goal expressed as a fixed or variable amount that is included in CVP analysis to determine the sales level necessary to earn that amount of net income.

SALES MIX. The relative quantities of each product sold by a multi product firm.

WEIGHTED-AVERAGE CONTRIBUTION MARGIN. The overall contribution margin based on the contribution margins of the individual products weighted by their relative quantities.

"WHAT IF" ANALYSIS. Use of CVP analysis to evaluate the effect of changes in selling price, sales volume, sales mix, or costs.

THE ANSWERS

MATCHING ATTRIBUTES

1. G
2. E
3. A
4. J

5. H
6. F
7. B

8. C
9. D
10. I

MULTIPLE CHOICE

1. e
2. c
3. b
4. e

5. b
6. a
7. d
8. c

9. b
10. e
11. b

ILLUSTRATIVE PROBLEMS

1. Current break-even point. (Income taxes are always zero at the break-even point.)

   Variable costs are 50% of sales price.

$$
\begin{aligned}
\text{Let } S &= \text{break-even sales} \\
S &= \text{variable costs} + \text{fixed costs} \\
S &= .5S + \$75{,}000 \\
.5S &= \$75{,}000 \\
S &= \$150{,}000
\end{aligned}
$$

2. The proposed changes would result in variable costs of $32 or 40% of the new sales price of $80.

$$
\begin{aligned}
S &= .40S + \$75{,}000 + \$66{,}000 \\
.6S &= \$141{,}000 \\
S &= \$235{,}000
\end{aligned}
$$

3. If the proposed changes are made, the sales volume necessary to produce a $42,000 *after tax* net income would be:

$$
\begin{aligned}
\text{Let } S &= \text{Sales required for \$42,000 after tax income} \\
S &= \text{Variable costs} + \text{fixed costs} + \text{after-tax income} \\
S &= .4S + \$141{,}000 + (\$42{,}000 / (1-.30)) \\
.6S &= \$141{,}000 + \$42{,}000 / .7 = \$201{,}000 \\
S &= \$335{,}000
\end{aligned}
$$

4.

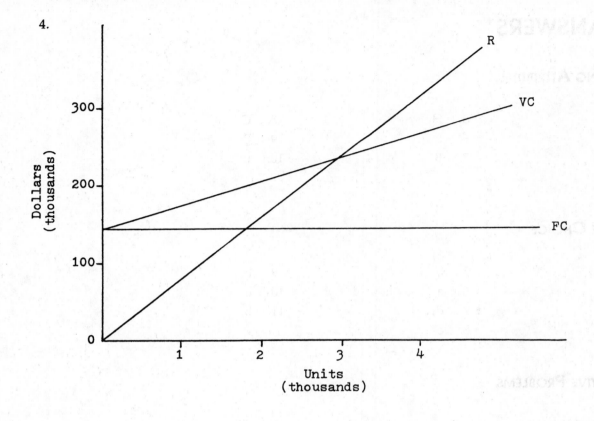

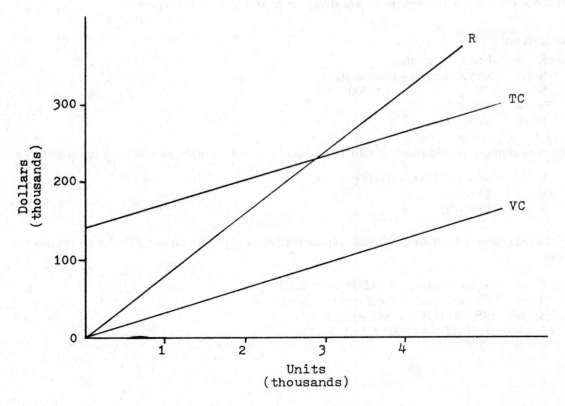

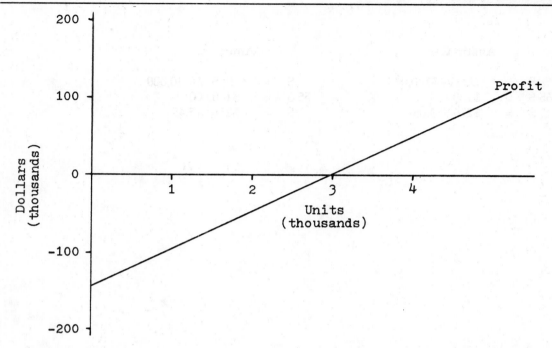

5. The margin of safety is the sales minus the break-even point, or $180,000 - $150,000 = $30,000. The margin of safety may also be expressed as a percentage of sales. In this case, it would be

$$\frac{\$30,000}{\$180,000} = 16.67\%$$

6a.

		Austin Co.		Ames Co.
Sales		$ 450,000	$	450,000
Variable costs				
$450,000 x .35		157,500		
$450,000 x .45				202,500
		———————		———————
Contribution margin		292,500		247,500
Fixed costs		180,000		140,000
		———————		———————
Net income		$ 112,500	$	107,500
		========		========

b.

Sales		$ 350,000	$	350,000
Variable costs				
$350,000 x .35		122,500		
$350,000 x .45				157,500
		———————		———————
Contribution margin		227,500		192,500
Fixed costs		180,000		140,000
		———————		———————
Net income		$ 47,500	$	52,500
		========		========

c.

	Austin Co.			Ames Co.	
S	=	.35 S + $180,000	S	=	.45 S + $140,000
.65 S	=	$180,000	.55 S	=	$140,000
S	=	$276,923.08	S	=	$254,545.45

CHAPTER 7

DECISION MAKING BASED ON RELEVANT INFORMATION

In this chapter, it helps to think like a manager. Managers are responsible for a lot of decision making. It has been said that a successful manager is one who makes more right decisions than wrong decisions.

What makes the difference between making correct and incorrect decisions? Well, it's good judgment, to be sure. Most managers know, though, that their correctness in decision making improves dramatically if they have good information. Good decisions are seldom made without it. And much of that information comes from the accountants.

It is very important that *that* information be relevant to the decision. Therefore, the accountant enters into the decision-making process by providing relevant information to management. Now, let's look at specific examples of that relevant information needed by managers.

LEARNING OBJECTIVES

1. Describe how the managerial decision-making process works and identify the relevant managerial accounting information required for good decisions.
2. Explain what is meant by differential analysis.
3. Describe how relevant costs (revenues), differential costs (revenues), unavoidable costs, sunk costs, and opportunity costs are used in decision making.
4. Evaluate a special order pricing situation.
5. Evaluate the addition or deletion of products.
6. Evaluate a make or buy decision.
7. Distinguish between the treatment of joint product costs for inventory valuation and for decision-making purposes.
8. Evaluate the replacement of equipment.
9. Recognize how product mix decisions should be made when a firm's scarce resources and other constraints are considered.
10. Explain and compare market demand-oriented pricing and cost-oriented pricing.
11. Understand three cost-oriented pricing methods: markup pricing, cost plus target income pricing, and target return on investment pricing.
12. Describe the basic legal implications of pricing decisions.

LEARNING TIPS

This chapter shows us how accounting information is used in various crucial management decisions. These decisions include:

    a.   Special sales order situations,

    b.   Add or delete a product (or product line),

    c.   Make-or-buy products,

    d.   Equipment replacement,

    e.   Product mix, and

    f.   Pricing.

This is a pretty jam-packed chapter. You may want to get a head start to get an understanding of these new techniques so you can be part of the management process.

REVIEW

1. **Describe how the managerial decision-making process works and identify the relevant managerial accounting information required for good decisions.**

Decision making is a process of choosing among alternatives. In business, decision making is often based on the highest-profit or lowest-cost alternative. Both quantitative and qualitative factors must be considered. The decision process usually involves four steps:

    a.   Define the problem to be solved (or the objective to be accomplished).

    b.   Determine the various alternatives.

    c.   Acquire and evaluate information which relates to the decision.

    d.   Make the decision.

2. **Explain what is meant by differential analysis.**

Differential analysis determines the effects of a particular course of action on revenues and costs. In other words, what difference does a decision make on those revenues and costs?

3. **Describe how relevant costs (revenues), differential costs (revenues), unavoidable costs, sunk costs, and opportunity costs are used in decision making.**

Relevant costs are those costs that change as the result of a decision or course of action. Similarly, relevant revenues are those revenues that change as the result of a decision or course of action. These are always future-oriented, since decisions cannot affect the past. A business person who plans to make a decision wants to know how this decision will change future costs and revenues. Managerial accounting provides means to answer those questions.

Differential costs are the differences between the relevant costs under two or more alternatives. Differential revenues are the differences between the relevant revenues under two or more alternatives.

Unavoidable costs are those costs that *must* be incurred, so they do not fit into the decision process. Similarly, sunk costs are not considered in a decision, because they are past costs that cannot be changed or recooped.

An opportunity cost is the benefit given up from one opportunity to accept another. For example, the opportunity cost involved with going to a football game might be the lost fun of going to a fraternity party that same evening. The opportunity cost connected with investing in common stocks might be the interest that could have been earned from investing in utility bonds with that same money.

4. **Evaluate a special order pricing situation.**

The Brite Spot Cookery manufactures a standard set of aluminum alloy cookware. The plant has been approached by a church group that wishes to purchase 10,000 sets for a special, lower-income home cooking assistance program for people who live outside the company's present marketing area. Proposed price on these sets is $40.00. No additional sales or administrative costs would be required for this order, but fixed production costs would increase $30,000 because of the hiring and training cost for additional labor. Differential analysis reveals the following:

The Brite Spot Cookery
Differential Analysis of Special Order

	With Church Order	Without Church Order	Differential Analysis
Sales:			
120,000 sets @ $55	$ 6,600,000	$ 6,600,000	
10,000 sets @ $40	400,000		$ 400,000
Variable costs:			
120,000 sets @ $18.50	2,200,000	2,200,000	
10,000 sets @ $18.50	185,000		185,000
Contribution margin	$ 4,615,000	$ 4,400,000	$ 215,000
Fixed costs:			
Manufacturing—regular	3,300,000	3,300,000	
Manufacturing—additional	30,000		30,000
Selling and administrative	220,000	220,000	
Net income	$ 1,065,000	$ 880,000	$ 185,000

In this case, we see that the average cost of producing the set is:

$$\$45.83 = \frac{(\$2,200,000 + \$3,300,000)}{(120,000)}$$

However, it is profitable to sell an additional 10,000 sets at $40 per set because normal fixed costs are unaffected by the proposed contract.

5. Evaluate the addition or deletion of products.

Below is the schedule of the present revenue and cost structure for toboggans and the proposed addition of bobsleds for the Marlbrough Company:

	Toboggans	Bobsleds	Combined
Sales:			
5,000 @ $75	$ 375,000		$ 375,000
1,500 @ $200		$ 300,000	300,000
Variable costs:			
5,000 @ $30	150,000		150,000
1,500 @ $120		180,000	180,000
Fixed costs:			
Production	75,000	55,000	130,000
Administration	25,000	20,000	45,000
Marketing	40,000	45,000	85,000
Other	3,000	5,000	8,000
Total fixed costs	143,000	125,000	268,000
Net income	$ 82,000	$ (5,000)	$ 77,000

The Marlbrough Company manufacturers and sells a complete line of surf boards for the summer season and toboggans for winter. The market for surf boards far exceeds the toboggan market, and so there is excess capacity for the latter. The marketing vice president, Mark Cunningham, has suggested that the company develop a bobsled to complement the toboggan business. Mr. Cunningham believes the company could penetrate the specialized, exclusive bobsled market.

Although the bobsled business appears to have a $5,000 loss projected, it is determined that $20,000 of the fixed production costs and $10,000 of the fixed administrative costs were allocated to the bobsled and that currently the toboggan bears these costs. Actual toboggan net income is $52,000. Therefore, the increment in net income because of the proposed bobsled line is $25,000. This is computed as:

Projected bobsled loss	$	(5,000)
Add back allocated fixed costs		30,000
Additional income based on actual bobsled costs	$	25,000

6. Evaluate a make or buy decision.

Goetz Bros. Camping Equipment Co. manufactures camp stoves among other products. There is some excess capacity. President Joseph Goetz wants to investigate whether it would be feasible to manufacture the stove housing for its most popular Model N. He asks controller Jim Kurtenbach to analyze the potential costs.

The following schedule results:

Goetz Bros. Camping Equipment Co.
Analysis of manufactured stove housing costs

		Cost
Direct materials	$	18,000
Direct labor		13,500
Variable manufacturing overhead		6,750
Fixed manufacturing overhead		33,000
Total manufacturing costs	$	71,250 (a)
Number of housings to be produced		15,000 (b)
Cost per unit produced (a)/(b)	$	4.75

Goetz is currently purchasing its stove housings from Martin Manufacturing Company for $4.40 each, when annual quantities are 10,000 or more. On the surface, it appears to be less costly to purchase the housings than to make them. Upon asking some probing questions, Mr. Goetz learns that of the fixed manufacturing overhead in the above schedule, one-half is considered incremental. That is, only $16,500 of the total fixed overhead is attributed to additional costs resulting from manufacturing the housings. The other $16,500 is allocated from the manufacture of other products. A complete analysis of the decision process reveals the following:

	Make Housings	Purchase Housings	Differential Analysis
Direct materials	$ 18,000		$ 18,000
Direct labor	13,500		13,500
Variable manufacturing overhead	6,750		6,750
Fixed manufacturing overhead	33,000	$ 16,500	16,500
Purchase cost of housings		66,000	(66,000)
Total costs	$ 71,250	$ 82,500	$ (11,250)

Hence, it is apparent that the cost to purchase the housings is actually $11,250 more than the cost of manufacturing them internally.

7. **Distinguish between the treatment of joint product costs for inventory valuation and for decision-making purposes.**

Joint product costs are those costs that result from producing two or more products from the same process, so that the same production costs apply to multiple products. The joint product costing techniques for inventory purposes do not work equally well for decision-making purposes.

For inventory costing purposes it is common to allocate joint product costs on the basis of pro rata share of market value of the products at the point of split-off. For example, if the Jackson Company produces two wax products, Slip and Zip, from a common process, and if the common costs of producing these waxes up to the point of product separation is $115,500, and if the market sales values of the products are $135,000 and $180,000 respectively, the joint product cost of $115,500 is assigned to the two products as follows:

$$\text{Slip} \quad \frac{135,000}{135,000 + 180,000} \quad \times \, \$115,500 = \$49,500$$

$$\text{Zip} \quad \frac{180,000}{135,000 + 180,000} \quad \times \, \$115,500 = \$66,000$$

Suppose now that each product above can be further processed, then sold at a higher price. For example,

	(1) Sale Price at Point of Split-off	(2) Sale Price After Further Processing	(3) Differential Revenue from Further Processing	
Slip	$ 135,000	$ 189,000	$ 54,000	Col (3) = (2) - (1)
Zip	180,000	207,000	27,000	

	(4) Differential Cost of Further Processing	(5) Profit (loss) from Further Processing	
Slip	$ 27,000	$ 27,000	Col (5) = (3) - (4)
Zip	36,000	(9,000)	

8. **Evaluate the replacement of equipment.**

Equipment is carried on the accounting records at original acquisition cost minus accumulated depreciation over the asset's life. The result is called "book value." Another term for the book value of existing equipment is "sunk cost." Sunk cost is not useful for decision making. However, many people are hesitant to ignore it.

Suppose the McRuiz Company has a computer that cost $950,000 that is 60% depreciated. The company has the opportunity of acquiring an entirely new microcomputer network, including required software for $600,000. The new system will save $125,000 per year in operating costs over the expected life of five years.

The old computer has a resale value of $90,000. The following analysis applies:

	Keep Old Machine	**Five-Year Performance** Buy New Network	Differential Analysis
Variable operating expense	$ 1,875,000	$ 1,250,000	($625,000)
Depreciation (or write-off) of present machine	380,000 *	380,000 *	-0-
Disposal value present unit		(90,000)	(90,000)
Depreciation of new network		600,000	600,000
Total costs	$ 2,255,000	$ 2,140,000	($115,000)

*Book value is 40% of $950,000.

Book value (sunk cost) of the present equipment is not relevant to the decision. If it were left out of the above analysis, the result would not be changed.

9. **Recognize how product mix decisions should be made when a firm's scarce resources and other constraints are considered.**

Frequently, analysis of contribution margin per unit of product sold or as a percentage of sales price will not indicate the most profitable product. It may be necessary to relate contribution margin to production or marketing constraints (or limitations). For example, the Goetz Bros. Camping Equipment Co. (referred to above) makes a camp stove and a lantern at its George, Iowa plant. Sales price, cost and production data follow:

	Stove	Lantern
Selling price per unit	$ 36.00	$ 24.00
Variable costs	18.00	15.00
Contribution margin	$ 18.00	$ 9.00
Contribution margin, % of sales	50%	37.5%
Maximum plant capacity (in hours)	180,000	180,000
Production hours per unit	1.5	.6
Maximum units producible	120,000	300,000
Contribution margin per unit	$ 18.00	$ 9.00
Production hours per unit	1.5	.6
Contribution margin per hour	$ 12.00	$ 15.00
Total production hours available	180,000	180,000
Total contribution margin	$ 2,160,000	$ 2,700,000

This analysis for the George plant of Goetz illustrates that in some cases, the total contribution margin provided by products may relate more to the contribution of that product per production hour than to contribution margin per unit sold.

10. **Explain and compare market demand-oriented pricing and cost-oriented pricing.**

The market forces of supply and demand frequently have more impact on pricing decisions than do product costs. For example, government controls over certain products may absolutely establish prices of products and services. This may be true of the cost of telephone calls or bus rides. Market competitive forces establish prices for agricultural products and commodity prices. A producer cannot sell above market on any given day and would be foolish to sell for less than market. As shown in the following section, cost-oriented prices are most common in business.

11. **Understand three cost-oriented pricing methods: markup pricing, cost plus target income pricing, and target return on investment pricing.**

The methods of establishing cost-oriented prices are demonstrated in the following paragraphs.

Markup pricing. Andrea's Fine Gifts is a retail store in Green Bay that marks up its Irish crystal 100% of cost, while the markup on linen napkins is 50% of cost. As an example, the following table shows the technique.

	Cost	Markup %	Markup Amount	Selling Price
Irish crystal lamp	$150	100%	$150	$300
Linen napkins, set	20	50%	10	30

A markup that is 100% of cost equals 50% of selling price. See the Irish crystal lamp above for an example. Markup is $150, which is 50% of selling price. When the markup on cost is 50% (on the linen napkins), this converts to 33.3% of selling price.

The formula is:

$$\text{Markup as a \% of selling price} = \frac{\text{Markup as a \% of cost}}{100\% + \text{markup as \% of cost}}$$

$$\text{For Irish crystal this is} = \frac{100\%}{100\% + 100\%} = \frac{100\%}{200\%} = 50\%$$

$$\text{For linen napkins this is} = \frac{50\%}{100\% + 50\%} = \frac{50\%}{150\%} = 33.3\%$$

The reverse process, i.e., to convert from a markup on selling price to a markup on cost, use the folowing procedure:

$$\text{Markup as a \% of cost} = \frac{\text{Markup as a \% of selling price}}{100\% - \text{markup as \% of selling price}}$$

$$\text{For Irish crystal this is} = \frac{50\%}{100\% - 50\%} = \frac{50\%}{50\%} = 100\%$$

$$\text{For linen napkins this is} = \frac{33.3\%}{100\% - 33.3\%} = \frac{33.3\%}{66.6\%} = 50\%$$

Markup with absorption costing. The Abramowicz Company manufactures class rings and other college-related jewelry. Its fixed and variable production costs per ring, based on a volume of 10,000 rings, is $120 per ring. Ken Abramowicz, president, has established 80% as a target markup on production cost. The selling price of each ring, following this approach, is $120 + .80 x $120 = $216. Mr. Abramowicz must be certain that the markup is sufficient to cover selling and administrative costs and desired profit. Fixed and variable production costs are included in the $120, by definition.

Markup with variable costing. Referring to the class rings of the Abramowicz Company, assume that the $120 of production cost includes $40 of fixed production costs (or $400,000, since the volume is 10,000 rings). Also, there is $43 of variable selling and administrative expenses. The variable cost of each ring, then, is $120 - $40 + $43 = $123. Target markup on variable cost is 75% or $92.25. Thus, the selling price of the class ring under this method is $123 + $92.25 = $215.25. In this case, the markup of $92.25 must cover manufacturing and other fixed costs and profit in addition to the variable costs.

Cost plus target income pricing. Judy Leaver, psychologist, has left her job at the state correctional institution to establish her professional office to counsel wayward young people and their families. After locating a prospective office and looking at furniture and supply costs, she estimates that her annual operating costs will approximate $36,000. She wants to earn a first year profit of $18,000. Realistically, she believes she can average 100 counseling hours with clients per month. Based on these data, Ms. Leaver calculates her hourly conseling rate as:

$$\text{Hourly rate for services} = \frac{\$36,000 + \$18,000}{1,200 \text{ hours}} = \$45$$

Price based on target return on investment. Referring again to the Abramowicz Company, assume that Mr. Abramowicz has a $500,000 investment in assets. Further, assume that total costs of the college rings, including selling and administrative costs, are $1,800,000. If Abramowicz expects a 20% return on investment, the selling price per ring is:

$$
\begin{aligned}
\text{Selling price} &= [\$1,800,000 + (.25 \times \$500,000)]/10,000 \text{ rings} \\
&= \$192.50
\end{aligned}
$$

12. Describe the basic legal implications of pricing decisions.

The Robinson-Patman Act, passed by Congress over a half century ago, requires that prices must be justified by costs of the products or services sold, under certain circumstances. Thus, it is important that businesses maintain good cost records and be in a position to present to the court, if challenged, that prices have an appropriate relationship to cost.

MATCHING ATTRIBUTES

Below, in Group A are listed attributes that may be identified with the terms included in Chapter 7, "Decision Making Based on Relevant Information," listed in Group B. Indicate, by use of the identifying letter of the appropriate Group B item, which description in Group A best matches which Group B term.

Group A

B___ 1. A formalized method for evaluating decisions, using quantitative data.

H___ 2. Expected future costs that will differ between alternatives considered.

K___ 3. Costs that won't make a difference in a decision, for example, book value of existing assets.

F___ 4. The benefit forfeited by rejecting one alternative in favor of another.

C___ 5. The difference between relevant revenues of one alternative and those of another alternative.

L___ 6. Future costs that will not differ with alternatives or sunk costs.

D___ 7. Common costs of production that result in two or more products.

J___ 8. Two or more products are produced together, then are finished as separate products.

I___ 9. Similar products must be sold for similar prices to different customers.

E___ 10. Add-on amount to determine sales value.

A___ 11. Sales value determined by other than economic forces.

G___ 12. Different proportions of products sold than in previous periods.

Group B

A.	Cost-oriented pricing	G.	Product mix
B.	Decision model	H.	Relevant costs
C.	Differential revenues	I.	Robinson-Patman Act
D.	Joint product cost	J.	Split-off point
E.	Markup pricing	K.	Sunk costs
F.	Opportunity costs	L.	Unavoidable costs

MULTIPLE CHOICE

For each of the following items choose the most appropriate completion phrase.

1. The Coover Company is a retail store that is planning to expand its business by adding a new product line. Resources available permit it to acquire only one new line. If it adds the Greenlawn brand of garden tools it cannot add the Roundwheel bicycle line. If the company adds the Greenlawn line, the profits it could have made on the Roundwheel line are:

    a. Sunk costs
    b. Opportunity costs
    c. Unavoidable costs
    d. Relevant costs
    e. Differential costs

2. Graber Equipment Co. handles two competing lines of lawn irrigation products. Because of special installation equipment, required inventory levels, and the training of personnel for both lines, the company is considering dropping one line.

	Shamrock	St. Andrew	Combined
Sales	$ 250,000	$ 80,000	$ 330,000
Variable costs	100,000	40,000	140,000
Contribution margin	150,000	40,000	190,000
Fixed costs	50,000	50,000	100,000
Net income	$ 100,000	$ (10,000)	$ 90,000

Fixed costs are divided equally between the two lines for ease of allocation. If the St. Andrew line is discontinued, it is anticipated that fixed costs would be reduced $20,000. Based on this analysis,

    a. St. Andrew line should be dropped because it loses $10,000.
    b. St. Andrew line should be retained because it breaks even.
    c. St. Andrew line should be retained because it produces a profit of $20,000.
    d. Shamrock line should be discontinued because it contributes to the loss of St. Andrew.
    e. St. Andrew should be retained because it provides Graber's customers with a choice of products.

3. Managers attempt to structure decision making in quantitative terms so choices can be made on a systematic basis. Which of the following steps would *not* be included in such a process? The decision maker:

    a. Follows a well-defined process.
    b. Can justify each step taken.
    c. Can evaluate the results achieved.
    d. Applies personal preferences to the process as much as possible.

4. Many managers follow the following decision-making process. (Indicate the *inappropriate* step.)

   a. Define problem, indicating objective to be accomplished.
   b. Identify alternatives.
   c. Obtain relevant information.
   d. Deal with personalities of all individuals involved.
   e. Make decision based on above data obtained.

5. The basic objective in differential analysis is:

   a. To maximize cost.
   b. To minimize revenue.
   c. To optimize manager's position.
   d. To determine difference of costs or revenues under each alternative.
   e. To compute difference each alternative has on sunk costs.

6. Evanston Company has unused capacity in its garment factory. It has a possible special one-time order to produce tennis shorts for a large retailer. This special order would result in a profit of $25,000. If the company decides to reject the special order and, instead, use the idle time for repair and maintenance of facilities, the $25,000 profit foregone is called:

   a. Incremental cost
   b. Opportunity cost
   c. Unavoidable cost
   d. Sunk cost
   e. A mistake

7. Ralph Butler is considering dropping one crop from farm production next year and concentrating on his other farm products. Basing his decision on differential analysis means he should

   a. Consider the incremental costs created by that one crop he is considering dropping.
   b. Consider the incremental revenues created by that one crop he is considering dropping.
   c. Consider all the incremental costs and revenues.
   d. Consider what the neighboring farmers will do and follow their lead.
   e. Consider the effects of his decision on unavoidable costs.

8. Whenever a manufacturer has both the productive capacity and the expertise to manufacture a certain part, the decision whether to make the part or buy it should be based on:

   a. The relevant costs of each alternative.
   b. The sunk costs of existing manufacturing equipment.
   c. Whether overtime pay is required.
   d. How much the part could be sold for separately.
   e. The revenue function squared divided by the cost function.

9. Joint product costs are most commonly allocated to the separate products based on:

   a.   Arbitrary assignment according to manager's judgment.

   b.   Each product's proportional direct cost.

   c.   Each product's relative sales value.

   d.   Whatever is best for taxes.

   e.   Each product's perceived worth.

10. Barclay Petroleum Company drilled a well for oil. When oil was hit, gas also was recovered. Total costs of exploration, drilling and required equipment was $760,000. Expected recoverable reserves of oil will have a net sales value of $1,200,000 and the expected recoverable reserves of gas will have a net sales value of $1,800,000. The $760,000 cost of the well should be:

   a.   Charged against oil revenues.

   b.   Charged against gas revenues.

   c.   Charged evenly against both oil and gas revenues.

   d.   40% against gas revenue and 60% against oil revenue.

   e.   60% against gas revenue and 40% against oil revenue.

ILLUSTRATIVE PROBLEMS

1. The Shakey Heights Iron Works manufactures a special vault-type filing cabinet that provides special security protection. During 1988 its revenues and costs for the unit were:

Sales price	$	110
Variable costs		65
Fixed costs:		
Production		750,000
Sales and administrative		650,000

The company received a one-time offer to sell 8,000 units @ $80 each in a market that would not interfere with current sales. This order would require $20,000 additional set-up and shipping costs, but otherwise would not increase other fixed costs. Should the company accept the offer? Show your analysis below.

640,000
520,000
120,000
20,000
100,000

2. Hayes Racquet Company makes a deluxe tennis racket (Tenny) and a high quality badminton racket (Bandy). The company's revenue and cost schedule for these products is below:

	Tenny	Bandy	Total
Sales:			
25,000 @ $28	$ 700,000		$ 700,000
32,000 @ $32		$ 1,024,000	1,024,000
Variable costs:			
25,000 @ $7.50	187,500		187,500
32,000 @ $9.00		288,000	288,000
Fixed costs:			
Production	400,000	400,000	800,000
Selling and administrative	150,000	150,000	300,000
Net income	$ (37,500)	$ 186,000	$ 148,500

Requested:

Should the Hayes Company discontinue Tenny? If the product is discontinued, total production costs will reduce to $700,000 and selling and administrative costs will decrease to $200,000. Show your analysis here.

	w	w/o	
Sales	700,000	1,024,000	700,000
	1,024,000		187,500
U Costs	187,500	288,000	512,500
	288,000	736,000	
F Costs	800,000	700,000	↑ 00,000
	300,000	200,000	↓ 00,000
	148,500	(164,000)	312,500

3. The Amos Fritz Skaters, Inc. manufactures and sells skateboards. The board itself is constructed of a special wood that requires extensive processing to insure proper shape and durability. Its costs of manufacture last year were:

Direct materials	$	50,000
Direct labor		88,000
Variable manufacturing overhead		36,000
Fixed manufacturing overhead		60,000
Total manufacturing costs	$	234,000
Number of units manufactured		40,000
Cost per unit	$	5.85

The Carolina Corporation has submitted a bid to sell the same quality skate board to Amos Fritz for $4.95 in an annual quantity of 40,000. If Amos Fritz discontinued production of the board, all production costs would be discontinued except $40,000 of manufacturing overhead which is made up of depreciation, taxes, insurance and maintenance of the building, for which there is no other current use. Should Amos Fritz continue to make the board, or should they buy it from the Carolina Corporation? Show your analysis.

4. Two Rivers Fabricating Co. makes two corn products which are Sweet 'N' Fluffy and Spicy Lean. Common costs for producing the two products are $120,000, at which point the market value of Sweet 'N' Fluffy is $90,000 and the market value of Spicy Lean is $60,000. If the two products are processed further, the additional costs for Sweet would be $48,000 and for Spicy would be $24,000. The market values of the two products after further processing would be $126,000 for Sweet and $104,000 for Spicy.

Requested:

a. What portion of the $120,000 common costs should be allocated to each product?

b. Should the company further process each product, or should it sell each at the point of joint product split-off? Show your computations.

5. Argyle Weavers, Inc. have a machine (#1) that has been operating very effectively for several years in the production of their main product. A sales engineer for Twyman Company says his company can supply a replacement machine (#2) that will save Argyle $500,000 per year in operating costs. Cost of the new machine is $2,000,000. John Osborn, controller for Argyle indicates that machine #1 still has a book value of $600,000 and it operates well, "so, why replace it?"

Requested:

Using differential analysis, determine the cost differentials over the next six years of operation, assuming both machines would operate efficiently during that period of time.

$$2,000,000$$
$$3,000,000$$
$$\overline{}$$
$$1,000,000$$

6. Vanderlind Beverage Co. makes and sells two soft drinks, Bubble and Bomb. Their respective contribution margins follow:

	Bubble	Bomb
Selling price	$ 0.18	$ 0.20
Variable cost	.06	.08
Contribution margin	.12	.12
Contribution margin percent	66.7%	60%
Units producible per hour	50,000	60,000

(handwritten: 350 under Bubble; 350 under Bomb; 17,500,000 under Bubble; 21,000,000 under Bomb)

There are 350 production hours possible per month. Based upon the preceding information, which of the two products is most profitable to produce? Show your computations.

(handwritten computations:)

17,500,000
× .12
———
2,100,000.00

21,000,000
× .12
———
2,520,000

VOCABULARY

COST-ORIENTED PRICING.   An approach used to price products and services by determining the actual or estimated costs involved and adding the amount of desired profit.

COST PLUS TARGET INCOME PRICING. The use of cost-volume-profit analysis to establish a selling price based on the costs involved and the firm's profit goals.

DECISION MAKING. Making a choice between alternative courses of action.

DECISION-MAKING PROCESS. Defining the problem and the objective to be achieved, selecting alternative courses of action, obtaining relevant information, and arriving at a decision.

DECISION MODEL. A formalized method for evaluating alternative courses of action.

DIFFERENTIAL ANALYSIS (INCREMENTAL ANALYSIS). A decision model used to evaluate the differences in relevant revenue and costs between alternative courses of action.

DIFFERENTIAL REVENUE. The difference between the relevant revenue of two alternatives.

JOINT PRODUCTS. The name given to multiple products produced from common raw materials or the same production process.

JOINT PRODUCT COSTS. Common costs required to produce joint products before they are identifiable as separate units.

MARKET DEMAND-ORIENTED PRICING. A theoretical approach to pricing in which the primary focus is on the relationship of supply and demand in the market place.

MARKUP PRICING. Determining selling prices by using a markup percentage that is large enough to cover the cost base involved and yield the amount of profit desired.

OPPORTUNITY COSTS. The potential benefit forfeited by rejecting one alternative while accepting another.

RELEVANT COSTS. Expected future costs that will differ between alternatives.

RELEVANT REVENUES. Expected future revenues that will differ between alternatives.

RETURN ON INVESTMENT (ROI). The comparison of profit results with the investment in assets required to earn them.

SPLIT-OFF POINT. The point in the production process at which joint products become separable products.

SUNK COSTS. Costs that are not relevant in decision making because they already have been incurred and cannot be changed.

TARGET RETURN ON INVESTMENT PRICING. A pricing method with which a desired return on investment is added to the cost base involved to establish a selling price.

UNAVOIDABLE COSTS. Either future costs that will not differ between alternatives or sunk costs.

THE ANSWERS

MATCHING ATTRIBUTES

1.	B	5.	C	9.	I
2.	H	6.	L	10.	E
3.	K	7.	D	11.	A
4.	F	8.	J	12.	G

MULTIPLE CHOICE

1.	b	5.	d	8.	a
2.	c	6.	b	9.	c
3.	d	7.	c	10.	e
4.	d				

ILLUSTRATIVE PROBLEMS

1.

Sales	$	640,000
Variable costs (8,000 @ $65)		520,000
Contribution margin		120,000
Fixed costs		20,000
Incremental income	$	100,000

Yes, the company should accept the offer because it will result in increased income of $100,000.

2.

	With Tenny	Without Tenny	Differential Analysis
Sales	$ 1,724,000	$ 1,024,000	$ 700,000
Variable costs	475,500	288,000	187,500
Contribution margin	1,248,500	736,000	512,500
Fixed costs:			
Avoidable, production	100,000		100,000
Avoidable, s and a	100,000		100,000
Unavoidable, product	700,000	700,000	-0-
Unavoidable, s and a	200,000	200,000	-0-
Total fixed costs	1,100,000	900,000	200,000
Net income	$ 148,500	$ (164,000)	$ 312,500

Hayes Company should *not* discontinue Tenny, because doing so would result in a reduction of net income of $312,500, creating a loss of $164,000.

3.

	Make Board	Buy Board	Differential Analysis
Direct materials	$ 50,000		$ 50,000
Direct labor	88,000		88,000
Variable overhead	36,000		36,000
Fixed overhead	60,000	$ 40,000	20,000
Purchase costs		198,000	(198,000)
Total costs	$ 234,000	$ 238,000	$ (4,000)

Amos Fritz should continue to *make* the board, because to do otherwise would result in increased costs of $4,000.

4a.

$$\text{Sweet:} \quad \frac{\$90,000}{\$90,000 + \$60,000} \times \$120,000 = \$72,000$$

$$\text{Spicy:} \quad \frac{\$60,000}{\$90,000 + \$60,000} \times \$120,000 = \$48,000$$

b.

	Sales Value at Split-Off	Sales Value if Processed Further	Differential Revenue from Further Processing
Sweet	$ 90,000	$ 126,000	$ 36,000
Spicy	60,000	104,000	44,000

	Differential Cost from Further Processing	Profit (Loss) from Further Processing
Sweet	$ 48,000	$ (12,000)
Spicy	24,000	20,000

Based on this analysis, the company should sell Sweet at the point of split-off and further process Spicy.

5.

	Keep Old Machine	Buy New Machine	Differential Analysis
Operating expenses	$ 3,000,000	$ -0-	$(3,000,000)
Depreciation of old	600,000	600,000	-0-
Depreciation of new	-0-	2,000,000	2,000,000
Total costs	$ 3,600,000	$ 2,600,000	$(1,000,000)

The company would save $1,000,000 by buying the replacement machine.

6.

	Bubble	Bomb
Maximum units producible:		
50,000 x 350 hours	17,500,000	
60,000 x 350 hours		21,000,000
Contribution margin per unit	$ 0.12	$ 0.12
Total contribution margin	$ 2,100,000	$ 2,520,000

Bomb is more profitable to produce.

Chapter 8

BUDGETING: A MANAGEMENT TOOL FOR FINANCIAL PLANNING AND CONTROL

As a novice in management accounting, you will find in this chapter that the budget is the vehicle used by management to assist in its performance of its planning, coordination and control objectives. Unfortunately, it is a tool often misunderstood by management at various levels. Used correctly, budgeting can assist in accomplishing the goals of the organization. It is important for the accounting student to understand the basic principles of budgeting as a management tool for financial planning and control. Try to master the following learning objectives.

LEARNING OBJECTIVES

1. Explain how a master budget is used as a management tool.
2. Define the need for goal congruence in an organization.
3. List the benefits and limitations of budgeting.
4. Identify the key steps involved in preparing a master budget.
5. Recognize the significance of an accurate sales forecast for the budgeting process and the methods used to predict sales.
6. Distinguish between an operating budget and a financial budget.
7. Prepare and use each of the individual budgets included in the master budget.
8. Discuss the importance of inventory level decisions made during the budgeting process.
9. See how budget performance reports are used for control purposes.
10. Describe the major considerations involved with budgeting in nonmanufacturing operations.

LEARNING TIPS

Put yourself in the position of the top management of an organization. You want to be sure that certain specified goals of the organization are accomplished. You want to be certain that all units (segments) of the organization work together to accomplish those goals. You want a united effort among managers in their planning to achieve established goals. Further, you want to have a way of measuring how closely the organization, and various units within the organization, come to actual attainment of the goals. What tool is there in the manager's "bag of tricks" that will do all these things? Why, it's the budget, of course!

REVIEW

Let's now look at Chapter 8 to see if we understand all of the learning objectives Professor Helmkamp has set out for us to accomplish.

1. **Explain how a master budget is used as a management tool.**

   First, management must set forth targets or objectives to be accomplished during the budget period (usually a year). Often these targets are expressed as dollars of profit, return on the organization's investment, or percentage of the industry's market for certain products. The master budget shows in dollars how the various parts fit together to make up that target. For example, how many dollars of labor, material and overhead are required to meet the sales expected for the period, and how the sales dollars, minus the cost and expense dollars, result in dollars of profit.

2. **Define the need for goal congruence in an organization.**

   Goal congruence refers to the agreement of goals of the various segments and people within the organization with those goals of the organization. Goals of the organization are established by the board of directors and top management personnel. Goals of operating units may be established by the managers of those units. It is essential that the goals of individual units be in agreement and compatible with the goals of the organization. Suppose, for example, that the organization's goals include maintaining a reputation for excellence and producing only top-quality products, such as bicycles. Obviously, it would *not* be appropriate for the sales department to establish the goal of flooding the market with bicycles by selling them in every discount store in the country. Only through considerable management effort can coordination of objectives, or goal congruence, be achieved.

3. **List the benefits and limitations of budgeting.**

   There are many benefits of business budgeting, but there are limitations as well. It is important for the manager to recognize both benefits and limitations in order to capitalize on the former and minimize the latter. Among the many benefits are:

   a.   Because of a formal budget program within an organization, because all managers are required to submit budget estimates, and because management performance is judged in comparison with the budgeted operations, all managers must formally plan their work. We all do some planning intuitively, but the budgeting process forces us to be more detailed and explicit in our planning.

   b.   Budgeting causes managers to be more organized in their planning and operations. A budget is, after all, an *organized* plan; therefore, users of the plan (the budget) become organized in the process of developing and using the budget.

   c.   Besides being a planning and organizing device, a budget is also very much of a control tool. Control occurs, not by accident, but by deliberate performance measurement and evaluation against the plan—the budget. Control essentially means creating conformance, and in a budgeting sense, control occurs when actual operations are in close agreement with the budget.

   d.   Coordination is a key management function and an important by-product of the budgeting process. Each segment manager sees how his or her segment fits into the overall picture, and how each segment relates to the others.

   e.   One of the most beneficial aspects of a budget is its communication properties. Because budgets are used throughout the organization and because segments of the organization are closely interrelated, the budget becomes a device for communicating information in all directions in the organization: up and down the organization and across—i.e., at the same level within the firm.

f.   If a budget is used effectively, it becomes a strong motivator for good performance. Managers should be involved with the establishment of the budget, and in so doing, they want to see the goals that are set forth in the budget attained. Involvement is an essential ingredient in motivation.

The organization must always keep in mind that there are certain limitations to budgeting, as well as benefits. If management is not mindful of the limitations, the budget may become a negative factor within the organization rather than a positive one. These limitations can be avoided or overcome with a well-planned education program for participants and constant vigilance on the part of management. Included in the limitations are:

a.   Oversimplification can result if management is not fully aware of the complexities of the marketplace, and the way in which world economic forces, labor, society and competition all impact upon the organization. For example, a rise in terrorist activities may cause consumer reactions not predicted in the budget.

b.   Because budgets tend to be results-oriented, underlying causes of increases in costs or reductions in sales may be ignored. Frequently the reasons for events are more important than the events themselves. The budget is composed of figures which are generally viewed as facts rather than explanations.

c.   Sometimes managers feel that budgets are *imposed* upon them. This happens when they are not involved in the preparation of the budget. Budgets, to be successful, must be supported by all levels of management, starting at the top of the organization.

d.   Budgets are prepared months before the beginning of the budget period, and, of course, more than a year prior to the end of the budget period (if an annual budget is assumed). Since it is difficult to anticipate all future events, strict adherence to the budget may prevent a manager from taking advantage of new opportunities. Thus, management initiative may be stifled.

e.   Because budgets tend to create pressure for performing within the budget, a manager may cut spending in one area to offset overspending in another. For example, a manager may hire cheap, inexperienced labor that might produce an inferior product or mishandle equipment in order to stay within a budgeted cost category.

f.   Because budgets deal with *future* periods, there is a certain amount of unknown involved. This discourages some who say, "We can't budget because we don't know what the future holds." Supporters of the budgeting concept say instead, "It is better to have an imperfect plan to guide us into the future than no plan at all." Seasoned management judgment produces better budgets than does wild guessing.

4. **Identify the key steps involved in preparing a master budget.**

The key steps involved in preparing a master budget are:

a.   List the goals of the organization that relate to the budget period.

b.   Communicate to managers of each segment of the organization their expected involvement in the preparation of the budget.

c.   Develop a sales forecast.

d.   Develop product costs and period costs based on the sales forecast.

e.   Determine the equipment and facilities acquisition requirements.

f.   Develop cash requirements from the accrual revenues and costs determined above. Prepare a projected cash receipts and disbursements schedule.

g.   Prepare a full set of projected financial statements.

h.   Compare the projected financial statements with the goals established for the period to determine whether they are in agreement. Some budget revisions may be necessary.

5. **Recognize the significance of an accurate sales forecast for the budgeting process and the methods used to predict sales.**

The sales forecast is the foundation upon which the balance of the master budget is built. If this foundation is not solid, the rest of the budget will be weak and ineffective. The purpose of the sales forecast is to estimate the total market potential for the product(s) of the firm and to determine the firm's expected share of that market.

Many methods of sales forecasting are used by businesses. Among them are:

   a.   Estimates by members of the sales force.

   b.   Test marketing of products.

   c.   Group estimates by company executives.

   d.   Statistical or mathematical models.

6. **Distinguish between an operating budget and a financial budget.**

A firm's master budget consists of both the operating budget and the financial budget. The operating budget includes detailed schedules of revenues and costs required to meet the firm's profit objectives. The financial budget indicates resources and financial position resulting from the budget.

The financial budget includes the following schedules: capital expenditures budget; cash budget; budgeted balance sheet; and budgeted statement of cash flows. All other budget schedules are part of the operating budget. See the next review item for a complete list.

7. **Prepare and use each of the individual budgets included in the master budget.**

Chapter 8 illustrates fourteen budget schedules. They are:

   1.   Sales Budget

   2.   Production Budget

   3.   Direct Labor Budget

   4.   Direct Materials Budget

   5.   Manufacturing Overhead Budget

   6.   Cost of Goods Sold Budget

   7.   Administrative Expenses Budget

   8.   Selling Expenses Budget

   9.   Capital Expenditures Budget

   10.   Schedule of Cash Receipts and Disbursements

   11.   Cash Budget

   12.   Budgeted Income Statement

   13.   Budgeted Balance Sheet

   14.   Budgeted Statement of Cash Flows

Each of the above budget schedules is illustrated in an extended illustrative problem following the multiple choice questions. It is recommended that the student complete each of these schedules.

8. **Discuss the importance of inventory level decisions made during the budget process.**

After the sales forecast is completed, it is necessary to set the desired inventory levels before production schedules can be determined. This is true because of the equation:

$$\begin{array}{llll}
\text{Production} = & \text{forecasted} + & \text{desired ending} - & \text{beginning} \\
\text{quantities} & \text{sales units} & \text{finished goods} & \text{finished goods} \\
& & \text{inventory} & \text{inventory}
\end{array}$$

Similarly, the quantities to be purchased cannot be determined without considering raw materials inventories. The purchase quantity formula is:

$$\begin{array}{llll}
\text{Purchase} = & \text{budgeted} + & \text{desired ending} - & \text{beginning} \\
\text{quantities} & \text{materials} & \text{materials} & \text{inventory} \\
& \text{usage} & \text{inventory} & \text{of materials}
\end{array}$$

We can see, then, that finished goods and raw materials inventories have a direct effect on production and purchase quantities in budget preparation. These inventory levels are set by management policy.

9. **See how budget performance reports are used for control purposes.**

Budgeting provides management with a tool for control as well as planning and coordination. The control aspect enters when actual performance is compared with the budget. This is followed with an identification of significant variances of actual data from the budget (the plan). The final step is the taking of corrective action by management.

The common form of a budget performance report is to set up a money column for the budget. Then, along side it is a column for actual, so that comparison can be made on a line-by-line basis. The third money column is for the variance, which indicates the amount over or under budget. Often these variances will be labeled U for unfavorable variance or F for favorable. Sometimes, in addition to absolute dollar variances, percentage values will also be calculated and shown. Frequently, percentage variances are more meaningful than absolute dollar amounts.

10. **Describe the major considerations involved with budgeting in nonmanufacturing operations.**

Most of the basic concepts and procedures of budgeting apply across the board, regardless of the type of organization involved. On the other hand, there are also significant differences.

Only manufacturing firms have the three types of inventories: raw materials, work in process and finished goods. Because of this, some aspects of budgeting for nonmanufacturing firms is less complex. Merchandising firms emphasize product inventory levels and inventory turnover rates in order to achieve target profit levels.

Service firms use the bottom-up approach to budget development. This is because their professional staff is more-or-less fixed in size in the short run. Therefore, based on the costs of operations, revenues are usually forecast on the basis of production of income by each professional staff person. Of course, inventories of product and supplies are virtually nonexistent in service firms.

Governmental organizations usually forecast revenues based on prior periods, then determine expenditures based on the revenues. Governmental units usually budget to break even, rather than to show a profit or loss. Often statute requires that the revenue levels are percentage changes from the prior period or have mandatory noncollection rates for taxes and other levels, to prevent overly optimistic or unrealistic projections.

MATCHING ATTRIBUTES

Below in Group A are listed attributes that may be identified with the budgeting terms in Group B. Indicate, by use of the identifying letter of the appropriate Group B item, which attribute best matches which Group B term.

Group A

G _____ 1. A management tool aimed at accomplishing company goals.

F _____ 2. Various segments of a company must have common purposes.

J _____ 3. Statistical technique used in sales forecasting.

L _____ 4. Sales are conducted in a limited area for determining public acceptance of the product.

E _____ 5. Shows the acquisition of facilities and equipment planned for the budget year.

A _____ 6. Contains the costs of operating the executive offices, accounting department, personnel office and other administrative costs.

C _____ 7. Budgeted direct materials usage, plus desired ending direct materials, less beginning direct materials.

H _____ 8. Forecasted sales units, plus desired ending finished goods, less beginning finished goods.

M _____ 9. Past costs are irrelevant, all costs for the budget period must be justified, from the ground up.

I _____ 10. Focuses on a cost/benefit evaluation of each service offered.

K _____ 11. Often developed on bottom-up approach because of rather fixed personnel staff size.

B _____ 12. Contains only controllable revenues and costs.

D _____ 13. Contains an analysis of annual cash flows.

Group B

A.	Administrative expenses budget	G.	Master budget
B.	Budget performance report	H.	Production units required
C.	Budgeted purchases in units	I.	Program budget
D.	Budgeted statement of cash flows	J.	Regression analysis
E.	Capital expenditures budget	K.	Service firm budget
		L.	Test market
F.	Goal congruence	M.	Zero-base budget

MULTIPLE CHOICE

For each of the following items, choose the most appropriate completion phrase.

1. A master budget, prepared and used by a business is:

    a. A control device that prevents people from straying from the company's way of doing things.

    b. A detailed plan that shows how resources are expected to be acquired and used during a certain period of time.

    c. A plan of how a specified department or division of the company will operate in a coming period.

    d. An informal summary of operations, with few details of people, expenses or assets.

2. Goal congruence with an organization refers to:

   a.   The desire by employees to end up with the same profit, or at least, profit percentage in each segment of the business.

   b.   The need for an organization to operate each of its segments the same.

   c.   The acceptance by managers of organizational goals as their own.

   d.   Creates the individuality of each manager by encouraging them to establish goals independently.

3. Budgeting has several significant benefits to a firm that effectively uses a budgeting system. Which of the following is *not* such a benefit?

   a.   Budgeting forces management to plan ahead, anticipating future events in some systematic way.

   b.   Budgeting assists management in using company resources most effectively and efficiently.

   c.   Budgeting causes managers to think imaginatively by creating their own direction, profit goals and objectives, without being concerned about the effects on other segments of the company.

   d.   Budgeting helps managers set realistic targets against which future performance can be measured.

4. A number of limitations may apply to business budgeting. Which of the following is considered such a limitation?

   a.   A budget creates a more relaxed, easy-going atmosphere in which to operate because everything is planned in advance.

   b.   Budgets usually show results and detailed explanations for those results.

   c.   A budget tends to oversimplify the facts, and does not represent the complexities faced by management.

   d.   Through the years budgeting has developed into a rather precise science, so that virtually all the guesswork is gone.

   e.   The budget encourages new developments and actions, thus increasing management incentive to be innovative.

5. Your text lists a number of major steps involved in the development of a budget. Which of the following would *not* be such a step?

   a.   Management identifies major organizational goals for the budget period, such as net income and return on investment.

   b.   The accounting department develops the details of the various segments of the budget and gives them to the operating managers to accomplish.

   c.   Sales for the budget period are forecast.

   d.   Capital expenditures for the period are assigned priorities.

   e.   Accrual accounting is converted to a cash basis to determine cash receipts and disbursements.

6. The sales forecast is the cornerstone of successful budgeting since so much of the budget depends upon it. Which of the following statements is *true* about the sales forecast?

   a.   A good sales manager can effectively forecast future periods' sales within 1% or 2% accuracy most of the time; there is little uncertainty involved.

   b.   Sales forecasts are developed without considering such outside factors as general economic conditions and industry matters.

   c.   Advertising and competitors' actions may have a significant effect on a company's sales forecast.

   d.   Sales forecasts are most frequently and realistically mainly extensions of prior period sales; e.g. adding a flat growth factor, such as 10%, to last year's sales.

7. Several methods of forecasting future sales are frequently used. These include:

   a.   Have the chief executive officer estimate sales for the budget period based on her or his best judgment.

   b.   Have people send in questionnaires from a newspaper ad indicating how much of the product they intend to buy during the budget period.

   c.   Hire a professional astrologer to give a scientific forecast.

   d.   Take an average of the best estimates of production personnel, since they have first-hand knowledge of what is being produced.

   e.   Use statistical or mathematical techniques such as trend analysis of current and past sales.

8. The budgeting process in the firm is started:

   a.   By operating personnel submitting the budget requests for the coming year.

   b.   By top management establishing guidelines for financial performance.

   c.   By operating managers telling the sales department what they must sell to meet production plans.

   d.   By the sales personnel providing their estimates of sales for the budget period.

   e.   By the personnel department indicating how many people will be available to work during the budget year.

9. Differences in budgeting for not-for-profit firms from for-profit firms include:

   a.   Not-for-profit firms can usually adjust the revenues for changes in levels or quality of services offered during the budget period.

   b.   Not-for-profit firms usually have more legalistic controls placed on them, thus limiting their flexibility once the budget has been approved.

   c.   For-profit firms usually employ program budgeting more extensively than not-for-profit firms.

   d.   Not-for-profit firms make extensive use of return on investment measures of capital expenditure performance.

10. The master budget consists of the operating budget and the financial budget. The operating budget includes (among others):

   a.   Sales budget, production budget, budgeted income statement, and the cash budget.

   b.   Capital expenditures budget, cash budget, budgeted balance sheet and budgeted statement of changes in financial position.

   c.   Selling expenses budget, administrative expenses budget and budgeted income statement.

   d.   Direct materials budget, direct labor budget, manufacturing overhead budget and budgeted balance sheet.

   e.   Sales budget, cost of goods sold budget, budgeted income statement, and capital expenditures budget.

ILLUSTRATIVE PROBLEM

Campus Apparel Company is a manufacturer of sweaters specializing in sales to college fraternities and sororities. It is the basis for this extended budget problem. The firm's headquarters and knitting mills are located in Cortez, Colorado, close to an abundant supply of virgin wool, a trained labor supply, and plentiful power. The company's test-market campuses are Fort Lewis College, University of Colorado, and Northern Arizona University.

The executive committee has established a goal of 20% of market share for the company for 1993-94 and a net-income-to-sales percentage of 5%. A new style fabric and design, with a cotton-wool blend, has been test-marketed during the current year. The budget for next year will be based on full exploitation of this new product, called Campus-Mode.

Sales for 1993-94 are expected to be 21,000 units at a selling price of $36 each. No beginning inventory of this new item will be on hand, although there will be 2,000 of a former product, called Mode-less, on hand, which will be sold for $12.50 each in the first quarter.

Costs of production of the new sweaters are:

Raw materials:

Wool thread, 20 yards @ $0.30	$	6.00
Cotton thread, 20 yards @ $0.16		3.20
Labor, 3/4 hour @ $6.40		4.80
Manufacturing overhead @ 125% of		
direct labor cost		6.00
Total cost	$	20.00

Additional data:

Advertising expense is equal to 2% of the current quarter sales, except for last year's product, which is not advertised. Sales commissions are 7% of current quarter sales. When borrowing cash, the company borrows in multiples of $10,000 and must maintain a minimum cash balance of $10,000. Interest is 10% per year and is paid for the number of quarters the loan is outstanding whenever a principal payment is made.

Sales collections are 60% in the quarter of sale, 30% in the quarter following sale, and 10% in the second quarter following sale. Accounts payable are paid 80% in the quarter of materials purchase, 20% in the following quarter. All costs and expenses other than material purchases are paid in the quarter incurred.

The corporate income tax rate is 20% of net income before taxes. Estimated payments in equal amounts ($1,000 increments) are paid in the final three quarters of the year.

Requested:

a. Develop a full set of master budget schedules for Campus Apparel Co. for the year ending March 31, 1994. The schedule outlines are presented on the following pages with some data included. It is strongly suggested that they be prepared in the order provided.

b. Test the final result with the profit goal.

Schedule 1

CAMPUS APPAREL COMPANY
Sales Budget
Year Ending March 31, 1990

| | Quarter | | | | |
	1	2	3	4	Total
Mode-less Sweaters					
Budgeted sales units					
x Budgeted price per unit	$12.50				
= Budgeted sales dollars					
Campus-Mode Sweaters					
Budgeted sales units					
x Budgeted price per unit	$36.00	$36.00	$36.00	$36.00	$36.00
= Budgeted sales dollars					
Total					
Budgeted sales dollars					

Schedule 2

CAMPUS APPAREL COMPANY
Production Budget
Year Ending March 31, 1990

| | Quarter | | | | |
	1	2	3	4	Total
Campus-Mode Sweaters					
Forecast sales units	3,000	8,000	7,500	2,500	21,000
+ Desired end. fin. goods	2,700	2,500	800	0	0
= Total units needed					
- Beginning finished goods					
= Production required, units					

Schedule 3   **CAMPUS APPAREL COMPANY**
                                    Direct Materials Budget
                                    Year Ending March 31, 1990

	Q u a r t e r				
	1	2	3	4	Total
Campus-Mode Sweaters					
Production units x yds wool thread/unit					
= Yards of thread required + yards ending materials	52,000	28,000	11,000	0	0
= Yards needed - Beginning materials					
= Purchase requirements x cost per yard	$0.30	$0.30	$0.30	$0.30	$0.30
= Cost of purchases					
Production units x yds cotton thread/unit					
= Yards of thread required + yards ending materials	28,500	39,000	29,000	8,500	8,500
= Yards needed - Beginning materials					
= Purchase requirements x cost per yard	$0.16	$0.16	$0.16	$0.16	$0.16
= Cost of purchases					
Total purchases					

Schedule 4

CAMPUS APPAREL COMPANY
Direct Labor Budget
Year Ending March 31, 1990

Q u a r t e r

	1	2	3	4	Total

Campus-Mode Sweaters

  Production units
x Direct labor hr per unit

= Total hours required
x Labor rate per hour

= Direct labor costs

Schedule 5

CAMPUS APPAREL COMPANY
Manufacturing Overhead Budget
Year Ending March 31, 1990

	Rate Per Hour	Q u a r t e r				Total
		1	2	3	4	
Variable Costs						
Indirect labor	$1.25					
Indirect materials	0.60					
Employee benefits	1.24					
Utilities	0.75					
Total variable costs	$3.84					
Direct labor hours		4,275	5,850	4,350	1,275	15,750
Predetermined overhead rate						
Fixed Costs						
Supervision	$7,500					
Property taxes	1,100					
Insurance	2,500					
Maintenance	3,250					
Utilities	8,800					
Depreciation	9,200					
Other	1,800					
Total	$4,150					
Total manufacturing overhead	$34,150					

Schedule 6

CAMPUS APPAREL COMPANY
Cost of Goods Sold Budget
Year Ending March 31, 1990

	Mode-less Sweaters	Campus-Mode Sweaters	Total
Beginning finished goods	$18,900	$0	
+ Direct materials used:			
Beginning direct material	0		
+ Budgeted purchases	0		
− Ending direct materials	0		
= Direct materials used			
+ Direct labor			
+ Variable manufacturing overhead (DLH x $3.84)			
= Total manufacturing costs			
− Ending finished goods			
= Cost of goods sold			

Unit costs per product:

Direct materials, wool	20 yds.	x	$0.30	=	$6.00
Direct materials, cotton	20 yds.	x	$0.16	=	3.20
Direct labor	.75 hrs.	x	6.40	=	4.80
Variable manufacturing overhead	.75 hrs.	x	3.84	=	2.88
Unit cost					$16.88

Schedule 7

CAMPUS APPAREL COMPANY
Administrative Expenses Budget
Year Ending March 31, 1990

Administrative Expenses	Quarter 1	2	3	4	Total
Management salaries	$9,680				
Clerical salaries	3,400				
Insurance	475				
Property taxes	245				
Utilities	290				
Supplies	275				
Depreciation	1,900				
Other	175				
Total	$16,440				

Schedule 8

CAMPUS APPAREL COMPANY
Selling Expenses Budget
Year Ending March 31, 1990

| | Quarter | | | | |
	1	2	3	4	Total
Variable Expenses					
Advertising					
Sales commissions					
Total variable expenses					
Fixed Expenses					
Sales salaries	9,500				
Travel	1,150				
Entertainment	750				
Insurance	125				
Property taxes	110				
Utilities	90				
Depreciation	1,100				
Other	150				
Total fixed expenses	12,975				
Total selling expenses					

Schedule 9

CAMPUS APPAREL COMPANY
Capital Expenditures Budget
Year Ending March 31, 1990

| | Quarter | | | | |
	1	2	3	4	Total
Office equipment			$21,500		$21,500
Sewing machines	$34,000				34,000
Total	$34,000	$0	$21,500	$0	$55,500

Note: This schedule is complete. It is for information purposes only.

Schedule 10

CAMPUS APPAREL COMPANY
Schedule of Cash Receipts and Disbursements
Year Ending March 31, 1990

	Quarter				
	1	2	3	4	Total
Cash Receipts					
From Begin A/R Balance	$10,500				$10,500
1st quarter sales	79,800				
2nd quarter sales					
3rd quarter sales					
4th quarter sales					
Total cash receipts	$90,300				
Cash Disbursements					
For Begin A/P Balance	$8,000				$8,000
1st quarter purchases					
2nd quarter purchases					
3rd quarter purchases					
4th quarter purchases					
Total cash disbursements					

Schedule 11   CAMPUS APPAREL COMPANY
                                     Cash Budget
                             Year Ending March 31, 1990

                                    Q u a r t e r
                        ----
                          1   2   3   4   Total
Beginning cash balance $15,000 $15,000
Cash Receipts

Cash collect from sales --

Total cash available   --

Cash Disbursements

 Payments for purchases
 Direct labor
 Manufacturing overhead
 Selling expenses
 Administrative expenses
 Capital expenditures
 Estimated tax payments ---

Total cash disbursements ---

Change in cash
 before borrowing
+Borrowing required   ---

-Loan repayment, principal
-Loan interest payment   ---

Ending cash balance   ===

Schedule 12

CAMPUS APPAREL COMPANY
Budgeted Income Statement
Year Ending March 31, 1990

	Campus-Mode Sweaters	Mode-less Sweaters	Total
Sales, in units	21,000	2,000	23,000
Sales, in dollars			
Cost of goods sold			
	---------	------------------	
Manufacturing margin			
Variable selling expenses			
	---------	------------------	
Contribution margin			
	---------	------------------	
Fixed costs:			
Manufacturing			
Selling			
Administrative			---------
Total fixed costs			---------
Net operating income			
Interest expense			

Net income before tax			
Estimated income tax			

Net income after tax			
			=========

Schedule 13   CAMPUS APPAREL COMPANY
                               Budgeted Balance Sheet
                                 March 31, 1990
                    (With comparative estimates as of March 31, 1989)

                                             1989   1990
Assets   --

Current Assets:
 Cash $15,000
 Accounts receivable   10,500
 Finished goods inventory   18,900
 Raw materials inventory   0
                                   ---------   ---------
Total current assets $44,400

Fixed assets:
 Building   220,000
 Machinery and equipment   390,000
 Accumulated deprec. and amort.   (305,000)
                                   ---------   ---------
Total fixed assets   305,000
                                             ---------   ---------
Total assets $349,400
                                             =========   =========

Liabilities and Stockholders' Equity

Current liabilities:
 Accounts payable $8,000
 Income taxes payable
 Notes payable to bank
                                   ---------   ---------
Total current liabilities $8,000

Stockholders' Equity:
 Common stock   150,000
 Retained earnings   191,400
                                   ---------   ---------
Total stockholders' equity   341,400
                                             ---------   ---------
Total liabilities and equity $349,400
                                             =========   =========

Schedule 14   CAMPUS APPAREL COMPANY
                          Budgeted Statement of Cash Flows
                             Year Ending March 31, 1990

Net income after tax
Adjustments to convert net income to net cash
  flows from operations:
  Increase in accounts receivable
  Decrease in finished goods inventory
  Increase in raw materials inventory
  Decrease in accounts payable
  Increase in accrued taxes
  Depreciation expense

Cash flow from operations
Cash flow from investing activities:
  Purchase of equipment
Cash flow from financing activities:
  Proceeds of loan
  Repayment of loan

Net increase in cash

VOCABULARY

ADMINISTRATIVE EXPENSES BUDGET. A schedule of the estimated administrative expenses for the budget period.

BUDGET. A quantitative plan showing how resources are expected to be acquired and used during a specified time period.

BUDGET PERFORMANCE REPORT. A management report comparing the actual and budgeted performance with an emphasis on any significantly large variances.

CAPITAL EXPENDITURES BUDGET. The budget showing the acquisition of long-term assets planned during a particular period.

CASH BUDGET. A projection of the cash receipts and disbursements expected during the budget period.

COST OF GOODS SOLD BUDGET. The cost of goods sold estimated for the budgeted income statement of a future period.

DIRECT LABOR BUDGET. An estimate of the direct labor needs of a budget period based on the expected production level.

DIRECT MATERIALS BUDGET. A projection of the direct materials that must be purchased to satisfy the production requirements of a budget period.

FINANCIAL BUDGET. The component of the master budget that shows the funding and financial position needed for the planned operations.

GOAL CONGRUENCE. The reconciliation of the goals of individual managers with those of the organization.

MANUFACTURING OVERHEAD BUDGET. A projection of the manufacturing overhead cost items required to support the expected production level.

MASTER BUDGET. A set of interrelated budgets representing a comprehensive plan of action for a specified time period.

OPERATING BUDGET. The component of the master budget that shows a detailed description of the revenues and costs required to achieve a firm's profit goals.

PRODUCTION BUDGET. A projection of the number of units that will be manufactured during the budget period to satisfy the requirements of the sales forecast and maintain adequate finished goods inventory levels.

PROGRAM BUDGETING. A budgeting approach used by not-for-profit organizations emphasizing the benefits of the services or programs involved rather than their costs.

SALES BUDGET. A translation of the sales forecast for a budget period into detailed information concerning the products or services expected to be sold.

SALES FORECAST. The projection of the potential sales for an entire industry as well as those expected for the firm preparing the forecast.

SELLING EXPENSES BUDGET. A schedule showing the estimated selling expenses needed to generate the expected sales volume for the budget period.

ZERO-BASE BUDGET. A budget prepared without allowing any consideration of past costs because each cost must be justified currently by the managers involved.

THE ANSWERS

MATCHING ATTRIBUTES

1.	G	6.	A	10.	I
2.	F	7.	C	11.	K
3.	J	8.	H	12.	B
4.	L	9.	M	13.	D
5.	E				

MULTIPLE CHOICE

1.	b	5.	b	8.	b
2.	c	6.	c	9.	b
3.	c	7.	e	10.	c
4.	c				

ILLUSTRATIVE PROBLEM

Schedule 1a

```
                        CAMPUS APPAREL COMPANY
                             Sales Budget
                       Year Ending March 31, 1990

                              Q u a r t e r
                   ------------------------------------
                      1        2        3       4       Total
Mode-less Sweaters
------------------
   Budgeted sales units     2,000                              2,000
 x Budgeted price per unit  $12.50                             $12.50
                           ---------                          ---------
 = Budgeted sales dollars   $25,000                            $25,000
                           ---------                          ---------
Campus-Mode Sweaters
--------------------
   Budgeted sales units     3,000    8,000    7,500    2,500   21,000
 x Budgeted price per unit  $36.00   $36.00   $36.00   $36.00  $36.00
                           -----------------------------------------------
 = Budgeted sales dollars  $108,000 $288,000 $270,000  $90,000 $756,000
                           -----------------------------------------------
Total
-----
   Budgeted sales dollars  $133,000 $288,000 $270,000  $90,000 $781,000
                           ===============================================
```

Schedule 2a

CAMPUS APPAREL COMPANY
Production Budget
Year Ending March 31, 1990

Q u a r t e r

Campus-Mode Sweaters	1	2	3	4	Total
Forecast sales units	3,000	8,000	7,500	2,500	21,000
+ Desired end. fin. goods	2,700	2,500	800	0	0
= Total units needed	5,700	10,500	8,300	2,500	21,000
- Beginning finished goods	0	2,700	2,500	800	0
= Production required, unit	5,700	7,800	5,800	1,700	21,000

Schedule 3a

CAMPUS APPAREL COMPANY
Direct Materials Budget
Year Ending March 31, 1990

Q u a r t e r

Campus-Mode Sweaters	1	2	3	4	Total
Production units	5,700	7,800	5,800	1,700	21,000
x yds wool thread/unit	20	20	20	20	20
= Yards of thread required	114,000	156,000	116,000	34,000	420,000
+ yards ending materials	52,000	28,000	11,000	0	0
= Yards needed	166,000	184,000	127,000	34,000	420,000
- Beginning materials	0	52,000	28,000	11,000	0
= Purchase requirements	166,000	132,000	99,000	23,000	420,000
x cost per yard	$0.30	$0.30	$0.30	$0.30	$0.30
= Cost of purchases	$49,800	$39,600	$29,700	$6,900	$126,000
Production units	5,700	7,800	5,800	1,700	21,000
x yds cotton thread/unit	20	20	20	20	20
= Yards of thread required	114,000	156,000	116,000	34,000	420,000
+ yards ending materials	28,500	39,000	29,000	8,500	8,500
= Yards needed	142,500	195,000	145,000	42,500	428,500
- Beginning materials	0	28,500	39,000	29,000	0
= Purchase requirements	142,500	166,500	106,000	13,500	428,500
x cost per yard	$0.16	$0.16	$0.16	$0.16	$0.16
= Cost of purchases	$22,800	$26,640	$16,960	$2,160	$68,560
Total purchases	$72,600	$66,240	$46,660	$9,060	$194,560

Schedule 4a

CAMPUS APPAREL COMPANY
Direct Labor Budget
Year Ending March 31, 1990

	Quarter				
	1	2	3	4	Total
Campus-Mode Sweaters					
Production units	5,700	7,800	5,800	1,700	21,000
x Direct labor hr per unit	0.75	0.75	0.75	0.75	0.75
= Total hours required	4,275	5,850	4,350	1,275	15,750
x Labor rate per hour	$6.40	$6.40	$6.40	$6.40	$6.40
= Direct labor costs	$27,360	$37,440	$27,840	$8,160	$100,800

Schedule 5a

CAMPUS APPAREL COMPANY
Manufacturing Overhead Budget
Year Ending March 31, 1990

	Rate Per Hour	Quarter				
		1	2	3	4	Total
Variable Costs						
Indirect labor	$1.25	$5,344	$7,313	$5,438	$1,594	$19,688
Indirect materials	0.60	2,565	3,510	2,610	765	9,450
Employee benefits	1.24	5,301	7,254	5,394	1,581	19,530
Utilities	0.75	3,206	4,388	3,263	956	11,813
Total variable costs	$3.84	16,416	22,464	16,704	4,896	60,480
Direct labor hours		4,275	5,850	4,350	1,275	15,750
Predetermined overhead rate		$3.84	$3.84	$3.84	$3.84	$3.84
Fixed Costs						
Supervision		$7,500	$7,500	$7,500	$7,500	$30,000
Property taxes		1,100	1,100	1,100	1,100	4,400
Insurance		2,500	2,500	2,500	2,500	10,000
Maintenance		3,250	3,250	3,250	3,250	13,000
Utilities		8,800	8,800	8,800	8,800	35,200
Depreciation		9,200	9,200	9,200	9,200	36,800
Other		1,800	1,800	1,800	1,800	7,200
Total		34,150	34,150	34,150	34,150	136,600
Total manufacturing overhead		$50,566	$56,614	$50,854	$39,046	$197,080

Schedule 6a

CAMPUS APPAREL COMPANY
Cost of Goods Sold Budget
Year Ending March 31, 1990

	Mode-less Sweaters	Campus-Mode Sweaters	Total
Beginning finished goods	$18,900	$0	$18,900
+ Direct materials used:			
Beginning direct material	0	0	0
+ Budgeted purchases	0	194,560	194,560
- Ending direct materials	0	1,360	1,360
= Direct materials used	0	193,200	193,200
+ Direct labor	0	100,800	100,800
+ Variable manufacturing overhead (DLH x $3.84)	0	60,480	60,480
= Total manufacturing costs	$0	$354,480	$354,480
- Ending finished goods	0	0	0
= Cost of goods sold	$18,900	$354,480	$373,380

Unit costs per product:
Direct materials, wool	20 yds. x $0.30 =		$6.00
Direct materials, cotton	20 yds. x $0.16 =		3.20
Direct labor	.75 hrs. x 6.40 =		4.80
Variable manufacturing overhead	.75 hrs. x 3.84 =		2.88
Unit cost			$16.88

Schedule 7a

CAMPUS APPAREL COMPANY
Administrative Expenses Budget
Year Ending March 31, 1990

	Quarter				
Administrative Expenses	1	2	3	4	Total
Management salaries	$9,680	$9,680	$9,680	$9,680	$38,720
Clerical salaries	3,400	3,400	3,400	3,400	13,600
Insurance	475	475	475	475	1,900
Property taxes	245	245	245	245	980
Utilities	290	290	290	290	1,160
Supplies	275	275	275	275	1,100
Depreciation	1,900	1,900	1,900	1,900	7,600
Other	175	175	175	175	700
Total	$16,440	$16,440	$16,440	$16,440	$65,760

Schedule 8a

CAMPUS APPAREL COMPANY
Selling Expenses Budget
Year Ending March 31, 1990

| | Quarter | | | | |
	1	2	3	4	Total
Variable Expenses					
Advertising	$2,160	$5,760	$5,400	$1,800	$15,120
Sales commissions	9,310	20,160	18,900	6,300	54,670
Total variable expenses	11,470	25,920	24,300	8,100	69,790
Fixed Expenses					
Sales salaries	9,500	9,500	9,500	9,500	38,000
Travel	1,150	1,150	1,150	1,150	4,600
Entertainment	750	750	750	750	3,000
Insurance	125	125	125	125	500
Property taxes	110	110	110	110	440
Utilities	90	90	90	90	360
Depreciation	1,100	1,100	1,100	1,100	4,400
Other	150	150	150	150	600
Total fixed expenses	12,975	12,975	12,975	12,975	51,900
Total selling expenses	$24,445	$38,895	$37,275	$21,075	$121,690

Schedule 9a

CAMPUS APPAREL COMPANY
Capital Expenditures Budget
Year Ending March 31, 1990

| | Quarter | | | | |
	1	2	3	4	Total
Office equipment			$21,500		$21,500
Sewing machines	$34,000				34,000
Total	$34,000	$0	$21,500	$0	$55,500

Schedule 10a

CAMPUS APPAREL COMPANY
Schedule of Cash Receipts and Disbursements
Year Ending March 31, 1990

Quarter

	1	2	3	4	Total
Cash Receipts					
From Begin A/R Balance	$10,500				$10,500
1st quarter sales	79,800	$39,900	$13,300	$0	133,000
2nd quarter sales		172,800	86,400	28,800	288,000
3rd quarter sales			162,000	81,000	243,000
4th quarter sales				54,000	54,000
Total cash receipts	$90,300	$212,700	$261,700	$163,800	$728,500
Cash Disbursements					
For Begin A/P Balance	$8,000				$8,000
1st quarter purchases	$58,080	$14,520			72,600
2nd quarter purchases		52,992	13,248		66,240
3rd quarter purchases			37,328	9,332	46,660
4th quarter purchases				7,248	7,248
Total cash disbursements	$66,080	$67,512	$50,576	$16,580	$200,748

Schedule 11a

CAMPUS APPAREL COMPANY
Cash Budget
Year Ending March 31, 1990

Quarter

	1	2	3	4	Total
Beginning cash balance	$15,000	$18,609	$21,608	$10,023	$15,000
Cash Receipts					
Cash collect from sales	90,300	212,700	261,700	163,800	728,500
Total cash available	105,300	231,309	283,308	173,823	743,500
Cash Disbursements					
Payments for purchases	66,080	67,512	50,576	16,580	200,748
Direct labor	27,360	37,440	27,840	8,160	100,800
Manufacturing overhead	41,366	47,414	41,654	29,846	160,280
Selling expenses	23,345	37,795	36,175	19,975	117,290
Administrative expenses	14,540	14,540	14,540	14,540	58,160
Capital expenditures	34,000		21,500		55,500
Estimated tax payments		5,000	5,000	5,000	15,000
Total cash disbursements	206,691	209,701	197,285	94,101	707,778
Change in cash before borrowing	(101,391)	21,608	86,023	79,722	35,722
+Borrowing required	120,000				120,000
-Loan repayment, principal			70,000	50,000	120,000
-Loan interest payment			6,000	1,250	7,250
Ending cash balance	$18,609	$21,608	$10,023	$28,472	$28,472

Schedule 12a

CAMPUS APPAREL COMPANY
Budgeted Income Statement
Year Ending March 31, 1990

	Campus-Mode Sweaters	Mode-less Sweaters	Total
Sales, in units	21,000	2,000	23,000
Sales, in dollars	$756,000	$25,000	$781,000
Cost of goods sold	354,480	18,900	373,380
Manufacturing margin	401,520	6,100	407,620
Variable selling expenses	68,040	1,750	69,790
Contribution margin	$333,480	$4,350	337,830
Fixed costs:			
Manufacturing			136,600
Selling			51,900
Administrative			65,760
Total fixed costs			254,260
Net operating income			83,570
Interest expense			7,250
Net income before tax			76,320
Estimated income tax			15,264
Net income after tax			$61,056

Schedule 13a

CAMPUS APPAREL COMPANY
Budgeted Balance Sheet
March 31, 1990
(With comparative estimates as of March 31, 1989)

	1989	1990
Assets		
Current Assets:		
Cash	$15,000	$28,472
Accounts receivable	10,500	63,000
Finished goods inventory	18,900	0
Raw materials inventory	0	1,360
Total current assets	$44,400	$92,832
Fixed assets:		
Building	220,000	220,000
Machinery and equipment	390,000	445,500
Accumulated deprec. and amort	(305,000)	(353,800)
Total fixed assets	305,000	311,700
Total assets	$349,400	$404,532
Liabilities and Stockholders' Equity		
Current liabilities:		
Accounts payable	$8,000	$1,812
Income taxes payable		264
Notes payable to bank		0
Total current liabilities	$8,000	$2,076
Stockholders' Equity:		
Common stock	150,000	150,000
Retained earnings	191,400	252,456
Total stockholders' equity	341,400	402,456
Total liabilities and equity	$349,400	$404,532

Schedule 14a   CAMPUS APPAREL COMPANY
                             Budgeted Statement of Cash Flows
                               Year Ending March 31, 1990

Net income after tax $61,056
Adjustments to convert net income to net cash
  flows from operations:
    Increase in accounts receivable $(52,500)
    Decrease in finished goods inventory   18,900
    Increase in raw materials inventory   (1,360)
    Decrease in accounts payable   (6,188)
    Increase in accrued taxes   264
    Depreciation expense   48,800   7,916

Cash flow from operations   68,972
Cash flow from investing activities:
  Purchase of equipment   (55,500)
Cash flow from financing activities:
  Proceeds of loan   120,000
  Repayment of loan   (120,000)   0

Net increase in cash $13,472
                                                             =========

CHAPTER 9

CAPITAL BUDGETING

Capital budgeting may seem like a strange name. It is the term used for the process of planning and controlling expenditures for fixed assets. It is an extremely important area of management. The accountant has some of the data and the techniques for providing the analysis for management's decisions regarding the firm's acquisitions of plant and equipment. Management will provide the data the accountant does not possess to insure an appropriate analysis. You should understand the following objectives of Chapter 9.

LEARNING OBJECTIVES

1. Explain why capital budgeting decisions are so important to management.
2. Identify the major characteristics of capital budgeting decisions.
3. Determine the role of cash flows in capital budgeting decisions.
4. List the typical cash inflows and cash outflows involved in capital budgeting decisions.
5. Explain how the time value of money is used in budgeting decisions.
6. Evaluate an investment with the net present value method and rank investments with the profitability index.
7. Define the essential features of a firm's cost of capital.
8. Evaluate an investment with the internal rate of return method.
9. Discuss the concept of depreciation as a tax shield and explain how different depreciation methods affect cash flows.
10. Compute an investment's payback period and recognize how this method is used in capital budgeting decisions.
11. Calculate an investment's average rate of return and explain how this method is used in capital budgeting.

LEARNING TIPS

Suppose that you are planning to buy a new car. How many choices do you have? What do you want the car for? How will you pay for it?

Now, put yourself in the position of a corporate executive whose company needs a new factory or several new expensive machines. There are many decisions to make. New plant and equipment decisions are made because the company

a.   Wants to expand capacity;

b.   Needs to replace old, worn equipment;

c.   Wants to improve operating efficiency;

d.   Has to improve its products to stay competitive; or

e.   Must meet EPA or other regulatory requirements.

Chapter 9 provides you with the tools for making these difficult decisions to maximize your company's profits.

REVIEW

Decisions! Decisions! They plague us wherever we go. Since we were children and our parents allowed us to make some of our own decisions, we found it wasn't always fun. As we have grown into adults, we find that many decisions are perplexing and difficult. Usually this is because we lack knowledge about the outcome of our decisions. Decisions always involve the future, and the future is filled with uncertainty.

Chapter 9 deals with relatively long-term decisions. Long-term decisions relate to a time period beyond our knowledge horizon. Thus, we anticipate a greater lack of information, and therefore a higher risk, than for short-term decisions. This chapter introduces special tools to help us become more comfortable with the long-term future decisions.

1.   **Recognize why capital budgeting decisions are so important to management.**

It takes years to plan for and build a new factory. The investment is large, and there is a great deal of uncertainty about such matters as:

a.   Will there be enough demand for the company's product to justify building a new factory to produce the product?

b.   Will the additional demand continue long enough so that the company will get its money back out of the factory and actually make a profit from it?

c.   Will the company have enough money, or will it be able to borrow enough money, to construct, equip and operate the new factory?

d.   Will there be an adequate supply of labor, raw materials and power to operate the factory efficiently and effectively?

With these and many other questions facing management before they make long-term capital acquisition decisions, it becomes more clear why management must have the best decision-making tools available to decide on long-term issues.

2.   **Identify the major characteristics of capital budgeting decisions.**

The most significant attributes of capital budgeting decisions are the following:

a.   Such decisions involve a lot of money—generally much more than normal operating capital. Because of this the future success of the business may well depend upon the successful planning for and execution of these decisions.

b.   The money spent on such projects will be committed for an extended period of time.

c. The investment decision cannot be changed. For example, a specially constructed factory for building bicycles could not easily be sold to another company (unless they also wanted to manufacture bicycles) in case the company changed its mind or found that building bicycles in the new factory was not profitable for that firm.

d. There is considerable risk involved because of the uncertainty of the future. The longer-term the decision, the greater the risk; that is, the further into the future we wish to project, the less we know about that time frame.

3. **Determine the role of cash flows in capital budgeting decisions.**

Cash flow analysis is involved in all but one of the commonly used capital budgeting techniques. Essentially what is being done in these methods is to compare, on a dollar and time basis, the effects a particular investment decision will have on the cash flow into and out of an organization. Since the cash flows occur over a substantial time period, they must be adjusted, through present value methods, so that they can be measured on an *equal time basis*. The exception is the average rate of return method that measures accounting income relative to the investment cost. Thus, this method is sometimes called the accounting method.

4. **List the typical cash inflows and cash outflows involved in capital budgeting decisions.**

The most common cash inflows associated with the capital budgeting decision are:

a. Additional revenues from the investment.
b. Cost savings resulting from the investment.
c. Sale value of the investment at the end of its life.
d. Reduction in working capital—e.g., decrease in inventory investment—that occurs at the end of the life of the investment.

The most common cash outflows associated with a capital budgeting decision are:

a. Initial cost of the investment.
b. Additional operating costs required by the investment.
c. Maintenance and repairs required for the new investment.
d. Additional working capital needed for the investment.

In the above lists of cash inflows and outflows, working capital changes relate to current assets minus current liabilities. If a new capital asset will increase business or add to the production capacity of a company, additional inventory of parts, work in process and finished goods will be necessary as long as the investment is useful. The increased business caused by the investment may also result in more accounts receivable. On the other hand, accounts payable used to purchase the inventory may also go up. This sum of additional current assets, less additional current liabilities, increases cash outflows when the investment is acquired and increases cash inflows when the working capital goes down at the end of the investment life.

5. **Explain how the time value of money is used in capital budgeting decisions.**

An old saying, "Today's dollar is worth more than tomorrow's dollar," indicates the time value of money. If I ask you whether you want your paycheck Thursday or a month from Thursday, you will probably say, "Thursday, for sure!" If you need the money now—and who doesn't?—you may have to borrow if your paycheck is late. If you borrow money to meet your needs, you will have to pay interest (rent) on the use of the money until you pay it back.

You may remember from grammer school math class that the interest formula is I = P x R x T; interest = principal x rate x time. If on April 1 you borrow $100 from a friend that you agree to pay back July 1 and your friend charges you interest at the rate of 12% a year you will calculate the interest as:

$$I = \$100 \times .12 \times 1/4 = \$3.00$$

12% is the annual interest rate, and the 1/4 represents the time (or term) of the loan, which is 3 months or 1/4 year. Your friend's $100 has a future value of $103 (principal plus interest) as of the repayment date, July 1.

6. **Evaluate an investment with the net present value method and rank investments with the profitability index.**

The net present value method involves calculating the present value of all present and future cash inflows and outflows using an appropriate interest rate. Suppose the Jenks Company buys a new machine that will produce buttons and badges. Neal Dancer, owner of Jenks Company, determines that he can earn $1,300 a year (part-time) from the machine, after paying all costs and expenses.

The machine costs $2,500 today and will have a life of five years. At the end of five years, the machine will have a $200 salvage value. What is the net present value of this investment?

Use Table A-3 in Appendix A of your text and a 15% rate.

Amount	Timing of Amount	Discount Factor	Present Value
$-2,500	Present	.0000	$ -2,500.00
1,300	1 year in future	.8696	1,130.48
1,300	2 years in future	.7561	982.93
1,300	3 years in future	.6575	854.75
1,300	4 years in future	.5718	743.34
1,300	5 years in future	.4972	646.36
	subtotal	3.3522	
200	5 years in future	.4972	99.44
	Net present value		$ 1,957.30

Instead of calculating the present value of each $1,300 item separately, by using Table A-4, the annuity of $1,300 a year for five years has a present value of

$1,300 x 3.3522 =	$ 4,357.86
Add the present value of the final salvage	99.44
Subtract the original investment cost	-2,500.00
This equals the net present value of	$ 1,957.30

The profitability index for this investment is calculated as

$$\frac{\$1,957.30}{\$2,500} = .7829$$

This profitability index should be compared with other possible investments available to Mr. Dancer. The decision rule for investments is: The investment with the largest (highest) profitability index is preferred over those with a smaller (lower) index.

7. **Define the essential features of a firm's cost of capital.**

Cost of capital refers to an organization's cost of obtaining debt and equity funds. This is not the same as the interest rate a company pays to borrow money, although the borrowing rate is included in the calculation of cost of capital. Cost of capital is a weighted average of the debt and equity funds obtained. Assume that Evans, Inc. has the following cost and mix of funds:

Type	Amount	Cost
Debt	$ 75,000	.14
Preferred stock	225,000	.09
Common equity	300,000	.18
Total funds	$ 600,000	

The Evans, Inc. cost of capital is calculated as a weighted average of each of the above components. Thus,

Type	Weight (Portion of Total)		Weight x Cost	
Debt	75/600 =	.125	.0175	(.125 x .14)
Preferred	225/600 =	.375	.03375	(.375 x .09)
Common	300/600 =	.500	.09	(.500 x .18)
		1.000		
Cost of capital			.14125	

8. **Evaluate an investment with the internal rate of return method.**

The internal rate of return method involves determining what rate will discount all present and future cash flows to exactly zero. The Johnson Cab Co. bought new maintenance equipment that will save hiring out cab maintenance work in the future. To outfit the garage cost $180,000. The equipment will have a ten-year life. It is anticipated that net savings on an annual basis will approximate $30,000. Dividing the initial cost by the projected annual savings, we get:

$$\frac{\$180,000}{\$30,000} = 6.00$$

This value, 6.00, is looked up in the ten-year row of Table A-4, and we find that it falls between 12% and 10%, being closest to 10%. To calculate the exact internal rate of return, interpolation may be accomplished as follows:

10-year factors from Table A-4

Factor for 10%	6.1446	6.1446
IRR factor above	6.0000	
Factor for 12%		5.6502
Difference	0.1446	0.4944

IRR = .10 + (.1446/.4944) x .02 = .10585 or 10.585%

The fraction .1446/.4944 represents the proportion of the distance between 10% and 12% that 6.0000 falls, and of course .02 is the difference between 10% and 12%.

9. **Discuss the concept of depreciation as a tax shield and explain how different depreciation methods affect cash flows.**

Depreciation is said to be a tax shield because it is a deductible expense for income tax purposes. When a business computes its taxable income it deducts depreciation and other operating expenses from revenues earned. Therefore, it is sometimes said that depreciation shields a certain portion of income from tax.

The reason that one depreciation method is preferable over another is that the fastest write-off, or the method that allows the depreciation shield to be taken earliest, is most advantageous, from a cash flow basis. It's that concept we ran into earlier—that a dollar now is better than a dollar next year. The comparison below should drive home the point.

The accelerated cost recovery system (ACRS) formerly used by the IRS for depreciation calculations, provides a rapid write-off of assets. The rate used in the first year is the same regardless of the time during the year that the asset is acquired. Under other depreciation methods, the first year's depreciation must be computed based on the proportion of the year the asset is held.

The Kenyon Kugler Company is considering the purchase of transportation equipment for its medical services division costing $48,000. Anticipated life, using straight line depreciation is five years, with an estimated salvage value of $8,000. Since it is to be bought July 1, 1988, one-half year's depreciation will be taken in 1990 and one-half year in 1995. The company's normal tax rate is 27%. Cost of capital is considered to be 16%. The annual tax shield from this investment is:

Year	Straight-line Depreciation	Tax Rate	Tax Shield	Discount Rate	Present Value
1990	$ 4,000	27%	$ 1,080	.8621	$ 931
1991	8,000	27%	2,160	.7432	1,605
1992	8,000	27%	2,160	.6407	1,384
1993	8,000	27%	2,160	.5523	1,193
1994	8,000	27%	2,160	.4761	1,028
1995	4,000	27%	1,080	.4104	443

Present value of depreciation tax shield $ 6,584
                                                                              ======

Calculating the present value of the tax shield using ACRS with a five-year life, 200% declining balance, ignoring the salvage value, and switching to straight line when this method results in a larger expense than 200% declining balance, the following table would apply:

Present Year	Book Value at Beginning of Year	Rate	Annual Depreciation	Book Value at End of Year	Discount Rate	Value
1990	$48,000	20%	$ 9,600	$38,400	.8621	$8,276
1991	38,400	40%	15,360	23,040	.7432	11,416
1992	23,040	40%	9,216	13,824	.6407	5,905
1993	13,824	40%	5,530	8,294	.5523	3,054
1994	8,294	**	5,529	2,765	.4761	2,632
1995	2,765	**	2,765	0	.4104	1,135

Present value of depreciation tax shield $32,418
                                                                              ======

**Straight-line depreciation results in a larger depreciation amount than 200% declining balance. Use $8,294/1.5 in 1994 and 1/2 of $5,529 in 1995.

In the above case it can be seen that the difference in the present values of the tax shields is $25,834 ($32,418 - $6,584). This illustrates the value in rapid write-off of assets through accelerated depreciation methods. (The above calculations are rounded to the nearest whole dollar.)

10. **Compute an investment's payback period and recognize how this method is used in capital budgeting decisions.**

The payback period is the length of time in which the enterprise recoups its cost of an investment. For example, Brooklyn Bridge Co. is considering an investment of $157,500 in a crane. The company expects to earn a net cash contribution of $35,000 per year from the crane. What is the crane's payback period?

$$\text{Payback period} \quad = \quad \frac{\text{Initial cost of investment}}{\text{annual net cash flows}}$$

$$= \quad \frac{\$157,500}{\$35,000} \quad = \quad 4.5 \text{ years.}$$

In this case, Brooklyn Bridge Co. expects to recover its initial investment in the equipment in 4.5 years. As indicated in the text, the chief weaknesses of this method are that no consideration is given to the total life of the investment and no consideration is given to the time value of money.

Many investment analysts use the payback method by going a step further and computing the payback reciprocal, which is one divided by the payback period. In this case that would be $1/4.5 = .2222$. This is useful because whenever the life of the investment is relatively long compared to the payback period, the payback reciprocal is approximately equal to, but always greater than, the internal rate of return.

The longer the life of the investment, relative to the payback period, the more closely the payback reciprocal approximates the internal rate of return. Thus, the payback reciprocal is often used as a technique for comparing different investment alternatives.

11. **Calculate an investment's average rate of return and explain how this method is used in capital budgeting.**

The average rate of return method uses accrual accounting data instead of the cash flow data used by the previous methods. The average rate of return is computed as:

$$\frac{\text{Average net income}}{\text{Average investment}}$$

Suppose the Tony Champion Bottled Gas Co. is considering the purchase of additional equipment to manufacture and store industrial gases that are not currently processed by the company, at a cost of $455,000. A projected income statement for this new line of business indicates the expected average net income, after taxes, that could be expected over the life of the investment is $45,000.

The first step is to calculate the average investment in the asset. If straight-line depreciation is used, the average investment is the initial cost plus the residual value divided by two. Suppose, then, that Tony Champion estimates the salvage (residual) value of the equipment to be $25,000. The average investment would be:

$$\frac{\$455,000 + \$25,000}{2} \quad = \quad \$240,000$$

Then, the average rate of return is calculated as:

$$\frac{\$45,000}{\$240,000} \quad = \quad .1875 \text{ or } 18.75\%$$

The average rate of return method may be used to compare alternative investments. This method, like the payback method, ignores the time value of money.

MATCHING ATTRIBUTES

Below, in Group A are listed attributes that may be identified with the capital budgeting terms listed in Group B. Indicate, by use of the identifying letter of the appropriate Group B item, which description in Group A best matches which Group B term.

Group A

_E_   1.   Type of decision for the purchase of an investment which should pay for itself and provide a profit.

_D_   2.   All methods of capital budgeting analysis involve the amount of the investment and _____.

_D_   3.   The capital budgeting analysis method that does not involve the measurement of cash flows.

_F_   4.   A company's cost of obtaining funds in the form of debt and equity capital.

_Q_   5.   Present cash flows are worth more than cash flows a year from now.

_J_   6.   Increase in current assets (less current liabilities) needed to support an investment.

_I_   7.   Process of reducing the value of a future amount into a present value.

_C_   8.   A series of equal amounts over a specified number of equal time periods.

_A_   9.   Method of computing depreciation for tax purposes.

_L_   10.   Cash inflows to a company minus cash outflows.

_O_   11.   One divided by the investment cost recovery period.

_N_   12.   Length of time to recoup investment cost through net cash flows.

_K_   13.   The rate that results in the discounted cash inflows exactly equalling the discounted cash outflows.

_H_   14.   Business is immediately able to reinvest cash inflow in another project with the same or greater rate of return.

_G_   15.   Tax shield example.

_P_   16. $\dfrac{\text{Present value of net cash flows}}{\text{Investment cost}}$

_M_   17.   The difference between the discounted value of the cash stream and the current investment cost.

Group B

A. ACRS
B. A measure of the yield (return) on an investment
C. Annuity
D. Average rate of return
E. Capital budgeting
F. Cost of capital
G. Depreciation
H. Discounted cash flow assumptions
I. Discounting
J. Incremental working capital
K. Internal rate of return
L. Net cash flows
M. Net present value
N. Payback period
O. Payback reciprocal
P. Profitability index
Q. Time value of money

MULTIPLE CHOICE

For each of the following items circle the letter indicating the most appropriate completion phrase or sentence.

1. Capital budgeting differs from operations budgeting in that:

    a. Operations budgeting tends to be long-term in nature, whereas capital budgeting tends to be short-term.

    b. Capital budgeting seeks optimum capital stock investment in the company to maximize stockholders' return on investment.

    c. Capital budgeting seeks to increase the value of the business through appropriate investment selection.

    d. Operations budgeting seeks an acceptable rate of return on various equipment and other asset purchases, to maximize annual net income.

2. Capital budgeting for businesses may be crucial to long-term profitability of a company because

    a. It often involves large amounts of money, and one bad decision could "sink" a company.

    b. The investment is committed for a long time.

    c. The investment normally can only be recovered through profitable operations over an extended period of time.

    d. The decisions affect the uncertain future, and the economy, and many other unknown factors may have a favorable or unfavorable impact on future profits.

    e. All of the above.

3. In the analysis of capital budgeting decisions, a number of techniques are commonly used. Each method involves the measurement of cash flows, except the

    a. Net present value method.

    b. Internal rate of return method.

    c. Payback period method.

    d. Average rate of return method.

4. Which of the following is an example of cash outflows involved with capital budgeting decisions?

    a. Depreciation of assets acquired.

    b. The initial cost of the investment.

    c. Revenues resulting from the investment.

    d. Salaries of the company executives who make the investment decisions.

5. Which of the following is an example of cash inflows involved with capital budgeting decisions?

    a. Incremental revenues resulting from the decision.

    b. Amortization of the asset costs.

    c. An increase in the working capital needed to support the investment.

    d. Interest earned on invested cash that would be used to acquire the investment if a favorable decision is made.

6. Assume the following after-tax costs of obtaining capital for the LaJolla Drive Wholesale Company:

Type	Amount	After-tax Cost
Debt	$400,000	8%
Equity	$600,000	12%

What is the cost of capital for this company?

a. 8%

b. 12%

c. 10.4%

d. 10%

7. Net present value method (NPV) is often used in evaluating investment decisions. Which of the following is true with respect to this method?

a. Negative NPV means the positive cash flows are less than the negative cash flows for this investment, on a discounted basis.

b. A negative NPV is a positive sign and a positive NPV is a negative sign with respect to making an investment decision.

c. The net present value method is the only capital budgeting method that does not depend on the use of a cost of capital or hurdle rate.

d. An NPV of zero indicates there is no cost of capital for the company's proposed investment.

[Note: For computing the solutions of some of the following questions, refer to the partial present value tables excerpted from Professor Helmkamp's textbook. These tables immediately follow this section.]

8. Lindbergh's Print Shop is planning the purchase of a new press for $160,000 which would have a useful life of eight years. The company's cost of capital is 16%, and it expects to save an average of $32,000 a year in cash operating costs (after taxes) with the new press. Assume a salvage value at the end of eight years to be $12,000. What is the net present value of this proposed investment, rounded to the nearest $100?

a. $139,000

b. $142,000

c. -$17,300

d. $160,000

e. None of the above.

9. Assume the same facts as in question 8. above, except that the $32,000 is after-tax net income. The average rate of return (to the nearest whole percent) is:

a. 20%

b. 40%

c. 37%

d. 32%

e. 8%

10. Assuming the same facts as in question 8 above, except ignoring salvage value, what is the internal rate of return, to the nearest .1%?

    a.   11.8%
    b.   12.0%
    c.   5.0%
    d.   11.7%
    e.   11.0%

11. Referring once again to item 8 above, compute the payback period for the new press.

    a.   8 years
    b.   7 years
    c.   6 years
    d.   5 years
    e.   some other period

12. The payback reciprocal is sometimes used as an approximation of the internal rate of return. Under what circumstances is this valid?

    a.   When the asset life is at least as long as the payback period.
    b.   When the cost of capital equals the inverse (reciprocal) of the payback period.
    c.   When the asset life is at least twice as long as the payback period.
    d.   As long as the total cash inflows exceed the total cash outflows.
    e.   If the internal rate of return is greater than 10%.

13. Huntsberry Landscaping Company is considering the purchase of a new earth-moving machine at a cost of $78,000. Its expected life is seven years, at which time its salvage value will approximate $3,500. After-tax cash savings in operating costs with the new machine are shown in the following table.

Year	After-tax Cost savings	Year	After-tax Cost savings
1	$12,000	5	$16,000
2	18,300	6	15,500
3	21,500	7	14,300
4	17,800	8	11,600

What is the approximate payback period for the above investment?

    a.   8 years
    b.   6 years
    c.   5 years
    d.   4 1/2 years
    e.   4 years

Partial Tables A-3 and A-4 from your text:

Periods	Present Value of An Annuity of $1				Present Value of $1			
	10%	12%	14%	16%	10%	12%	14%	16%
1	0.9091	0.8929	0.8772	0.8621	0.9091	0.8929	0.8772	0.8621
2	1.7355	1.6901	1.6467	1.6052	0.8264	0.7972	0.7695	0.7432
3	2.4869	2.4018	2.3216	2.2459	0.7513	0.7118	0.6750	0.6407
4	3.1699	3.0373	2.9137	2.7982	0.6830	0.6355	0.5921	0.5523
5	3.7908	3.6048	3.4331	3.2743	0.6209	0.5674	0.5194	0.4761
6	4.3553	4.1114	3.8887	3.6847	0.5645	0.5066	0.4556	0.4104
7	4.8684	4.5638	4.2883	4.0386	0.5132	0.4523	0.3996	0.3538
8	5.3349	4.9676	4.6389	4.3436	0.4665	0.4039	0.3506	0.3050
9	5.7590	5.3282	4.9464	4.6065	0.4241	0.3606	0.3075	0.2630
10	6.1446	5.6502	5.2161	4.8332	0.3855	0.3220	0.2697	0.2267

ILLUSTRATIVE PROBLEM

1. Darin Bruce is a new member of the executive committee of Diane's Fashion Swimwear, a company specializing in beach and pool garments. His background is design and high fashion. However, he will be involved in many executive decisions about investments and company expansion. He has no background in capital budgeting, so the president, Sue Pullar, has asked you to give Mr. Bruce a brief outline of the steps involved in making capital expenditure decisions.

Requested:

Develop written notes in preparation for your discussion with Mr. Bruce. Do not detail the various analysis methods.

2. H. V. Kultenbird is the production manager for the Blue Network, a communications company. She has proposed the purchase of $275,500 of new communications equipment to improve the transmission of signals received from satellites. She indicates that the acquisition of such equipment will result in additional net cash after-tax revenues or cost reductions as follows:

First year	$ 62,000
Second year	106,800
Third year	134,300
Fourth year	158,300
Fifth year	75,000

At the end of the fifth year, the equipment would be sold for $35,000.

Requested:

Assuming a cost of capital of 12%, compute the net present value of this proposed investment, using the present value schedule preceding this section and the following table.

Year	Description	Cash Flow	12% Present Value of $1	PV of Cash Flows
0	Investment	$(275,500)	1.0000	$(275,500)
1	Cost saving	62,000		
2	Cost saving	106,800		
3	Cost saving	134,300		
4	Cost saving	158,300		
5	Cost saving	75,000		
5	Salvage	35,000		

3. Assume the same set of circumstances as in the Blue Network case above, except that the cash inflows from the investment would be $80,000 per year for five years with no equipment salvage value.

Requested:

Compute the internal rate of return for this investment.

4. Assume the same facts as in problem 2 above. Compute the average return on investment.

VOCABULARY

ACCELERATED COST RECOVERY SYSTEM (ACRS). A form of accelerated depreciation used to depreciate assets purchased after 1980 for federal income tax purposes. ACRS was modified by the Tax Reform Act of 1986 for depreciable property purchased after 1986.

ANNUITY. A series of equal payments over a specified number of time periods, with a particular interest rate or discount rate included in the payments.

AVERAGE RATE OF RETURN. A capital budgeting method that provides a rough approximation of an investment's profitability as measured with net income from the income statement.

CAPITAL BUDGETING. The process used to evaluate capital expenditures.

CAPITAL EXPENDITURES. Expenditures made for long-term assets that determine a firm's operating capacity.

COST OF CAPITAL (HURDLE RATE). A firm's cost of obtaining funds in the form of debt or owners' equity, which represents the firm's minimal rate of return from an investment that is acceptable to management.

DISCOUNTED CASH FLOWS. Use of present values to convert the cash inflows and cash outflows from an investment to equivalent or current dollars.

DISCOUNTING. Applying a discount rate to convert future values to present values.

DISCOUNT RATE. The rate used to convert future values to present values.

INTERNAL RATE OF RETURN (IRR) METHOD. The use of a discount rate that will exactly equate the discounted cash outflows from an investment with its discounted cash inflows, thus making the net present value zero.

INTERPOLATION. A mathematical technique used to compute an interest or discount rate bracketed by two known rates.

NET PRESENT VALUE (NPV) METHOD. A capital budgeting method used to evaluate the discounted cash flows associated with an investment.

PAYBACK PERIOD METHOD. A capital budgeting method used to determine the length of time required to recover the cost of an investment from the net cash flows it generates.

PRESENT VALUE. The current value of some future sum of money or series of payments, discounted with a specific discount rate.

PROFITABILITY INDEX. The present value of the net cash flows from an investment divided by its cost.

TAX SHIELD. A tax deductible item, such as depreciation, which shields income that otherwise would be taxed.

TIME VALUE OF MONEY. Money held at an early date such as today is more valuable than the same amount of money available at a later date such as next year because of the interest that can be earned on the money over time and the uncertainty associated with receiving it in the future.

THE ANSWERS

MATCHING ATTRIBUTES

1.	E	6.	J	10.	L	14.	H
2.	B	7.	I	11.	O	15.	G
3.	D	8.	C	12.	N	16.	P
4.	F	9.	A	13.	K	17.	M
5.	Q						

MULTIPLE CHOICE

1.	c	5.	a	9.	c	13.	d
2.	e	6.	c	10.	a		
3.	d	7.	a	11.	d		
4.	b	8.	c	12.	c		

ILLUSTRATIVE PROBLEMS

1. Steps involved in making capital expenditure decisions:

   a. Identify manager's requested capital expenditures for achieving the firm's long-term goals.
   b. Obtain information about the cost of the investments and their expected return.
   c. Select a capital budgeting method to evaluate each investment.
   d. Evaluate each investment using the capital budgeting method chosen.
   e. Rank investment opportunities by risk and return.
   f. Select best investments, given opportunities and resources available.
   g. Reevaluate each capital expenditure as new information becomes available.

2.

Year	Description	Cash Flow	12% Present Value of $1	PV of Cash Flows
0	Investment	$(275,500)	1.0000	$(275,500)
1	Cost saving	62,000	.8929	55,360
2	Cost saving	106,800	.7972	85,141
3	Cost saving	134,300	.7118	95,595
4	Cost saving	158,300	.6355	100,600
5	Cost saving	75,000	.5674	42,555
5	Salvage	35,000	.5674	19,859
	Net present value			$123,610

3.

$$\text{IRR factor} \quad = \quad \frac{\text{Cost of investment}}{\text{Annual net cash flows}} \quad = \quad \frac{\$275,500}{\$80,000} \quad = \quad 3.4438$$

Per Table A-4, using the 5 year line,

Factor for 12%	3.6048	3.6048
IRR factor	3.4438	
Factor for 14%		3.4331
Difference	0.1610	0.1717

$$\text{IRR} \quad = \quad .12 + \frac{0.1610}{0.1717} \times .02 \quad = .139 \quad = 13.9\%$$

4.

$$\frac{.2 \times (\$62,000 + 106,800 + 134,300 + 158,300 + 75,000)}{.5 \times (\$275,500 + 35,000)} = .691$$

CHAPTER 10

STANDARD COSTS: DIRECT MATERIALS AND DIRECT LABOR

Managers need to know. Budgets tell what happened—compared to the plan—after the period is over. Budgets report on a company-wide or segment basis. How about each individual job or operation? The answer for many firms is a standard cost system. Standard costs are established for each operation and product, so that *as production occurs* management can evaluate actual performance against the standard. This is a management tool that is widely used in manufacturing, and to a lesser extent, in service industries. It is a must for the management accountant.

LEARNING OBJECTIVES

1. Recognize why standard costs are used by a manufacturing firm.
2. List the benefits and limitations of standard costs.
3. Describe the different ways standard costs are developed.
4. Distinguish between ideal standards and attainable standards.
5. Explain how price and quantity standards are developed for direct materials.
6. Explain how rate and efficiency standards are developed for direct labor.
7. Identify the basic steps taken in cost variance analysis.
8. Develop a general model for direct cost variance analysis.
9. Compute cost variances for direct materials and direct labor.
10. Identify potential causes of direct cost variances and the managers responsible for them.
11. Determine what is a significant cost variance.
12. Analyze cost performance with a control chart.
13. Prepare journal entries to record a standard cost performance.

LEARNING TIPS

Standard costs create a lot of extra work for the accountant and the manager, but they also provide valuable information for management at all levels. When actual costs vary from the standard, cost variance analysis helps determine whose responsibility it is, and how and where corrections can be made. There are certain rules for computing variances that you can pick up if you are observant. First learn the rules, and you will be able to calculate any variance easily. But be sure also to study the reason for each variance and what management might do to improve performance in the future.

REVIEW

1. **Recognize why standard costs are used by a manufacturing firm.**

   Standard costs are employed by manufacturing firms in order to establish a predetermined cost for each product for the measurement of manufacturing efficiency. Standard costs are used for planning and controlling manufacturing cost performance for the purpose of achieving profit goals.

2. **List the benefits and limitations of standard costs.**

   Among the benefits of standard costs are:
   a. Standard costs are useful in developing a profit plan of operations, called a budget. In this sense, standard costs are reliable estimates of what costs should be.
   b. Standard costs are very useful in measuring performance. Since standard costs are targets to attain by operating personnel, any variance from them is used as a measure of performance efficiency.
   c. Use of standard costs reduces recordkeeping costs. Inventory costs and production costs are recorded at standard, or predetermined, costs, rather than actual costs, which tend to vary considerably, thus making the recordkeeping a simpler process.
   d. Standard costs may be used effectively for managerial decision making. Since these costs are readily available (whereas actual costs are time-consuming to gather) decision-making can be accomplished easier and more quickly.
   e. Employees become aware of what costs should be when standard costs are used. In this way, they become more cost conscious and can be motivated to be more efficient in their work performance.

   The limitations of standard costs are as important as the benefits. These limitations are listed below:
   a. Sometimes standard costs are established through judgment, which can be faulty, rather than being based on fact. Faulty standards cause plans and performance evaluation to be in error.
   b. Poorly established standard costs may on one hand cause frustration and irritation on the part of employees, or, on the other hand, employees may dismiss the standards as meaningless, and ignore them.
   c. Standard costs require frequent updating in order for them to be useful. In periods of rapidly changing prices, this updating becomes particularly time-consuming.
   d. Managers pay particular attention to variances from standards, or the exceptions. This concentration on exceptions often means managers do not acknowledge performance that is on target. This can be annoying to the person being reviewed or criticized for exceptions.

3. **Describe the different ways standard costs are developed.**

   The three most commonly used methods of developing standard costs are:
   a. *Engineering approach* involves studies of the time it takes for an experienced employee to perform each task in the production process, as well as developing the proper techniques for performing the work. In this way, a standard is established for each segment of the process.
   b. *Analysis of historical performance* establishes a beginning point for determining what a particular standard should be. However, to use historical performance blindly—i.e., without analysis—is not wise.
   c. *Management judgment concerning the future* is a method that employs the judgment and experience of the managers who know the operations best to set the standards of future performance.

4. **Distinguish between ideal standards and attainable standards.**

Ideal standards assume maximum efficiency, without allowing for employee fatigue, errors or spoilage. Such standards are not realistic. Although they presumably can be reached for short periods of time, in the long run they cannot be maintained.

Attainable standards, on the other hand, make an appropriate allowance for the human factors of fatigue, errors and spoilage, but only to a limited extent. Thus, these standards may not be attained without considerable effort, but by being within reach, provide an incentive for employees to attain them.

5. **Explain how price and quantity standards are developed for direct materials.**

For this purpose, assume the manufacture of picnic tables by the Gold Medal Furniture Company. The company has designed a new line of wood and metal patio furniture, with the following specifications for the picnic table:

Redwood lumber		
15 board feet of 2" x 6" x 6'	@	$0.87 bd ft
15' 5/8" wrought iron rod	@	1.10 ft
12' 3/8" wrought iron rod	@	0.65 ft
8 ea. 1 3/4" black lag bolts	@	0.185 ea
1 quart SuniDay redwood stain	@	1.95 qt

These constitute the standard quantities and costs of materials for the new Gold Medal Picnicker table. Assume that spoilage and waste allowances have already been included in these quantities, and that the costs are net of discounts, but include transportation and other costs of acquisition. After considering these discounts and associated costs, the planned material costs for one Picnicker table are:

15 bd. ft., redwood lumber	@	$0.87	=	$13.05
15 linear ft. 5/8" wrought iron rod	@	1.10	=	16.50
12 linear ft. 3/8" wrought iron rod	@	0.65	=	7.80
8 ea. 1 3/4" lag bolts, black	@	0.185	=	1.48
1 qt. SuniDay redwood stain	@	1.95	=	1.95
Total material cost				$40.78

6. **Explain how rate and efficiency standards are developed for direct labor.**

Continuing with the example of the Gold Medal Furniture Company, let us assume the following facts for direct labor for each Picnicker table:

Cutting time for lumber and rods	0.30	hrs.
Sanding and smoothing cut components	0.25	hrs.
Painting and staining	0.50	hrs.
Inspection	0.25	hrs.
Packaging and moving to warehouse	0.40	hrs.
Idle time	0.30	hrs.
Total labor time	2.00	hrs.

Although there is some variation in direct labor rates depending upon experience and abilities, the Gold Medal Company uses $8.50 as a uniform standard direct labor rate. Therefore, standard direct labor cost for the Picnicker table is:

$$2.00 \text{ hrs.} \times \$8.50 \text{ per hr.} = \$17.00$$

Total direct manufacturing costs of producing the Picnicker table are:

Direct materials	$40.78
Direct labor	17.00
Total direct manufacturing costs	$57.78

7. Identify the basic steps taken in cost variance analysis.

What must be done to identify cost variances is to determine actual costs of production as soon as they occur, and pair actual costs with standard costs for those material and labor items. The differences between actual costs incurred and standard cost constitute standard cost variances. If these variances are to be recorded in the ledger, unfavorable cost variances are recorded as debits (additional costs) and favorable cost variances are recorded as credits (lower costs).

8. Develop a general model for direct cost variance analysis.

There are two variances that can be calculated for each product cost category, direct materials and direct labor. The two variances are quantity variance and price variance. If the quantity of materials used is different from the standard quantity of materials for that product, a materials quantity (or usage) variance results. Similarly, if the quantity of direct labor actually used differs from the standard quantity of direct labor, there will be a labor efficiency (or usage) variance.

If the price paid for direct materials differs from the standard cost, a materials price variance occurs. Also, if the actual labor rate incurred is different from the standard labor rate, there will be a labor rate variance. The sum of the materials variances is called the total materials variance, and the sum of the direct labor variances is the total labor variance.

The general model for the direct materials cost variance analysis is:

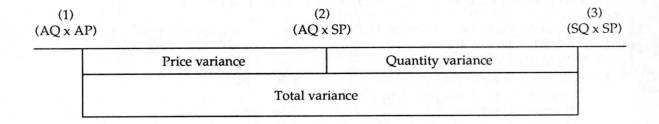

(1)	(2)	(3)
(AQ x AP)	(AQ x SP)	(SQ x SP)

Price variance	Quantity variance
Total variance	

AQ	=	actual quantity
AP	=	actual price
SP	=	standard price
SQ	=	standard quantity

Using this model:

price variance	=	(1) - (2)	=	(AQ x AP) - (AQ x SP),
quantity variance	=	(2) - (3)	=	(AQ x SP) - (SQ x SP),

and

total variance	=	(1) - (3)	=	(AQ x AP) - (SQ x SP).

9. **Compute cost variances for direct materials and direct labor.**

Using the Gold Medal Furniture Company example above, suppose actual quantities and prices of materials are as shown below for the month of May, when 1,000 Picniceer tables were manufactured.

	Actual	
Material	**Quantity**	**Price**
Redwood lumber, bd. ft.	15,750	.865
5/8" wrought iron rod, ft.	14,900	1.12
3/8" wrought iron rod, ft.	12,400	.65
1 3/4" black bolts, ea.	8,250	.17
SuniDay redwood stain, qt.	1,040	1.875

By using the general standard cost variance model above, the variances are calculated as shown on Figure 10-1.

FIG 10-1

GOLD METAL FURNITURE COMPANY
VARIANCE ANALYSIS
PICNICEER TABLES

MATERIAL	UNIT	ACTUAL QUANTITY	ACTUAL PRICE	(1) (AQ x AP)	ACTUAL QUANTITY	STANDARD PRICE	(2) (AQ x SP)	STANDARD QUANTITY	STANDARD PRICE	(3) (SQ x SP)
Redwood lumber	bd. ft.	15,750	0.865	13,623.75	15,750	0.870	13,702.50	15,000	0.870	13,050.00
5/8" wrought iron rod	ft.	14,900	1.120	16,688.00	14,900	1.100	16,390.00	15,000	1.100	16,500.00
3/8" wrought iron rod	ft.	12,400	0.650	8,060.00	12,400	0.650	8,060.00	12,000	0.650	7,800.00
1 3/4" black bolts	ea.	8,250	0.170	1,402.50	8,250	0.185	1,526.25	8,000	0.185	1,480.00
Suniday redwood stain	qt.	1,040	1.875	1,950.00	1,040	1.950	2,028.00	1,000	1.950	1,950.00
				----------			----------			----------
				41,724.25			41,706.75			40,780.00
				==========			==========			==========

Materials price variance = (1) - (2) = 41724.25 -41706.75 =   17.50

Materials quantity variance = (2) - (3)=41706.75 -40780.00 =   926.75

Total materials cost variance = (2) - (3) =   944.25
                                                              =========

Next let us consider the actual labor for the month. Suppose that actual direct labor hours for the month of May were 2,120 at a total cost of $17,808. The average actual labor rate was $8.40 ($17,808/2,120). The direct labor cost variances are computed as follows:

Labor rate variance:

$$(AQ \times AP) - (AQ \times SP) =$$
$$(2{,}120 \times \$8.40) - (2{,}120 \times \$8.50) = \quad -- \$ \quad 212.00$$

Labor efficiency variance:

$$(AQ \times SP) - (SQ \times SP) =$$
$$(2{,}120 \times \$8.50) - (2{,}000 \times \$8.50) = \quad \$ \quad 1{,}020.00$$

Total labor variance:

$$(AP \times AP) - (SQ \times SP) =$$
$$(2{,}120 \times \$8.40) - (2{,}000 \times \$8.50) = \quad \$ \quad 808.00$$

10. **Identify potential causes of direct manufacturing cost variances and the managers responsible for them.**

The two types of direct manufacturing cost variances are price and quantity. Direct materials price variances are the responsibility of the purchasing agent, or purchasing manager. The causes of variances in direct materials prices are (a) purchasing from the wrong supplier; (b) purchase of the wrong quality of materials; (c) normal materials price changes; (d) rush orders that increase shipping costs; (e) purchase of wrong quantity lots, thus affecting normal quantity discounts; and (f) outdated standard costs.

The materials quantity variance is the responsibility of the manager of the production activity involved. This variance measures the efficiency with which direct materials are used in manufacturing the product. One or more of the following causes create direct materials quantity variances: (a) materials that are of poor quality; (b) laborers who lack experience in this manufacturing process; (c) poor or inadequate supervision of labor; (d) faulty or poorly adjusted manufacturing equipment; (e) especially efficient manufacturing performance; (f) errors in the manufacturing process; and (g) outdated standards of production.

Looking next at the labor rate (price) variance, we see that the difference between the standard wage rate and the actual wage rate causes the rate variance. This variance is the responsibility of either the personnel department or the production manager, depending upon who authorizes the use of workers with different wage rates than those specified. It is this use of laborers who are paid a different rate from the standard that causes the labor rate variance. On the other hand, if standard direct labor rates are obsolete, so that people are not available at the specified rate, the cause of the rate variance may actually be an outdated direct labor rate standard.

The direct labor efficiency (quantity) variance is created by using a different quantity of direct labor hours in the manufacturing process than specified in the labor standard for the product. This variance, like all the others, can be positive or negative. The manager in charge of the production process is responsible for the direct labor efficiency variance. Causes of this variance include: (a) faulty equipment; (b) inexperienced workers; (c) inferior quality materials; (d) poor or inadequate supervision of workers; (e) especially high quality work performance; (f) changes in production methods; and (g) outdated labor standards.

11. Determine what is a significant cost variance.

Management usually wants to investigate only those variances from standard that are significant. "Significant" may be defined in terms of a certain dollar amount or a certain percentage of standard. Sometimes both are used. For example, variances of at least 10% of standard will be investigated as to cause and responsibility *if* the variance is at least $100 for the period. In this way, management time will not be wasted on the investigation of insignificant variances. Each company may establish its own minimum levels for scrutiny.

12. Analyze cost performance with a control chart.

Standard cost variances may be expressed in dollar terms or percentage terms, as discussed above. Either measure may be indicated on a control chart, which is a graph that shows the variances from standard of each item sampled. For example, the manufacturing of Picniceer tables by the Gold Medal Company may be monitored by choosing sample tables randomly, or, for example, every tenth table made could be chosen. The total labor cost charged to each table selected could then be plotted on the standard labor cost chart as shown in Figure 10-2.

This control chart is based on a standard direct labor cost of producing Picniceer tables, as indicated in a previous example, of $17.00 (rounded), with upper and lower control limits indicated as plus and minus 10% respectively. Ten random sample observations are shown. Although none of these observations exceeds either the upper or lower control limits, it is apparent that the later observations show a trend upward. This is a sign that the supervisor may wish to investigate the trend before the process goes out of cost control. Although costs lower than standard are generally considered to be favorable, usually management will investigate any cost that goes either higher than the upper control limit or below the lower control limit. This procedure permits the correction of cost variances as the manufacturing process occurs, rather than waiting until the end of the month, when all of the accounting data is reported.

Figure 10-2
Direct Labor Cost Control Chart
Labor Efficiency Variance

Upper control limit	$18.70		
Standard cost	$17.00		
Lower control limit	$15.30		

```
Upper control limit   $18.70  ─────────────────────────────────
                                                        x
                                                    x   x
                                          x       x
Standard cost         $17.00          x           x
                                  x           x
                                      x
Lower control limit   $15.30  ─────────────────────────────────
                              1 2 3 4 5 6 7 8 9 10
                              Sample observation
```

13. **Prepare journal entries to record a standard cost performance.**

The following entries record in general journal form some of the cost variances shown above.

<u>Materials purchased</u>

(a)	Debit	Credit
Direct materials inventory		
(15,750 bd ft x $0.87)	13,702.50	
Materials price variance (15,750 x $0.005)		78.75
Accounts payable (15,750 x $0.865)		13,623.75
(To record the purchase of redwood lumber.)		
(b)		
Direct materials inventory (14,900 ft x $1.10)	16,390.00	
Materials price variance (14,900 ft x $0.02)	298.00	
Accounts payable (14,900 ft x $1.12)		16,688.00
(To record the purchase of 5/8" wrought iron rods.)		

<u>Direct materials usage</u>

(c)		
Work in process inventory (15,000 bd ft x $0.87)	13,050.00	
Materials quantity variance (750 bd ft x $0.87)	652.50	
Raw materials inventory (15,750 x $0.87)		13,702.50
(To record the usage of redwood for 1,000 tables.)		
(d)		
Work in process inventory (15,000 ft x $1.10)	16,500.00	
Materials quantity variance (100 ft x $1.10)		110.00
Raw materials inventory (14,900 ft x $1.10)		16,390.00
(To record the usage of 5/8" wrought iron rods.)		

<u>Direct labor cost recorded</u>

(e)		
Direct labor payroll (2,120 hrs x $8.50)	18,020.00	
Accrued payroll (2,120 hrs x $8.40)		17,808.00
Labor rate variance (2,120 hrs x $0.10)		212.00
(To record the actual direct labor payroll.)		

<u>Direct labor hours used</u>

(f)		
Work in process inventory (2,000 hrs x $8.50)	17,000.00	
Labor efficiency variance (120 hrs x $8.50)	1,020.00	
Direct labor payroll (2,120 hrs. x $8.50)		18,020.00
(To record the direct labor hours used for 1,000 tables.)		

MATCHING ATTRIBUTES

Below in Group A are listed attributes that may be identified with the terms in Group B. Indicate, by use of the identifying letter of the appropriate Group B item, which attribute best matches which Group B term.

Group A

_____ 1. The difference between the actual amount paid for labor and the standard amount expected to be paid for labor.

_____ 2. Standards that include allowances for departures from maximum efficiency.

_____ 3. Function as performance targets in the production of goods in a manufacturing operation.

_____   4.   They tend to balance out over time and are not controllable by management.

_____   5.   Measures the efficiency of direct materials utilization.

_____   6.   The result of using a different number of labor hours than the standard hours allowed. ⌐

_____   7.   Results in variances that are identifiable and controllable. ·

_____   8.   Output of products actually produced divided by number of labor hours required to achieve that output.

_____   9.   This can be caused by using the wrong supplier, having an outdated standard price, or an incorrect choice of quality.

_____   10.   The difference between actual costs and standard costs.

_____   11.   Show the range of cost performance resulting from random fluctuations.

_____   12.   Requires the highest possible amount of effort to be achieved.

Group B

A.	Attainable standards	G.	Materials quantity variance
B.	Ideal standards		
C.	Labor efficiency variance	H.	Nonrandom fluctuations
D.	Labor productivity	I.	Random fluctuations
E.	Labor rate variance	J.	Standard costs
F.	Materials price variance	K.	Standard cost variances
		L.	Standard cost variance control limits

MULTIPLE CHOICE

1.   Standard costs offer several advantages or benefits to the user. Which of the following is *not* a true advantage or benefit?

   a.   Standard costs provide reliable estimates for developing a budget.

   b.   Standard costs provide targets for managers to attain or exceed, as well as yardsticks against which to measure actual performance.

   c.   Standard costs help make employees and managers more aware of costs of operation, creating greater efficiency by employees.

   d.   Standard costs make it unnecessary to keep actual costs which saves record-keeping, especially in periods when actual costs change rapidly and standards remain the same.

   e.   Standard costs are usually more readily available than actual costs, thus aiding managerial decision-making.

2.   Standard costs may be established by one or more methods. Which of the following is *not* an appropriate method for establishing standards?

   a.   Engineering studies such as time analysis and work sampling establish economical combinations of labor and materials for a particular product.

   b.   Analysis of past performance data provide insights into what future costs should be.

   c.   Managerial judgment may often provide the skilled analysis of what will happen in the future based on years of experience with operating costs of the past.

   d.   Borrowing the standards used by other companies often permits the use of data from leaders in the industry that may be more experienced than we are.

3. Only one of the following statements reflects the author's ideas about the establishment of standard costs.

    a.   Ideal standards are the best standards for a company to establish because they indicate what costs should be (and could be) under the best of circumstances.

    b.   Ideal standards encourage employees to "reach for the top," thus creating peak performance and lowest actual labor cost.

    c.   Attainable standards generally promote a more relaxed atmosphere in the company, and, although higher costs may ensue than under ideal standards, everyone is happier, which is, after all, what it's all about.

    d.   Attainable standards are generally preferred because they represent realistic targets that can be obtained with a reasonable effort on the part of employees.

4. Your text suggests five basic questions answered by standard cost variance analysis. Which of the following is *not* included among these questions?

    a.   How much is the total variance?

    b.   When did the variance occur?

    c.   Where did the variance occur?

    d.   Why did the variance occur?

    e.   Who is responsible for the variance?

5. Standard cost variances are often incorporated directly into the general accounting system. In this regard, which of the following statements is true?

    a.   Favorable cost variances are debits in the accounts, indicating an unused cost balance.

    b.   Favorable cost variances are credits in the accounts, representing a reduced cost of production.

    c.   Unfavorable cost variances are credits in the accounts, because they represent cost overruns.

    d.   Neither favorable nor unfavorable variances appear in the accounts as such, because they get into the financial statements through the cost accountant's worksheet entries at the time of statement preparation.

6. When computing standard cost variances, it is important to know that

    a.   When the actual price paid for materials to be used in production differs from the standard cost, the variance is called a cumulative cost variance.

    b.   The most useful calculation of standard cost variances is the aggregate, or total cost variance, so the manager knows how much the total actual cost exceeds or is lower than total standard cost for the product.

    c.   When the quantity of materials used differs from the standard quantity, the difference is called materials quantity variance.

    d.   The algebraic sum of the materials quantity variance and the labor quantity variance equals the total product quantity variance.

    e.   Combining the variances into one figure for the product helps to identify the variance as early as possible for the product.

7. The use of a standard cost control chart can be helpful to determine:

   a.   When total actual costs exceed total standard costs for the product.

   b.   When a product cost variance exceeds a predetermined limit such as a 10% cost overrun.

   c.   When the price variance exceeds the quantity variance.

   d.   When the quantity variance exceeds the price variance.

   e.   If the cost variance is greater than the standard cost.

8. When determining the direct materials price variance, the following calculation is applicable:

   a.   (AQ x AP) - (AQ x SP)

   b.   SQ(AP - SP)

   c.   AP - SP

   d.   (AQ x SP) - (SQ x SP)

   e.   AP(AQ x SQ)

9. When determining the direct materials usage variance, the following calculation is applicable:

   a.   (AQ x AP) - (AQ x SP)

   b.   (AQ x SP) - (SQ x SP)

   c.   AQ - SQ

   d.   (AQ x SQ) - (AP x SP,

   e.   AP - SP

10. When analyzing the importance of variances from standard costs, the following concerns should be evident:

   a.   The principle of management by exception should be used; all costs different from standard should be investigated.

   b.   Some acceptable percentage variance should be chosen, and all percentage variances that exceed this minimum should be investigated.

   c.   A specified dollar variance from standard should be chosen, and all dollar variances that exceed this minimum should be investigated.

   d.   Since neither dollar nor percentage variance limits are always appropriate, a percentage minimum variance that exceeds an absolute minimum dollar amount should be investigated.

11. Another way of determining which variances from standard should be investigated, is to follow the rule:

   a.   Investigate unfavorable variances only since favorable variances are desirable, and there is no benefit in looking into a good thing.

   b.   Management should investigate the favorable variances, since it is the operating personnel who are responsible for the unfavorable variances.

   c.   Favorable and unfavorable variances are equally worthy of investigation.

   d.   Primary investigative efforts should be evaluating random variances, since it is essential to know the pattern in which they occur in order to prevent recurrence.

ILLUSTRATIVE PROBLEMS

1. The Burlington Company has established the following standards for one jar of its new food supplement, V-44:

	Standard Quantity	Price	Standard Cost
Direct materials	7.5 ozs.	$2.00 per oz.	$15.00
Direct labor	.4 hrs.	$8.25 per hr.	3.30

During April, 21,500 ozs. of material were purchased at a cost of $1.90 per oz. All of the materials were used to manufacture 2,900 jars of product V-44. 1189 hours of direct labor were consumed to produce the product, with a total direct labor cost of $9,630.90.

Requested:

a. Compute the materials price and quantity variances for April.

b. Compute the labor rate and efficiency variances for April.

2. Waukesha Toy Shop manufactures a plastic puzzle, called Twistler, for insertion into boxes of inexpensive candy. The puzzles are mass produced at the following standard costs:

Direct materials	.15 oz.	@ $0.20 per oz.
Direct labor	.005 hrs.	@ $3.35 per hr.

During August, Waukesha produced 1,500,000 puzzles. 14,250 pounds of plastic were used at a total cost of $44,916.00. 7,200 direct labor hours were employed at a cost of $24,480.

Requested:

a.   Compute the direct materials variances for Twistler for August.

b.   Compute the direct labor variances for Twistler for August.

c. Write a memorandum to management explaining the significance and possible causes of the variances.

Vocabulary

ATTAINABLE STANDARDS. Cost performance targets that can be achieved with a reasonably efficient effort.

CONTROL CHART ANALYSIS. The use of a graphic display to evaluate whether cost results are within acceptable control limits.

IDEAL STANDARDS. Cost performance targets that can be achieved only with an optimal effort.

LABOR EFFICIENCY (USAGE) VARIANCE. The difference between the actual labor hours used and the standard hours allowed multiplied times the standard labor rate. It is used to measure the productivity of the labor force.

LABOR PRODUCTIVITY. The output of products actually produced divided by the number of labor hours required to achieve that output.

LABOR RATE VARIANCE. The difference between the actual labor rate and the standard labor rate multiplied by the actual hours worked. It is used to measure how well a firm stayed within its labor rate limits.

MATERIALS PRICE VARIANCE. The difference between the actual price paid for raw materials and the standard price that should have been paid multiplied by the actual quantity of materials purchased or used. It is used to measure the performance of the purchasing department and evaluate the effect of price changes on profits.

MATERIALS QUANTITY (USAGE) VARIANCE. The difference between the actual direct materials used for production and the standard quantity expected multiplied by the standard price of the materials. It is used to measure the efficiency of direct materials utilization.

NONRANDOM FLUCTUATIONS. Causes of variances that should be investigated because they are identifiable and controllable.

PRICE STANDARD. The amount that should be paid for a unit of direct materials or an hour of direct labor.

QUANTITY STANDARD. The amount of input in the form of direct materials or direct labor that should be used for a specified output of products.

RANDOM FLUCTUATIONS. Causes of variances resulting from chance that are not controllable by management because they are inevitable in every repetitive process.

STANDARD COSTS. Carefully predetermined costs that should be incurred to produce a product or perform an operation.

STANDARD COST VARIANCE CONTROL LIMITS. The upper and lower boundaries of a control chart defining a range of cost performance that is assumed to be the result of random fluctuations uncontrollable by management.

STANDARD COST VARIANCES. The differences between actual costs and standard costs, which can be used to control cost performance with management by exception.

STANDARD QUANTITY ALLOWED. The input units of direct materials that should have been used for the production of a specified amount of output.

THE ANSWERS

MATCHING ATTRIBUTES

1. E   5. G   9. F
2. A   6. C   10. K
3. J   7. H   11. L
4. I   8. D   12. B

MULTIPLE CHOICE

1. d   5. b   9. b
2. d   6. c   10. d
3. d   7. b   11. c
4. a   8. a

ILLUSTRATIVE PROBLEMS

1a. Materials price variance   =   AQ(AP - SP)
                                   =   21,500 ($1.90 - $2.00)
                                   = $ (2,150) Favorable

     Materials quantity variance   =   SP(AQ - SQ)
                                   = $2.00 (21,500 - 21,750)
                                   = $(500) Favorable

b.   Labor rate variance   =   AQ(AP - SP)
                                     =   1,189 ($8.10 - $8.25)
                                     = $(178.35)F

Labor efficiency variance   =   SP(AQ - SQ)
                                     = $8.25 (1,189 - 1,160)
                                     = $239.25

2a. Direct materials price variance =   AQ(AP - SP)
                                     =   228,000 oz. ($0.197 - $0.20)
                                     = $(684) Favorable

Direct materials quantity variance   =   SP(AQ - SQ)
                                     = $0.20 (228,000 - 225,000)
                                     = $600 Unfavorable

b.   Direct labor rate variance   =   AQ(AP - SP)
                                     =   7,200 ($3.40 - $3.35)
                                     = $360 Unfavorable

Direct labor efficiency variance   =   SP(AQ - SQ)
                                     = $3.35 (7,200 - 7,500)
                                     = $(1,005) Favorable

c.   The significance of variances depends on the type of operation and whether the variances are repetitive or nonrecurring. Repetitive operations characteristically have random fluctuations which tend to balance out over time. As long as the variances are within a range of random fluctuations, there is acceptable control and further investigation is not worthwhile. Some of the variances found here are probably due to random fluctuations. Some, however, could be attributed to the following causes: defective materials, equipment breakdowns, changes in product design, production scheduling problems, inexperienced workers, or inadequate supervision.

CHAPTER 11

FLEXIBLE BUDGETS AND STANDARD MANUFACTURING OVERHEAD COSTING

LEARNING OBJECTIVES

1. Explain why a fixed budget is of limited value to management for control purposes.
2. Prepare a flexible budget and discuss how it is used.
3. Describe how a flexible budget performance report is used to control costs.
4. Discuss how standard manufacturing overhead is applied to the products produced.
5. Determine how a manufacturing overhead flexible budget is developed based on some measure of standard production activity.
6. Evaluate how the choice of production activity level affects the predetermined overhead rate.
7. Distinguish among the four definitions of production capacity.
8. Account for over- and underapplied manufacturing overhead.
9. Compute and evaluate standard manufacturing overhead cost variances with the two-variance method.
10. Compute and evaluate standard manufacturing overhead cost variances with the three-variance method.
11. Prepare journal entries to record manufacturing accounts.
12. Recognize how standard cost variances are presented in an income statement used for internal reporting.

REVIEW

1. **Explain why a fixed budget is of limited value to management for control purposes.**

   A fixed budget establishes costs at a specified level or volume of production. For example, costs for materials, labor and overhead items would all be detailed for the production of, say, 1,000 picnic tables. If 1,000 tables are produced during the period, *then*, the fixed budget would be a useful standard against which to compare actual costs.

   However, what if 950 tables are made? Or 1,100 tables? Would the fixed budget then be a good standard for evaluating the costs of production? No, of course not. Because the fixed budget sets costs for 1,000 tables, naturally some, but not all, costs for 950 tables should be less. Some, but not all, costs for 1,100 tables should be more. It is always true of fixed budgets that their usefulness is limited to evaluating and controlling costs *only* at the production level at which the fixed budget is established.

2. **Prepare a flexible budget and discuss how it is used.**

   A flexible budget is composed of both variable and fixed costs set at differing levels of activity. Let's refer back to Chapter 10 to pick up the costs of the Picnicker table for the Gold Medal Furniture Company in order to prepare a flexible budget. We will have to add overhead costs to the direct costs of Chapter 10.

Gold Medal Furniture Company
Flexible Budget—Picnicker Tables
For the Year Ending June 30, 1992

	Per Unit	Levels of Activity		
		1,000	1,200	1,500
Variable costs:				
Direct materials	$ 40.78	$ 40,780	$ 48,936	$ 61,170
Direct labor	17.00	17,000	20,400	25,500
Indirect materials	1.25	1,250	1,500	1,875
Indirect labor	0.95	950	1,140	1,425
Utilities	0.80	800	960	1,200
Total variable costs	$ 60.78	60,780	72,936	91,170
Fixed costs:				
Supervision		24,000	24,000	24,000
Property taxes		1,450	1,450	1,450
Insurance		950	950	950
Maintenance		1,000	1,000	1,000
Depreciation		1,800	1,800	1,800
Total fixed costs		29,200	29,200	29,200
Total manufacturing costs		$ 89,980	$102,136	$120,370

The flexible budget above is designed to accommodate three levels of production: 1,000, 1,200, and 1,500 units. With this budget, target costs are established for each production level. The 1,500 level is maximum capacity, and 1,000 is considered to be the minimum level of profitable production. Thus, the spread from 1,000 to 1,500 units is called the relevant range of production activity. No matter which of the three production levels is actually reached, the cost schedule is available. If some different level is attained, the costs for that level can easily be computed from the data presented.

3. **Describe how a flexible budget performance report is used to control costs.**

The flexible budget provides budgeted costs for alternate levels of activity. Actual costs for the level of production attained are compared with the budgeted costs to determine the variances from budget. Cost variances over budget are called "unfavorable" and variances under budget are labeled "favorable". Suppose the actual level of production achieved is 1,200 units, and the actual costs attained and the cost variances from budget are as shown in the schedule below.

The flexible budget performance report below is used by management to evaluate performance after the fact, by comparing actual costs attained with the budgeted amounts for the level of production achieved. Both absolute variances from budget and percentage variances are used to determine the areas of greatest critical concern—those areas that are most out of control, and thus needing the most management attention. The variances in the example below are all relatively insignificant—both in absolute and percentage terms—thus not warranting great management concern.

Gold Medal Furniture Company
Flexible Budget Performance Report
For the Year Ending June 30, 1992

	Budget	Actual	Variance
Production units—>	1,200	1,200	-0-

Variable costs:

Direct materials	$ 48,936	$ 48,960	$ 24	U
Direct labor	20,400	20,160	240	F
Indirect materials	1,500	1,584	84	U
Indirect labor	1,140	1,104	36	F
Utilities	960	960	0	
Total variable costs	72,936	72,768	168	F

Fixed costs:

Supervision	24,000	24,000	0	
Property taxes	1,450	1,560	110	U
Insurance	950	980	30	U
Maintenance	1,000	950	50	F
Depreciation	1,800	1,800	0	
Total fixed costs	29,200	29,290	90	U
Total manufacturing costs	$102,136	$102,058	$ 78	F

4. **Discuss how standard manufacturing overhead is applied to the products produced.**

   Standard manufacturing overhead is applied to production by first determining a base for application, such as direct labor hours, then by dividing that base into the budgeted overhead costs to arrive at an overhead cost per direct labor hour. The budgeted overhead for the period, then, equals the budgeted direct labor hours times the budgeted overhead cost per direct labor hour. Direct machine hours could have been chosen as the base, rather than the direct labor hours.

5. **Determine how a manufacturing overhead flexible budget is developed based on some measure of standard production activity.**

   Let's assume that we are going to use direct labor hours as the basis for applying manufacturing overhead to production. Given that 1,150 tables are to be manufactured, we would determine the total variable manufacturing overhead for that level of production by multiplying the activity level, 1,150, by the total of variable overhead costs per unit. In the above example, we see that variable overhead unit costs are:

Indirect materials	$	1.25
Indirect labor		0.95
Utilities		0.80
Variable overhead per unit	$	3.00

Here we see that the variable overhead per unit manufactured is $3.00. However, when applying the overhead to production costs, we must use a base, such as direct labor hours, as described above. Since there are two direct labor hours budgeted per table made, we would apply variable manufacturing overhead at the rate of $3.00/2 = $1.50 per standard direct labor hour. The total overhead budget for Picnicker tables, then, is $29,200 per year plus $1.50 per standard direct labor hour. If the budgeted production for the year is 1,150 tables, the manufacturing overhead budget will be $29,200 + ($1.50 × 2)1,150 = $32,650.

6. **Evaluate how the choice of production activity level affects the predetermined overhead rate.**

The variable manufacturing overhead is a constant rate per direct labor hour. However, the fixed overhead per hour is constantly changing. That is, as the production level increases the fixed rate per hour decreases. Thus, there is an inverse relationship between volume and fixed overhead rate. This can be illustrated as follows:

Budgeted fixed overhead = $29,200 per year. Dividing this amount by the number of budgeted direct labor hours (2 per picnic table produced) gives us:

Number of Tables Produced	Direct Labor Hours Budgeted	Rate Per Direct Labor Hour
1,000	2,000	$ 14.60*
1,100	2,200	13.27
1,200	2,400	12.17
1,300	2,600	11.23
1,500	3,000	9.73

*Computed as $29,200/2,000 hours = $14.60 per hour. The other rates are computed in a similar manner.

We can see from this illustration that as production increases, budgeted direct labor hours increase in a corresponding fashion, but the fixed manufacturing overhead rate decreases.

7. **Distinguish among the four definitions of production capacity.**

The four definitions of production capacity are: maximum capacity, practical capacity, expected capacity and normal capacity.

Maximum capacity is the highest level of production that can be achieved by the company with the present manufacturing plant size and equipment. Maximum capacity does not allow for any considerations for inefficiency.

Practical capacity is that level of production that makes normal allowances for the efficiency of people, plant and equipment. That is, no one can operate at peak efficiency on a continuous basis. Therefore, practical capacity recognizes this fact and builds in a "practical" level of operations.

Expected capacity is that level of production that is planned or anticipated for a particular budget year. This level includes coordination with the sales budget for the number of units to be sold, and with the desired inventory levels at the beginning and end of the year.

Normal capacity is an average of several years'—frequently three to five years—production levels. The attempt is to even out the ups and downs—sometimes called the cyclical swings—of business. Since there are good years and bad years—high production years and low production years—a normal capacity concept develops an average capacity approach.

The following example illustrates how the normal capacity idea is applied in developing and applying fixed overhead rates. The Gold Medal Furniture Company finds that demand for its Picnicker tables varies from year to year because of the economy, competition, and even weather conditions in the company's distribution area. Some years they produce at maximum capacity, 1,500 tables, and other years at even below their desired minimum, or 800 tables. However, total fixed overhead remains fairly constant at $29,200 per year. At these various levels, the fixed overhead rates would vary. By dividing the $29,200 by the actual production levels, we get the following results:

PRODUCTION LEVELS

	900	1,000	1,200	1,400	1,500
Fixed overhead rates:					
Per table	$32.44	$29.20	$24.33	$20.86	$19.47
Per hour	$16.22	$14.60	$12.17	$10.43	$ 9.73

In order to avoid recording standard fixed overhead costs at these widely varying rates, the company decides to use a normal capacity of 1,200 units produced each year which results in a $12.17-per-hour rate.

8. **Account for over- and underapplied manufacturing overhead.**

Actual overhead each year differs from the overhead applied to production, partially because of varying levels of production, as explained above. If the overhead applied is greater than the actual overhead incurred, the result is overapplied overhead. On the other hand, if overhead applied is less than actual overhead, the result is underapplied overhead. This over- or underapplied overhead must be accounted for.

Assume the Gold Medal Company produces 1,150 Picnicker tables in 1991. They apply to work in process inventory the standard fixed overhead at the rate of $12.17 per hour for the standard direct labor hours applicable to the 1,150 tables. 1,150 x 2 hours = 2,300 hours. 2,300 x $12.17 = $27,991. Therefore, $27,991 of fixed overhead would be applied. Suppose actual fixed overhead equals $29,000. This will result in underapplied overhead of $29,000 - $27,991, or $1,009.

If, on the other hand, the company produces 1,325 Picnicker tables during the year, they would apply fixed overhead as follows:

$$1,325 \text{ units x 2 hours x } \$12.17 = \$32,250.50.$$

If the actual overhead equals $29,350, overhead would be overapplied to the extent of $32,205.50 - $29,350.00 = $2,900.50.

9. **Compute and evaluate standard manufacturing overhead cost variances with the two-variance method.**

Referring to the example in item 8 above, let us now compute the overhead cost variances using the two-variance method, with a production of 1,150 tables and an actual fixed overhead of $29,000 and variable overhead of $3,648.

(1)	(2)	(3)	(4)
Manufacturing overhead	Actual Amount	Flexible Budget based on 2,300 hours	Manufacturing Overhead applied to 2,300 hours
Variable overhead	$ 3,648	$ 3,450	$ 3,450
Fixed overhead	29,000	29,200	27,991
Total overhead	$ 32,648	$ 32,650	$ 31,441

Actual Manufacturing Overhead		Flexible Budget based on Standard Hours Allowed		Manufacturing Overhead applied to Standard Hours Allowed
	Budget Variance		Capacity Variance	
$32,648	$2 F	$32,650	$1,209 U	$31,441

Over- or Underapplied Manufacturing Overhead

$32,648	$1,207 U	$31,441

The budget variance is shown to be	$ 2	F, while the
capacity variance is	1,209	U; thus the
underapplied manufacturing overhead is	$ 1,207	U.

10. Compute and evaluate standard manufacturing overhead cost variances with the three-variance method.

Continuing with the previous example, the three-variance method will now be illustrated. Let us assume that 2,400 direct labor hours were consumed in producing the 1,150 units. The three-variance method provides the following results.

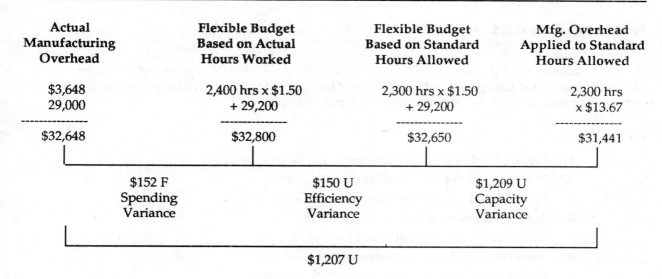

Actual Manufacturing Overhead	Flexible Budget Based on Actual Hours Worked	Flexible Budget Based on Standard Hours Allowed	Mfg. Overhead Applied to Standard Hours Allowed
$3,648 29,000	2,400 hrs x $1.50 + 29,200	2,300 hrs x $1.50 + 29,200	2,300 hrs x $13.67
$32,648	$32,800	$32,650	$31,441

$152 F
Spending
Variance

$150 U
Efficiency
Variance

$1,209 U
Capacity
Variance

$1,207 U

Underapplied Manufacturing Overhead

11. **Prepare journal entries to record manufacturing overhead cost variances in general ledger accounts.**

Manufacturing overhead cost variances are recorded in the general journal as a debit if the variance is unfavorable and as a credit if the variance is favorable. Thus, the three variances shown in item 8 above would be recorded as:

	Debit	Credit
Overhead efficiency variance	150	
Overhead capacity variance	1,209	
Overhead spending variance		152
Manufacturing overhead		1,207

(To close the underapplied manufacturing overhead for the month into the appropriate variance accounts.)

12. **Recognize how standard cost variances are presented in an income statement used for internal reporting.**

Standard overhead cost variances are shown in the income statement, for internal purposes, as increases to standard cost of goods sold if the variances are unfavorable, and as reductions from standard cost of goods sold if the variances are favorable.

MATCHING ATTRIBUTES

Below, in Group A are listed attributes that may be identified with the flexible budget and manufacturing overhead terms listed in Group B. Indicate, by use of the identifying letter of the appropriate Group B item, which description in Group A best matches each Group B term.

Group A

_____   1.   Highest level of production achievable with present facilities.
_____   2.   Planned level of production for the budget year.
_____   3.   Level of production that makes efficiency allowances.
_____   4.   Average of several years' production levels.
_____   5.   Shows costs for a range of future business activity.
_____   6.   Shows budgeted costs, actual costs and variances for the period.
_____   7.   Actual overhead exceeds overhead applied to production.
_____   8.   Actual overhead is less than overhead applied to production.
_____   9.   Shows budgeted costs at a single level of production activity.
_____   10. Calculates budget, capacity and total overhead variances.
_____   11. Includes fixed, variable and mixed costs, using an established rate of application.
_____   12. Results from dividing the budgeted amount by the budgeted hours.
_____   13. Includes calculation of efficiency variance.

Group B

A.   Expected capacity
B.   Fixed budget
C.   Flexible budget
D.   Maximum capacity
E.   Normal capacity
F.   Overapplied overhead
G.   Performance report

H.   Practical capacity
I.   Predetermined overhead rate
J.   Standard manufacturing overhead
K.   Three-variance method
L.   Two-variance method
M.   Underapplied overhead

MULTIPLE CHOICE

For each of the following items choose the most appropriate completion phrase.

1.   A fixed budget is of limited usefulness to management because

   a.   It relates to the budgeted and actual data only at the point at which the company's income is fixed.
   b.   Fixed budgets relate only to a single level of activity.
   c.   Fixed budgets contain only fixed cost data.
   d.   Fixed budgets are very helpful in budgeting fixed assets, but not for non-fixed items.

2. As a standard cost, manufacturing overhead is treated differently from direct materials and direct labor. Which of the following items is *not* true with respect to manufacturing overhead as a standard cost of production?

   a.   Unlike direct materials and direct labor, manufacturing overhead cannot be traced directly to the products produced.

   b.   Manufacturing overhead is homogeneous in nature; that is, it consists of several very similar items.

   c.   Manufacturing overhead consists of fixed, variable and mixed costs.

   d.   Manufacturing overhead is periodically applied to production costs, usually on a predetermined basis, as opposed to charging these costs to production as they are incurred.

3. A flexible budget is a budget that is adjusted for the activity level of the firm in the time period in question.

   a.   A flexible budget is established at the one level of activity thought to be most likely.

   b.   If more than one level of activity is used, those chosen are the highest and lowest levels considered likely.

   c.   Once the actual activity level is known, the budget can be revised to reflect this activity.

   d.   The flexible budget is prepared for overhead costs only, since other costs remain the same for the relevant range.

4. The Utica Producers has the following variable cost schedule for the manufacture of Model 1020 pump:

Direct materials	$ 7.50	per unit
Direct labor	11.25	per unit
Indirect materials and labor	5.25	per unit
Other indirect costs	4.50	per unit
Variable manufacturing costs	$ 28.50	per unit

Also, $11,550 of fixed overhead costs are budgeted for the month of April. What are the total manufacturing costs that should be budgeted for April, if the planned production volume is 1,200 pumps?

   a. $34,200

   b. $11,550

   c. $45,750

   d. $11,700

5. When using flexible budgets, calculation of the appropriate budget variances includes:

   a.   Subtracting actual costs from fixed budget amounts.

   b.   Comparing actual variable costs with variable cost budgets and actual fixed costs with fixed cost budgets.

   c.   Comparing variable *and* fixed actual costs with flexible cost budget data.

   d.   Dividing total actual costs by total budgeted costs to arrive at budget variance rates.

6. When recording applied manufacturing overhead in a standard cost system, the predetermined overhead rate times the standard production activity is
   a. Debited to work in process inventory and credited to manufacturing overhead.
   b. Debited to manufacturing overhead and credited to work in process inventory.
   c. Debited to cost of goods sold and credited to work in process inventory.
   d. Debited to finished goods inventory and credited to work in process inventory.

7. When choosing a basis for applying manufacturing overhead,
   a. Standard direct labor hours is the best basis.
   b. Standard machine hours is the best basis.
   c. Actual direct labor hours is the best basis.
   d. Actual machine hours is the best basis.
   e. The best basis is that activity that is the best predictor of variable manufacturing overhead costs.

8. Because of the behavior of cost components, flexible budgets are able to compensate for the fact that
   a. Variable costs per unit increase as production volume increases.
   b. Fixed costs per unit increase in direct proportion to the increase in production volume.
   c. Variable costs per unit decrease inversely with production volume increases.
   d. Fixed costs per unit decrease as production volume increases.

9. Once a predetermined overhead rate is selected and applied, the overhead will be underapplied if:
   a. Actual production is less than standard production.
   b. Actual production is greater than standard production.
   c. Standard hours for the production attained are more than budgeted production hours.
   d. Standard hours for the production attained are fewer than budgeted production hours.

Use the following information for items 10 through 14 below.

The Trenton Trunk Company has the following actual manufacturing overhead costs for August:

Actual variable manufacturing costs	$	24,650
Actual fixed manufacturing costs		19,000
Actual total manufacturing costs	$	43,650

Standard manufacturing overhead rates for Trenton Trunk are:

Variable,	$8.25 per direct labor hour
Fixed,	$18,000 per month

Assume a normal capacity of 1,200 trunks per month and three standard direct labor hours per trunk produced.

10. What is the budget variance for August, using the two-variance method, if 1,000 trunks are produced?

   a. $900 unfavorable.
   b. $900 favorable.
   c. $4,050 favorable.
   d. $3,900 unfavorable.
   e. $3,900 favorable.

11. What is the capacity variance for August, if 1,000 trunks are produced?

   a. $3,900 unfavorable.
   b. $3,900 favorable.
   c. $4,050 favorable.
   d. $3,000 unfavorable.
   e. $3,000 favorable.

12. What is the total overhead variance, if 1,000 trunks are produced?

   a. $4,050 favorable.
   b. $3,900 favorable.
   c. $3,900 unfavorable.
   d. $3,000 unfavorable.
   e. $3,000 favorable.

13. If the actual direct labor hours were 2,900, what is the efficiency variance for August?

   a. $900 unfavorable.
   b. $75 unfavorable.
   c. $75 favorable.
   d. $825 favorable.
   e. $825 unfavorable.

14. If the actual direct labor hours were 2,900, what is the spending variance for August?

   a. $1,725 favorable.
   b. $1,725 unfavorable.
   c. $900 unfavorable.
   d. $825 favorable.
   e. $825 unfavorable.

15. Which of the following terms best describes the production level that makes specific allowances for the efficiency of workers?

   a.   Normal capacity.
   b.   Expected capacity.
   c.   Maximum capacity.
   d.   Desired capacity.
   e.   Practical capacity.

Illustrative Problems

1. Carlisle Company makes stereo speakers for cars and other vehicles. The cost schedule for speaker VR10 is as follows:

Direct materials	$ 1.40	per unit
Direct labor	3.00	per unit
Variable overhead	1.80	per direct labor hour
Fixed overhead	$ 3,600	per month

Direct labor averages $6.00 per hour. During June, Carlisle Company produced 900 speaker VR10's, requiring 470 direct labor hours at an average cost of $5.90 per hour, $1,300 in direct materials, $795 in variable overhead, and $3,750 in fixed overhead.

Requested:

Prepare a flexible budget performance report for speaker VR10 for June by completing the following schedule:

Carlisle Company
Flexible Budget Performance Report—Speaker VR10
June, 1992

	Budget	Actual	Variance
Production units - - - - ->	900	900	-0-
Variable costs:			
Direct materials			
Direct labor			
Variable overhead			
Total variable costs	_____	_____	_____
Fixed costs:			
Fixed overhead			
	_____	_____	_____
Total manufacturing costs	======	======	====

2. Referring to **Carlisle Company in problem 1**, prepare for overhead costs for June:

   a.   A two-variance analysis.

   b.   A three-variance analysis.

Assume fixed overhead is applied to production based on normal capacity of 500 direct labor hours.

3. Referring again back to the Carlisle Company, record the journal entries for booking the variances in problem 2.

	Debit	**Credit**

a.   Two-variance analysis

b.   Three-variance analysis

VOCABULARY

BUDGET (CONTROLLABLE) VARIANCE. The difference between the actual manufacturing overhead incurred and the flexible budget based on the standard hours allowed (or whatever measure of standard production activity is being used.)

CAPACITY (DENOMINATOR) VARIANCE. The difference between the flexible budget based on the standard hours allowed and the standard amount of manufacturing overhead applied to the work in process inventory.

DENOMINATOR ACTIVITY. The production activity level chosen for the denominator of the predetermined overhead rate used to apply manufacturing overhead.

EFFICIENCY VARIANCE (OVERHEAD). The difference between the flexible budget based on actual hours and the flexible budget for standard hours allowed.

EXPECTED CAPACITY. The level of production activity expected for a specific year, given the firm's operating conditions and market demand for its products.

FIXED (STATIC) BUDGET. A budget prepared for only one level of sales or production activity.

FLEXIBLE BUDGET. A series of budgets for a range of business activity.

FLEXIBLE BUDGET PERFORMANCE REPORT. A management report showing the variances between actual costs and budgeted costs with the budgeted amounts are revised to the level of business activity attained, whenever necessary.

MAXIMUM CAPACITY. The highest level of production activity possible if optimal operating conditions exist.

NORMAL CAPACITY. The average annual production activity that will satisfy the market demand over a relatively long time period, such as three to five years.

PRACTICAL CAPACITY. The maximum production capacity of a firm less reasonable allowances for departures from an optimal performance.

PRODUCTION CAPACITY. Some measure of the production activity a firm can achieve with its existing physical facilities and organizational structure. The four measures of production capacity are maximum, practical, expected, and normal.

SPENDING VARIANCE. The difference between the actual manufacturing overhead incurred and the flexible budget based on the actual production activity level worked.

STANDARD MANUFACTURING OVERHEAD. The predetermined overhead rate multiplied by some measure of standard production activity, such as standard direct labor hours or standard machine hours.

THREE-VARIANCE METHOD. The division of an over/under applied manufacturing overhead variance into three components: a spending variance, an efficiency variance, and a capacity variance.

TWO-VARIANCE METHOD. The division of an over/underapplied manufacturing overhead variance into two components: a budget variance and a capacity variance.

THE ANSWERS

MATCHING ATTRIBUTES

1.	D	5.	C	8.	F	11.	J
2.	A	6.	G	9.	B	12.	I
3.	H	7.	M	10.	L	13.	K
4.	E						

MULTIPLE CHOICE

1.	b	7.	e	10.	a
2.	b	8.	d	11.	d
3.	c	9.	a	12.	c
4.	c	10.	a	13.	d
5.	c	11.	d	14.	b
6.	a	12.	c	15.	e

Illustrative Problems

1.

Carlisle Company
Flexible Budget Performance Report—Speaker VR10
June, 1992

	Budget	Actual	Variance	
Production units - - - - ->	900	900	-0-	
Variable costs:				
Direct materials	$ 1,260	$ 1,300	$ 40	U
Direct labor	2,700	2,773	73	U
Variable overhead	810	795	15	F
Total variable costs	$ 4,770	$ 4,868	$ 98	U
Fixed costs:				
Fixed overhead	3,600	3,750	150	U
Total manufacturing costs	$ 8,370	$ 8,618	$ 248	U

2a.

Manufacturing overhead	Actual Amount	Flexible Budget Based on Std Hrs Allowed	Manufacturing Overhead Applied to Standard Hours Allowed
Variable overhead	$ 795	$ 810	$ 810
Fixed overhead	3,750	3,600	3,240
	$ 4,545	$ 4,410	$ 4,050

Budget Variance $135 U

Capacity Variance $360 U

Underapplied Overhead $495 U

2b.

Overhead	Actual Amount	Flexible Budget Based on Actual Hours	Flexible Budget Based on Std. Hours Allowed	Manufacturing Overhead Applied to Standard Hours Allowed
Variable overhead	$ 795	$ 846	$ 810	$ 810
Fixed overhead	3,750	3,600	3,600	3,240
	$ 4,545	$ 4,446	$ 4,410	$ 4,050

Spending Variance $99 U	Efficiency Variance $36 U	Capacity Variance $360 U

Underapplied Manufacturing Overhead
$495 U

3. The journal entries to record the variances in problem 2 are as follows:

	Debit	Credit
a. Two-variance analysis:		
Overhead budget variance	135	
Overhead capacity variance	360	
Manufacturing overhead		495
(To close out the underapplied manufacturing overhead to the appropriate variance accounts.)		
b. Three-variance analysis:		
Overhead spending variance	99	
Overhead efficiency variance	36	
Overhead capacity variance	360	
Manufacturing overhead		495
(To close out the underapplied manufacturing overhead to the appropriate variance accounts.)		

CHAPTER 12

PROFIT VARIANCE ANALYSIS

In Chapter 11 we learned the value of flexible budgets and standard costing systems. Variances were presented as the differences between actual costs and budgeted or standard costs. As a result of these variances, management asks, "What caused these variances, and whose responsibility are they?" With this question in mind, we approach Chapter 12 to deal with these issues.

You may see variance analysis as a somewhat mechanical process. However, keep in mind how important these analyses are to management in their continuing effort to control costs.

LEARNING OBJECTIVES

1. Discuss the nature and importance of profit variance analysis.
2. Identify the major sources of a profit variance.
3. Realize why variable costs and fixed costs should be separated in profit variance analysis.
4. Describe how contribution margin variance analysis is performed with a single product.
5. Distinguish among a sales volume variance, a selling price variance, and a variable cost variance.
6. Explain how fixed cost variance analysis is performed.
7. Consider a sales mix variance while performing contribution margin variance analysis with more than one product.
8. Report profit variances to managers and advise them of potential causes of the variances.
9. Combine contribution margin variances with standard cost variances to inform mangers about the different sources of deviations from a planned profit performance.

LEARNING TIPS

In this chapter you will learn how to compute certain variances. Notice the form in which they are presented. See that the set-up of the analysis is very similar in each case. This will help you "get the hang of" these computations. Remember, though, the importance to management of these analyses. Cost control is impossible unless the accountant can pinpoint the exact nature of each variance and the responsibility for each.

REVIEW

1. **Discuss the nature and importance of profit variance analysis.**

   In previous chapters we discussed cost variances. We found that a cost variance is the difference between actual cost and the planned (or budgeted) cost. Similarly, a profit variance is the difference between the actual profit and the planned (or budgeted) profit. A manager is responsible for the costs incurred in (by) his or her department, and that manager is accountable for the profit (or loss) that occurs in his or her department. The profit, of course, is the revenues minus the expenses for the period. Profit variance analysis then is the analysis of the difference, or variance, in the actual profit from the planned profit.

2. **Identify the major sources of profit variance.**

   There are five major sources of profit variance. They are variances in the actual (from the planned):
   a.   Sales volume,
   b.   Sales price per unit,
   c.   Sales mix of products sold,
   d.   Variable costs of each product, and/or
   e.   Fixed costs of the period.

3. **Realize why variable costs and fixed costs should be separated in profit variance analysis.**

   We found from our earlier discussion that fixed costs and variable costs behave differently. Variable costs, in total, vary in direct proportion to the volume of activity of the period. Fixed costs, on the other hand, remain approximately the same each period, regardless of the volume of activity, if the business remains within the relevant activity range. Since these costs act differently, it is important, in analyzing the profit variance, to separate the variable costs from the fixed costs.

4. **Describe how contribution margin variance analysis is performed with a single product.**

   Contribution margin variance analysis is begun by separating the parts of contribution margin—sales and variable costs—and computing the variance of each from their budgeted amounts. Proper analysis involves the consideration of one factor at a time, while holding the others constant. The details are described in the next section.

5. **Distinguish among a sales volume variance, a selling price variance, and a variable cost variance.**

   Each of these variances is described below:
   a.   *Sales volume variance* is the actual sales volume minus the budgeted sales volume multiplied by the budgeted contribution margin per unit.
   b.   *Selling price variance* is the actual selling price minus the budgeted selling price times the actual number of units sold.
   c.   *Variable cost variance* is the difference between actual costs per unit and budgeted costs per unit times the actual number of units sold.

   The following example of the Springfield Casket Company illustrates the above definitions. Springfield makes a model of casket called Easirest. Following are sales and cost data for 1991.

Springfield Casket Company
Income Statement
Year Ended December 31, 1991

	Budget	Actual	Variance	
Sales, units	1,100	1,000	100	U
Sales, amount	$ 660,000	$ 620,000	$ 40,000	U
Variable cost of goods sold	330,000	297,000	33,000	F
Variable selling and administrative expense	52,800	52,700	100	F
Contribution margin	277,200	270,300	6,900	U
Fixed costs:				
Manufacturing	82,000	80,000	2,000	F
Selling and administrative	105,000	110,000	5,000	U
Total fixed costs	187,000	190,000	3,000	U
Net income before tax	$ 90,200	$ 80,300	$ 9,900	U

a.   **Sales volume variance**

Actual units sold		1,000	
Budgeted unit sales	-	1,100	
Volume variance	=	100	units
Budgeted contribution Margin per unit	x	$252	($277,200/1,100)
Sales volume variance	=	$25,200	U

b.   **Selling price variance**

Actual selling price	=	$620	($620,000/1,000 units)
Budgeted selling price	=	600	($660,000/1,100 units)
Price variance	=	$ 20	per unit
Actual units sold	x	1,000	
Selling price variance	=	$20,000	F

c.   **Variable cost variance**

$$\text{Actual costs per unit} = \$349.70 \quad \frac{(\$297,000 + \$52,700)}{1,000 \text{ units}}$$

$$\text{Budgeted costs per unit} = 348.00 \quad \frac{(\$330,000 + \$52,800)}{1,100 \text{ units}}$$

Variable cost variance	=	1.70 per unit
Actual units sold	x	1,000
Variable cost variance	=	$1,700 U

In the aggregate, these variances equal the contribution margin summary of $6,900, unfavorable, shown in the following schedule:

Sales volume variance	$ 25,200	U
Variable cost variance	1,700	U
Subtotal	26,900	U
Selling price variance	20,000	F
Contribution margin variance	$ 6,900	U

6. **Explain how fixed cost variance analysis is performed.**

Fixed cost variance analysis can be performed by comparing the actual fixed costs and budgeted fixed costs in detail, as shown in the schedule that follows:

Springfield Casket Company
Fixed Cost Variance Analysis
Year Ended December 31, 1991

	Budget	Actual	Variance	
Manufacturing:				
Salaries	$ 53,700	$ 52,700	$ 1,000	F
Insurance	2,500	3,400	900	U
Depreciation	11,500	12,600	1,100	U
Utilities	14,300	11,300	3,000	F
Total	82,000	80,000	2,000	F
Selling and administrative:				
Salaries	84,000	87,500	3,500	U
Insurance	4,500	6,000	1,500	U
Depreciation	8,500	8,500	-0-	
Utilities	8,000	8,000	-0-	
Total	105,000	110,000	5,000	U
Total fixed costs	$187,000	$190,000	$ 3,000	U

7. **Consider a sales mix variance while performing contribution margin variance analysis with more than one product.**

   Let us assume for this purpose that the Springfield Casket Company produces a second model of casket, called the Divine model. The revenue and variable cost budget data for each model are as shown in the following schedule:

	Easirest	Divine
Selling price	$ 600	$ 1,000
Variable production costs	300	425
Variable selling and administrative expense	48	75
Total variable costs	348	500
Contribution margin	$ 252	$ 500
Contribution percentage	42%	50%

Springfield Casket Company
Budgeted Contribution Margin Performance
Year Ended December 31, 1991

	Easirest	Divine	Total
Sales, units	1,100	900	2,000
Sales, amount	$ 660,000	$ 900,000	$ 1,560,000
Variable production costs	330,000	382,500	712,500
Variable selling and administrative expense	52,800	67,500	120,300
Total variable costs	382,800	450,000	832,800
Contribution margin	$ 277,200	$ 450,000	$ 727,200
Contribution percentage	42%	50%	46.62%

Springfield Casket Company
Actual Contribution Margin Performance
Year Ended December 31, 1991

	Easirest	Divine	Total
Sales, units	1,000	600	1,600
Sales, amount	$ 620,000	$ 600,000	$ 1,220,000
Variable production costs	297,000	258,000	555,000
Variable selling and administrative expenses	52,700	48,000	100,700
Total variable costs	349,700	306,000	655,700
Contribution margin	$ 270,300	$ 294,000	$ 564,300
Contribution percentage	43.6%	49%	46.25%

The sales mix variance for each product is computed as:

Sales mix variance = (actual sales units - budgeted sales units) x (budgeted contribution margin per unit - budgeted average contribution margin per unit)

For the Easirest casket this becomes:

Sales mix variance	=	(1,000 - 1,100) x ($252.00 - $363.60)
	=	100 x $111.60
	=	$11,160 Favorable
		======

For the Divine casket:

Sales mix variance	=	(600 - 900) x ($500.00 - $363.60)
	=	300 x $136.40
	=	$40,920 Unfavorable
		======

When two or more products are produced, the sales volume variance must be computed differently from the single product computation shown previously. The two-product analysis is:

Sales volume variance	=	(actual sales volume - budgeted sales volume) x budgeted average contribution margin per unit

For both products combined this shows:

Sales volume variance	=	(1,600 - 2,000) x $363.60 ($727,200/2,000 units)
	=	$145,440 U
		======

This number is the sum of the two individual product variances:

Easirest

Sales volume variance	=	(1,000 - 1,100) x $363.60
	=	$36,360 U
		======

Divine

Sales volume variance	=	(600 - 900) x $363.60
	=	$109,080 U
		======

Now, it is desirable to compute the other variances for both products, using the formulas previously presented.

Selling price variance:

Selling price variance	=	(actual selling price - budgeted selling price) x actual units sold
Easirest s.p.v.	=	($620 - $600) x 1,000 units
	=	$20,000 F
		======

$$\text{Divine s.p.v.} \quad = \quad (\$1,000 - \$1,000) \times 600 \text{ units}$$
$$= \quad \$\text{-0-}$$

Variable cost variance, production:

Variable cost variance = (actual costs per unit - budgeted costs per unit) × actual units sold

Easirest:	Actual cost per unit	$= \dfrac{\$297,000}{1,000}$	=	$297.00	
	Budgeted cost per unit		=	300.00	
	Variable cost variance, unit		=	3.00	
	Actual units sold			1,000	
	Variable cost variance		=	$3,000	F

Divine:	Actual cost per unit	$= \dfrac{\$258,000}{600}$	=	$430.00	
	Budgeted cost per unit		=	425.00	
	Variable cost variance, unit		=	5.00	
	Actual units sold			600	
	Variable cost variance		=	$3,000	U

Variable cost variance, selling and administrative:

Easirest:	Actual cost per unit	$= \dfrac{\$52,700}{1,000}$	=	$ 52.70	
	Budgeted cost per unit		=	48.00	
	Variable cost variance, unit		=	4.70	
	Actual units sold			1,000	
	Variable cost variance		=	$4,700	U

Divine:

Actual cost per unit	=	$\dfrac{\$48{,}000}{600}$	=	$ 80.00
Budgeted cost per unit			=	75.00
Variable cost variance, unit			=	5.00
Actual units sold				600
Variable cost variance			=	$3,000 U

8. **Report profit variances to managers and advise** them of potential causes of the variances.

The following report consolidates all of the previously discussed and computed variance analyses.

Springfield Casket Company
Contribution Margin Variance Analysis
Year Ended December 31, 1991

Budgeted contribution margin	$727,200	
Actual contribution margin	564,300	
Unfavorable contribution margin variance	$162,900	

Source of variance	Favorable	Unfavorable
Sales mix:		
Easirest caskets	$11,160	
Divine		$40,920
Sales volume:		
Easirest		36,360
Divine		109,080
Selling price:		
Easirest	20,000	
Divine		-0-
Variable cost, production:		
Easirest	3,000	
Divine		3,000
Variable cost, selling and admin:		
Easirest		4,700
Divine		3,000
Total	$34,160	$197,060
Net unfavorable contribution margin variance		$162,900 U

9. **Combine contribution margin variances with standard cost variances to inform managers about the different sources of deviations from a planned profit performance.**

For this discussion we look at the San Luis Wax Company, and we will refer back to a prior chapter to combine the six standard variable cost variances we previously learned with the sales volume and sales price variances from this chapter.

San Luis Wax Company produces only one product, a ski and toboggan wax called Spread. Budgeted sales and costs of Spread for 1992 are as follows:

Production and sales	2,000,000 lbs.
Selling price per pound	x 2.40
Total sales	$4,800,000
	=========

Standard cost per pound of production:

Direct materials, .8 gallons @ $0.80	=	$0.64
Direct labor, .10 hours @ 6.00	=	.60
Variable overhead, .10 hours @ 3.50	=	.35
Total variable costs of production	=	$1.59
		====

During 1992, San Luis produced and sold 2,200,000 pounds of Spread for total sales revenue of $4,400,000. (Average selling price, $2.00 per pound.) Actual variable production costs for 1992 are shown below, followed by a contribution margin performance report. Average cost per pound of finished product (calculated by dividing total costs by 2,200,000 pounds produced and sold) is shown in parentheses.

Direct materials (1,650,000 gal. x $0.84)	$1,386,000	($0.63)
Direct labor (264,000 hrs. x $5.90)	1,557,600	(0.708)
Variable overhead	792,000	(0.36)
Total variable costs	$3,735,600	($1.698)
	========	======

San Luis Wax Company
Contribution Margin Performance Report, Budget vs. Actual
Year Ended December 31, 1992

		Budget	Actual
Sales, in pounds		2,000,000	2,200,000
Sales, amount	(2,000,000 x $2.40)	$4,800,000	
	(2,200,000 x $2.00)		$4,400,000
Variable cost of goods sold:			
Direct materials	(2,000,000 x $0.64)	1,280,000	
	(2,200,000 x $0.63)		1,386,000
Direct labor	(2,000,000 x $0.60)	1,200,000	
	(2,200,000 x $0.708)		1,557,600
Variable overhead	(2,000,000 x $0.35)	700,000	
	(2,200,000 x $0.36)		792,000
Total variable cost of goods sold		3,180,000	3,735,600
Contribution margin		$1,620,000	$ 664,400
Unfavorable contribution margin variance		$955,600	

With this information we are now in a position to compute the variances.

Sales volume variance

Actual units sold		2,200,000	
Budgeted unit sales	-	2,000,000	
Volume variance	=	200,000	pounds
Budgeted contribution margin per unit	x	$0.81	($2.40 - $1.59)
Sales volume variance	=	$ 162,000	F

Selling price variance

Actual selling price	=	$ 2.00	
Budgeted selling price	=	2.40	
Price variance	=	$ 0.40	per pound
Actual units sold	x	2,200,000	pounds
Selling price variance	=	$ 880,000	U

Direct materials variances

There are two direct materials variances: quantity and price.

Quantity variance

Quantity variance	=	(standard quantity - actual quantity) x standard price
	=	(1,760,000 - 1,650,000) x $0.80
	=	-110,000 x $0.80
	=	-$88,000 F

[Note: standard quantity = 2,200,000 lbs. x .8 gal. per lb. = 1,760,000]

Price variance

Price variance	=	(standard price - actual price) x actual quantity
	=	($0.80 - $0.84) x 1,650,000
	=	$66,000 U

Direct labor variances

There are also two direct labor variances: rate and efficiency.

Labor rate variance

Labor rate variance	=	(standard rate - actual rate) x actual direct labor hours
	=	($6.00 - $5.90) x 264,000 hours
	=	$26,400 F

Labor efficiency variance

Labor efficiency variance	=	(standard hours - actual hours) x standard labor rate
	=	(220,000 -264,000) x $6.00
	=	$264,000 U

Variable manufacturing overhead variances

The variable overhead variances are spending and efficiency.

Overhead spending variance

Flexible budget for actual direct hours	=	$ 924,000 (264,000 x $3.50)
Actual variable overhead	=	792,000
Overhead spending variance	=	$ 132,000 F

Overhead efficiency variance

Flexible budget for standard hours allowed	=	$ 770,000	(220,000 x $3.50)
Flexible budget for actual direct hours	=	924,000	(264,000 x $3.50)
Overhead efficiency variance	=	$ 154,000 U	

San Luis Wax Company
Contribution Margin Variance Analysis
Year Ended December 31, 1992

Budgeted contribution margin	$1,620,000
Actual contribution margin	664,400
Unfavorable contribution margin variance	$ 955,600

Source of variance	Favorable	Unfavorable
Sales volume	$ 162,000	
Selling price		$ 880,000
Direct materials:		
Price		66,000
Quantity	88,000	
Direct labor:		
Rate	26,400	
Efficiency		264,000
Variable overhead:		
Spending	132,000	
Efficiency		154,000
Totals	$ 408,400	$1,364,000

Unfavorable contribution margin variance	$ 955,600 U

MATCHING ATTRIBUTES

Below in Group A are listed attributes that may be identified with the variance analysis terms listed in Group B. Indicate, by use of the identifying letter of the appropriate Group B item, which description in Group A best matches which Group B term.

Group A

_E_ 1. Results from differences between actual variable costs and budgeted variable costs.

_P_ 2. Results from differences between planned price and actual price.

_A_ 3. Difference between actual and planned net income for a period.

_C_ 4. Results from the difference between actual numbers of units sold and numbers of units planned.

_B_ 5. Results from actually selling relative quantities of products different from that which was planned.

Group B

A. Profit variance
B. Sales mix variance
C. Sales volume variance
D. Selling price variance
E. Variable cost variance

MULTIPLE CHOICE

For each of the following items choose the most appropriate completion phrase.

1. There are many variables that influence a company's net income. Which of the following is *not* a major accounting factor for computing net income?

    a. Volume of sales.
    b. Selling price of the products.
    c. Sales mix of products sold.
    d. The variety of products sold.
    e. Variable costs of production and sales.

2. When analyzing profit variance certain factors or rules can be very helpful. Which of the following is such a factor or rule?

    a. It is best to analyze all contributing factors simultaneously.
    b. Variable and fixed costs must be treated separately.
    c. Fixed costs remain fixed *per unit* of sales, within the relevant range.
    d. A variable cost *per unit* varies with the sales volume.
    e. Contribution margin is computed as sales minus variable and fixed costs.

3. Sales volume variance refers to the difference in actual quantities of product sold from the quantities planned in the budget. Which of the following is *not* a cause of sales volume variance?

    a. Changes in prices.
    b. Competitors' actions affecting market share.
    c. Employee productivity.
    d. A downturn in the economy.
    e. General industry sales decline.

4. Sales volume variance is an analysis of the dollar effect on contribution margin by a variance in sales volume. This variance is computed as:

   a. (Actual sales units - budgeted sales units) x budgeted contribution margin per unit.
   b. Actual sales units - budgeted sales units.
   c. (Actual sales units - budgeted sales units) x actual contribution margin per unit.
   d. (Actual sales units - budgeted sales units) x budgeted sales price per unit.
   e. (Actual sales units - budgeted sales units) x actual sales price per unit.

5. There are several causes of selling price variances. Which of the following is *not* a cause of selling price variance?

   a. Unplanned price discounts.
   b. A weak economy.
   c. A change in management's pricing policy.
   d. Using a different marketing channel.
   e. Inefficiency of labor producing the product.

6. Selling price variance is an analysis of the dollar effect on contribution margin because of a variance in selling price. This variable is computed as:

   a. Actual selling price - budgeted selling price.
   b. (Actual selling price - budgeted selling price)/budgeted number of units sold.
   c. (Actual sales - budgeted sales)/actual number of budgeted sales units.
   d. (Actual selling price - budgeted selling price) x budgeted number of units sold.
   e. (Actual selling price - budgeted selling price) x actual number of units sold.

7. Causes of variable cost variances include all of the following except one. Which is *not* a cause of variable cost variances?

   a. Higher supervision cost and property taxes than planned.
   b. Inefficient use of direct materials.
   c. Low productivity of direct labor.
   d. Less promotional cost than the amount planned.
   e. Higher sales commissions than those planned.

8. Variable cost variance analysis measures the dollar effect on contribution margin of a variance in variable costs from those planned costs. This variance is computed as:

   a. Total actual variable cost - budgeted costs, in total.
   b. (Actual variable costs per unit - budgeted variable costs per unit) x actual units sold.
   c. (Actual variable costs per unit - budgeted variable costs per unit) x budgeted units sold.
   d. (Actual variable costs per unit - budgeted variable costs per unit) x budgeted contribution margin per unit.
   e. (Actual variable costs per unit - budgeted variable costs per unit) x actual contribution margin per unit.

9. Fixed cost variance analysis is presented as

    a. (Actual fixed costs per unit - budgeted fixed cost per unit) x actual sales volume.

    b. (Actual fixed costs per unit - budgeted fixed cost per unit) x budgeted sales volume.

    c. (Total fixed costs - budgeted fixed costs)/actual sales volume.

    d. (Total fixed costs - budgeted fixed costs)/budgeted sales volume.

    e. Actual fixed costs - budgeted fixed costs.

10. Sales mix variance measures the effect on contribution margin of a different actual sales mix from that planned. The sales mix variance is computed as:

    a. (Actual sales units - budgeted sales units) x actual sales price per unit.

    b. (Actual sales units - budgeted sales units) x (budgeted contribution margin per unit - budgeted average contribution margin per unit).

    c. (Actual sales units - budgeted sales units) x actual contribution margin per unit.

    d. (Actual sales units - budgeted sales units) x budgeted contribution margin per unit.

    e. (Actual sales units - budgeted sales units) x budgeted average contribution margin per unit.

11. A variable overhead spending variance is computed as:

    a. (Budgeted variable overhead + fixed overhead)/flexible budget hours.

    b. Actual variable manufacturing overhead - flexible budget for actual direct labor hours.

    c. Actual variable manufacturing overhead - flexible budget for direct labor hours allowed.

    d. Flexible budget for actual direct labor hours - flexible budget for direct labor hours allowed.

    e. Total manufacturing overhead variance/actual direct labor hours.

12. Overhead efficiency variance is computed as:

    a. (Budgeted variable overhead + fixed overhead)/flexible budget hours.

    b. Actual variable manufacturing overhead - flexible budget for actual direct labor hours.

    c. Actual variable manufacturing overhead - flexible budget for direct labor hours allowed.

    d. Flexible budget for actual direct labor hours - flexible budget for direct labor hours allowed.

    e. Total manufacturing overhead variance/actual direct labor hours.

Illustrative Problems

1. The Lake Charles Equipment Co. makes a fishing rod that has the following price and cost schedule.

	Big One
Selling price	$10.00
Variable production costs	2.50
Variable selling and admin. costs	1.50
Total variable costs	4.00
Contribution margin	$6.00
Contribution percentage	60%

Lake Charles Equipment Co.
Statement of Income
Year Ending June 30, 1991

	Budget	Actual	Variance	
Sales, units	1,000,000	900,000	100,000	U
Sales, amount	$10,000,000	$8,100,000	$1,900,000	U
Variable costs:				
Production costs	2,500,000	2,160,000	340,000	F
Selling and administrative costs	1,500,000	1,440,000	60,000	F
Total variable costs	4,000,000	3,600,000	400,000	F
Contribution margin	6,000,000	4,500,000	1,500,000	U
Fixed costs:				
Production	1,800,000	1,800,000	0	
Selling and administrative	1,200,000	1,200,000	0	
Total fixed costs	3,000,000	3,000,000	0	
Net income	$3,000,000	$1,500,000	$1,500,000	U

Requested

Based upon the data presented above, prepare:

    a.   Sales volume variance analysis.

    b.   Selling price variance analysis.

    c.   Variable cost variance analysis report.

    d.   Contribution margin variance analysis report.

2. Referring to problem 1 above, now assume that Lake Charles Equipment Co. has a second product, called Slick One. Its price and cost schedule follows:

	Slick One
Selling price	$20.00
Variable production costs	2.50
Variable selling and admin. costs	2.50
Total variable costs	5.00
Contribution margin	$15.00
Contribution percentage	75%

The budgeted and actual contribution margin performance reports follow.

Lake Charles Equipment Co.
Budgeted Contribution Margin Performance
Year Ending June 30, 1991

	Big One	Slick One	Total
Sales, units	1,000,000	500,000	1,500,000
Sales, amount	$10,000,000	$10,000,000	$20,000,000
Variable costs:			
Production	2,500,000	1,250,000	3,750,000
Selling and administrative	1,500,000	1,250,000	2,750,000
Total variable costs	4,000,000	2,500,000	6,500,000
Contribution margin	$6,000,000	$ 7,500,000	$13,500,000
Contribution percentage	60.0%	75.0%	67.5%

Lake Charles Equipment Co.
Actual Contribution Margin Performance
Year Ending June 30, 1991

	Big One	Slick One	Total
Sales, units	900,000	600,000	1,500,000
Sales, amount	$8,100,000	$10,800,000	$18,900,000
Variable costs:			
Production	2,160,000	1,440,000	3,600,000
Selling and administrative	1,440,000	1,560,000	3,000,000
Total variable costs	3,600,000	3,000,000	6,600,000
Contribution margin	$4,500,000	$7,800,000	$12,300,000
Contribution percentage	55.56%	72.22%	65.08%

Requested:

Based upon the data presented above and in item 1 above, prepare for each product:

a.   Sales mix variance analysis.

b.   Sales volume variance analysis.

c.   Selling price variance analysis.

d.   Variable cost variance analysis.

e.   Contribution margin variance analysis report.

3. The Webster High Junior Achievement Company, Ortega, Inc. developed a nonalcoholic, low-calorie beverage called **Screem**. It was so successful that two of the students produced and marketed the product throughout the Southwest under the corporate name Ortega, Ltd. As the company grew, it established a standard cost system with the following 1991 production plan:

Production and sales in gallons		800,000
Budgeted selling price per gallon		x $1.50
Budgeted sales in dollars		$1,200,000
		========

Variable production costs per 10-gallon keg:
   Direct materials:

Material A (10 gal. @ $0.05 per gal.)	$ 0.50
Material B (5 lbs. @ $0.35 per lb.)	1.75
Direct labor (.2 hr. @ $5.50 per hr.)	1.10
Variable manufacturing overhead (.2 hr. @ $4.00 per hr.)	.80
Budgeted variable production costs	$ 4.15
	====

Budgeted contribution margin per gal. ($1.50 - $.415) = $1.085 per gal. During 1991, Ortega, Ltd. actually produced and sold 820,000 gallons of Screem with the following results:

Actual selling price per gallon	$ 1.40
	=====

Actual variable production costs:
   Direct materials purchased and used:

Material A (902,000 gal. @ $0.055 per gal.	$ 49,610
Material B (492,000 lbs. @ $.37 per lb.	182,040
Direct labor (20,500 hrs. @ $5.60 per hr.)	114,800
Variable mfg. overhead (20,500 hrs. @ $3.80)	77,900
Total actual variable production costs	$424,350
	=======

The company's contribution margin performance report follows:

Ortega, Ltd.
Contribution Margin Performance Report-Budget vs. Actual
Year Ended December 31, 1991

	Budget	Actual
Sales, units	800,000 gal.	820,000 gal.
Sales, dollars	$1,200,000	$1,148,000
Variable cost of goods sold:		
Direct material A	40,000	49,610
Direct material B	140,000	182,040
Direct labor	88,000	114,800
Variable mfg. overhead	64,000	77,900
Total variable costs	332,000	424,350
Contribution margin	$868,000	$723,650
Unfavorable variance	$144,350	

Requested:

Compute the following variances for Ortega, Ltd. for 1991.

a.   Sales volume variance

b.   Selling price variance

c.   Direct materials variance

d.   Direct labor variance.

e.   Variable manufacturing overhead variances

f.   Summary schedule of contribution margin variance analysis.

Vocabulary

CONTRIBUTION MARGIN VARIANCE ANALYSIS. A technique used to evaluate the sources of the difference between the actual contribution margin for a given period and the contribution margin budgeted for the same period or one for the previous period.

FIXED COST VARIANCE. The difference between the actual fixed costs incurred for the manufacturing, selling, and administrative functions during a particular period and the fixed costs budgeted for the same period.

FIXED COST VARIANCE ANALYSIS. A technique used to evaluate the actual fixed cost performance compared with the fixed costs budgeted.

PROFIT VARIANCE. The difference between the actual net income earned and the planned net income for the same period.

PROFIT VARIANCE ANALYSIS. A technique used to evaluate differences between actual and planned net income.

SALES MIX VARIANCE. A variance affecting contribution margin that is caused by actual relative quantities of multiple products that are different from those planned.

SALES VOLUME VARIANCE. A variance affecting contribution margin that results from actually selling more total units than the amount planned.

SELLING PRICE VARIANCE. A variance affecting contribution margin that occurs when the actual selling price is different from the planned selling price.

VARIABLE COST VARIANCE. A variance affecting contribution margin that arises whenever the actual variable costs incurred to produce or sell a product are not the same as the variable costs planned.

THE ANSWERS

Matching Attributes

1.	E	3.	A	5.	B
2.	D	4.	C		

Multiple Choice

1.	d	4.	a	7.	a	10.	b
2.	b	5.	e	8.	b	11.	b
3.	c	6.	e	9.	e	12.	d

ILLUSTRATIVE PROBLEMS

1.
   a. **Sales volume variance.**

Budgeted units sold	1,000,000
Actual units sold	900,000
Volume variance	100,000
Budgeted contribution margin per unit	$6.00
Sales volume variance	$600,000 U

   b. **Selling price variance.**

Actual selling price ($8,100,000/900,000)	$9.00
Budgeted selling price	10.00
Price variance	$1.00 U
Actual units sold	900,000
Selling price variance	$ 900,000 U

   c. **Variable cost variance, production.**

Actual costs per unit ($2,160,000/900,000)	$ 2.40
Budgeted costs per unit	2.50
Variable cost variance	0.10 F
Actual units sold	900,000
Variable cost variance, production	$ 90,000 F

   Variable cost variance, selling and administrative.

Actual costs per unit ($1,440,000/900,000)	$ 1.60
Budgeted costs per unit	1.50
Variable cost variance	0.10 U
Actual units sold	900,000
Variable cost variance, sell. & admin.	$ 90,000 U

d.

Lake Charles Equipment Co.
Contribution Margin Variance Analysis
Year Ended June 30, 1991

Budgeted contribution margin	$6,000,000
Actual contribution margin	4,500,000
Unfavorable contribution margin variance	$1,500,000

Source of variance	Favorable	Unfavorable
Sales volume		$600,000
Selling price		900,000
Variable cost:		
Production cost	$90,000	
Selling and administrative		90,000
	$90,000	$1,590,000

Net unfavorable contribution margin variance $1,500,000 U

2.

a. The sales mix variance for Lake Charles is computed as:

Big One

Sales mix variance
$=$ (actual sales units - budgeted sales units) x
(budgeted contribution margin per unit -
budgeted average contribution margin per unit)
$=$ (900,000 - 1,000,000) x ($6.00 - $9.00)
$=$ -100,000 x -$3.00
$=$ $300,000 F

[Budgeted average contribution margin per unit = total budgeted contribution margin ($13,500,000) divided by total budgeted unit sales (1,500,000), or $9.00.]

Slick One

Sales mix variance	=	(600,000 - 500,000) x ($15.00 - $9.00)
	=	100,000 x $6.00
	=	$600,000 F

b. **Sales volume variance.**

Big one

Sales volume variance	=	(actual sales volume - budgeted sales volume) x (budgeted average contribution margin per unit)
	=	(900,000 - 1,000,000) x $9.00
	=	-$900,000 U

Slick One

Sales volume variance	=	(600,000 - 500,000) x $9.00
	=	$900,000 F

c. **Selling price variance.**

Big one

Selling price variance	=	(actual selling price - budgeted selling price) x actual units sold
	=	($9.00 - $10.00) x 900,000
	=	-$900,000 U

Slick One

Selling price variance	=	($18.00 - $20.00) x 600,000
	=	$-1,200,000 U

d. **Variable cost variance.**

Big one

Cost variance, production	=	(actual cost per unit - budgeted cost per unit) x actual units sold
	=	($2.40 - $2.50) x 900,000
	=	-$90,000 F

Cost variance, selling and administrative	=	($1.60 - $1.50) x 900,000
	=	$90,000 U

Slick One

Cost variance, production = ($2.40 - $2.50) x 600,000
                          = -$60,000 F

Cost variance, selling
and administrative = ($2.60 - $2.50) x 600,000
                    = $60,000 U

e.

Lake Charles Equipment Co.
Contribution Margin Variance Analysis
Year Ended June 30, 1991

Budgeted contribution margin	$13,500,000
Actual contribution margin	12,300,000
Unfavorable contribution margin variance	$1,200,000

Source of variance	Favorable	Unfavorable
Sales mix:		
Big One	$ 300,000	
Slick One	600,000	
Sales volume:		
Big One		$ 900,000
Slick One	900,000	
Selling price:		
Big One		900,000
Slick One		1,200,000
Variable cost, production:		
Big One	90,000	
Slick One	60,000	
Variable cost, selling and administrative:		
Big One		90,000
Slick One		60,000
	$1,950,000	$3,150,000

Net unfavorable contribution margin variance $1,200,000

3.

a. **Sales volume variance.**

=   (Actual sales volume - budgeted sales volume) x budgeted contribution margin per unit

=   (820,000 - 800,000) x $1.085

= $21,700 F
=======

b. **Selling price variance.**

=   (Actual selling price - budgeted selling price) x actual sales volume

=   ($1.40 - $1.50) x 820,000

= $82,000 U
=======

c. **Direct materials price variances.**

Material A

=   (Actual price per gallon - budgeted price per gallon) x actual volume

=   ($0.055 - 0.05) x 902,000 gallons

= $4,510 U
======

Material B

=   ($0.37 - 0.35) x 492,000 pounds

= $9,840 U
======

Direct materials quantity variances.

Material A

=   (Actual quantity - budgeted quantity) x standard price

=   (902,000 gallons - 820,000 gallons) x $0.05

= $4,100 U
======

Material B

=   (492,000 lbs. - 410,000 lbs.) x $0.35

= $28,700 U
=======

d.   **Direct labor variances.**

Rate variance

=   (Actual rate - budgeted rate) x actual hours
=   ($5.60 - $5.50) x 20,500 hours
= $2,050 U
      ======

Efficiency variance

=   (Actual hours - standard hours allowed) x standard rate
=   (20,500 hours - 16,400 hours) x $5.50
= $22,550 U
      =======

e.   **Variable manufacturing overhead variances.**

Actual Variable Manufacturing Overhead $77,900		Flexible Budget for Actual Direct Labor Hours (20,500 x $4.00) $82,000		Flexible Budget for Standard DLH Allowed (16,400 x $4.00) $65,600
	$4,100 F		$16,400 U	
	Spending Variance		Efficiency Variance	

f.

Ortega, Ltd.
Contribution Margin Variance Analysis
Year Ended December 31, 1991

Budgeted contribution margin		$868,000
Actual contribution margin		723,650
Unfavorable contribution margin variance		$144,350
		=======

Source of variance	Favorable	Unfavorable
Sales volume	$21,700	
Selling price		$ 82,000
Direct materials:		
Price—Material A		4,510
Material B		9,840
Quantity—Material A		4,100
Material B		28,700
Direct labor:		
Rate		2,050
Efficiency		22,550
Variable overhead:		
Spending	4,100	
Efficiency		16,400
Total	$25,800	$170,150
Unfavorable variance		$144,350
		======

CHAPTER 13

ACCOUNTING FOR DECENTRALIZED OPERATIONS

Until now, we have assumed the firm is altogether under one roof, or at least in a centralized and unified organization. Large organizations, however, are often widely dispersed and segmented into geographic, product line or functional divisions. In Chapter 13 we learn the special problems of decentralized operations—both management and accounting problems. It is an exciting and challenging new vista.

LEARNING OBJECTIVES

1. Explain the major characteristics of a decentralized organization.
2. Identify the benefits and limitations of decentralization.
3. Describe the nature and role of responsibility accounting in a decentralized operation.
4. Distinguish between cost centers, profit centers, and investment centers.
5. Realize how allocated costs should be treated for performance evaluation purposes.
6. Prepare and evaluate a segmented income statement with a contribution report format.
7. Recognize how return on investment (ROI) analysis is used to evaluate profit performance.
8. Determine how residual income (RI) analysis is used to evaluate profit performance.
9. Explain the importance of intrafirm transfer pricing in a decentralized organization.
10. Discuss three approaches to transfer pricing—cost-based, market-based, and negotiated market-based.

LEARNING TIPS

It is one thing to manage an operation that you can see, and where you can readily visit with the various department managers. It is quite another to oversee a widely dispersed or far-flung company. How do you know what the various division managers are doing? Again, accounting is the language of business. Special reports are demonstrated in Chapter 13 to show how division managers and top management keep in touch.

Try to place yourself in the position of a division manager two thousand miles from the home office. What does top management want to know from you? How can you communicate with them to assure them you are on top of everything and carrying out company policies? This chapter tells the story.

REVIEW

1. Explain the major characteristics of a decentralized operation.

A decentralized business operation is characterized by having authority and responsibility delegated to the lowest level of management feasible. In this way, the management personnel closest to the operations have both the authority to make decisions and the responsibility to attain the results planned by management.

2. Identify the benefits and limitations of decentralization.

Among the benefits of decentralized management are the following:

a. Better decisions are possible (and likely) because the persons making the decisions are close to the operations and the personnel to be effected by those decisions.

b. Higher-level management have more time to deal with long-term planning and higher-level decisions if the day-to-day operations are decided upon by operating personnel.

c. Managers who have increased levels of authority and responsibility also have greater incentive to perform to their maximum.

d. Managers in a decentralized company receive better on-the-job training in management skills; therefore they are preparing for advancement to higher levels of management as they perform their management roles.

e. Measurement of the performance of the managers and their staffs is improved because it is possible to evaluate both individual management effort and group performance.

f. Decentralization sometimes is the only way to effectively deal with the problems of great size, in order that the company can respond to change and stay in contact with its operating environment.

Limitations of decentralization are as numerous as are its benefits. They must be considered. They are listed below:

a. Accounting becomes more complex and more costly with decentralized operations and the quantity of data to be collected and processed is much greater than under centralized operations.

b. When operations are decentralized some staff and service functions, such as accounting, personnel and computer services, might be duplicated, and therefore, more expensive to the entire organization.

c. Under decentralization, certain problems in evaluating performance occur because of the interrelationship among segments. For example, determining exact costs and prices of transferred and shared goods and services frequently occurs.

d. Decentralized managers are often less experienced than central, higher-level managers. These decentralized managers are more prone to error, and such errors may be costly to the organization.

e. Because decentralized managers are aware that they are being evaluated based upon their performance, they may make decisions that enhance their own performance as measured by accounting reports and forego some things that may not be easily measured by those reports in the short run, such as employee training and development and equipment repair and maintenance.

f. Coordination of all operations may become more difficult when decision making is decentralized throughout the organization.

3. **Describe the nature and role of responsibility accounting in a decentralized operation.**

Responsibility accounting is a subset of the general accounting system that provides timely perform-ance reports for each segment of the enterprise. These reports compare actual performance with planned performance (the budget). Variances from the plan are clearly indicated. Responsibility accounting is essential for evaluation of performance.

4. **Distinguish among cost centers, profit centers, and investment centers.**

These three terms are included under the more general caption "responsibility center." Each is defined below:

Cost center is a business department or segment that does not have revenues attributed to it. Costs incurred in that segment's operations are accumulated and reported, in comparison with that segment's budget, in order to measure the segment's performance against the plan.

Profit center applies to a segment that generates measurable revenue from the products and services it provides. From these activities, a mini-income statement can be developed from the responsibility accounting function, indicating the revenues earned, costs incurred, and the income produced by the segment, compared to the budgeted amounts for these categories.

Investment center is the term that relates to a center that has resource (asset) responsibility as well as cost and revenue responsibility. The investment center manager chooses the assets needed for her division, and has full responsibility and, therefore, accountability for performance.

The responsibility accounting system accumulates revenue, cost and asset information "tagged" according to the appropriate segment that has responsibility for them. This is usually done by the assignment of specific account number codes designating to which segment these items belong.

5. **Realize how allocated costs should be treated for performance evaluation purposes.**

Allocated costs occur when common costs that cannot be traced to a single segment of the business are assigned to segments on some predetermined basis. Cost allocation is arbitrary and not consistent with the notion of controllability. When evaluating management performance, allocated costs should be ignored.

6. **Prepare and evaluate a segmented income statement with a contribution report format.**

The following report of Graceland Park employs four measures of operating performance:
a.   Contribution margin
b.   Controllable income
c.   Segment income
d.   Net income before tax for the firm as a whole.

Graceland Park
Segmented Income Statement—Contribution Report Format
Year Ended December 31, 1990

	Rides	Gifts	Food	Total
Sales	$ 850,000	$ 320,000	$ 480,000	$ 1,650,000
Variable costs:				
Operating	102,000	9,600	28,200	139,800
Cost of goods sold	-	80,000	126,900	206,900
Total	102,000	89,600	155,100	346,700
Controllable fixed costs:				
Salaries and wages	255,000	64,000	211,500	530,500
Promotion	34,000	16,000	23,500	73,500
Total	289,000	80,000	235,000	604,000
Controllable income	459,000	150,400	89,900	699,300
Uncontrollable fixed costs:				
Depreciation	120,000	30,000	14,900	164,900
Taxes	119,000	9,000	12,000	140,000
Insurance	136,000	9,000	15,000	160,000
Total	375,000	48,000	41,900	464,900
Segment income	$ 84,000	$ 102,400	$ 48,000	234,400
Common fixed costs:				
Administration				48,000
Advertising				55,000
Other				21,300
Total				124,300
Net income before taxes				$ 110,100

7. **Recognize how return on investment (ROI) analysis is used to evaluate profit performance.**

   Referring again to Graceland Park in the preceding example, the operating asset amounts, per investment center, are used to compute the important return on investment (ROI) ratio.

	Code	Rides	Gifts	Food	Total
Segment income	a	84,000	102,400	48,000	234,400
Sales	b	850,000	320,000	480,000	1,650,000
Operating assets	c	$3,000,000	$120,000	$80,000	$3,200,000
Margin earned	d = a/b	.099	.32	.10	.1421
Turnover of assets	e = b/c	.283	2.667	6.0	.5156
ROI	d x e	.028	.853	.60	.07327

8. **Determine how residual income (RI) analysis is used to evaluate profit performance.**

Using residual income analysis, it is necessary to designate a target or minimum ROI. Suppose the Graceland Park board of directors decides that the minimum acceptable ROI for the park is 15% for future projects. It is apparent that the park as a whole earns a much lower rate and that the Gifts and Food divisions earn much higher rates, as shown in the preceding table. Although it would be virtually impossible to increase the ROI of the entire park's operations to 15%, all new proposals could be held to that test. For example, a new ride might be considered with an investment of $250,000 and a projected segment income of $52,500. Would this meet the test?

$$\text{ROI} = \frac{\$52,500}{\$250,000} = 21\%$$

A managerial decision to add this ride would meet the board's ROI criterion, but of course other factors would have to be considered, such as the impact the new ride would have on the revenues from other rides, and alternate investment opportunities.

An interesting side note should be considered. Since the Rides division as a whole falls far below the board's ROI minimum for new investments, should the current rides be abandoned? Probably not, since the Gifts and Foods divisions would have no reason to exist without the Rides. However, individual rides might be examined in detail to determine if some could be eliminated or replaced.

9. **Explain the importance of intrafirm transfer pricing in a decentralized organization.**

When division managers' performance is evaluated (at least partially) on the basis of the division's profitability, transfer prices become a source of conflict and debate. This is because the selling division wants the highest price possible (to enhance that division's profit); the buying division wants the lowest price possible (to reduce that division's costs); and top management wants transfers between (and among) divisions if such transfers enhance the total company's overall profit.

10. **Discuss three approaches to transfer pricing—cost-based, market-based, and negotiated market-based.**

The three approaches to intrafirm pricing decisions are discussed in the following paragraphs.

Cost-based prices These prices are simply the costs of the producing divisions, without any attempt to calculate a profit on the intrafirm transfer. These cost-based prices may consist of actual cost, standard cost, full (absorption) cost or variable cost, each according to the division's cost accounting system. A substitute for standard cost may be budgeted cost. Sometimes a combination of (or compromise between) two or more of these costs might be used.

Market-based prices These prices are related to what a willing buyer would pay and a willing seller would charge for the particular product on the open market. This market price provides the selling division an opportunity to earn a profit and leaves the buyer no worse off than if it acquired the product from another vendor.

Negotiated market-based prices Many actual prices in the market place result from buyer and seller discussing, haggling or negotiating the price based on supply and demand, costs, alternatives and whatever other factors are relevant. Thus, a negotiated market price is not looked-up and determined, but results from normal buyer-seller negotiations.

Matching Attributes

Below in Group A are listed attributes that may be identified with the decentralized accounting terms listed in Group B. Indicate, by use of the identifying letter of the appropriate Group B item, which description in Group A best matches which Group B term.

Group A

K 1. Involvement of each management level in the preparation of budget estimates for his/her own segment.

F 2. A segment of the firm that does not have revenue attributed to it.

Q 3. A business segment for which accounting reports are prepared relative to that segment's activities.

M 4. A business segment to which is attributed both revenues and costs, permitting preparation of its own income statement.

I 5. A business segment that has responsibility for choosing its own assets and is accountable for them as well as income statement responsibility.

L 6. Accounting report that shows the results of activities for a period of time by a business segment, comparing actual results with planned results, showing variances.

J 7. Principle that directs management's attention to those items where actual performance varies from planned performance by a significant degree.

G 8. Downward distribution of job assignments and corresponding decision-making powers.

C 9. Right to make decisions to perform certain tasks.

O 10. Obligations to attain certain results.

A 11. System that provides information for managing segments of a business.

P 12. Reports measuring managers' accomplishments.

B 13. Common costs that cannot be traced to a single business segment are assigned to segments on a predetermined basis.

E 14. Contribution margin minus controllable fixed costs.

R 15. Controllable income less the uncontrollable fixed costs that can be traced as direct costs to the divisions.

D 16. Revenue minus variable costs.

N 17. Amount earned in excess of minimum ROI.

H 18. Amount charged one division by another division for a product sold within the firm.

Group B

A.	Accountability	J.	Management by exception
B.	Allocated cost	K.	Participative management
C.	Authority	L.	Performance report
D.	Contribution margin	M.	Profit center
E.	Controllable income	N.	Residual income
F.	Cost center	O.	Responsibility
G.	Delegation	P.	Responsibility accounting
H.	Intrafirm transfer price	Q.	Responsibility center
I.	Investment center	R.	Segment income

MULTIPLE CHOICE

For each of the following items choose the most appropriate completion phrase.

1. Two key dimensions of controllability are:

   a. Size and volume of a segment's business.
   b. Level of management and the given time period.
   c. Time period and cost incurrence.
   d. Management level and number of employees.
   e. Investment in assets and sales volume.

2. With respect to responsibility accounting reports,

   a. Higher-level management get more detailed reports than lower level management.
   b. Each higher level manager receives reports on his/her own activities as well as reports on subordinates' performance.
   c. Management by exception is more related to financial reporting than responsibility accounting reports.
   d. Management is held responsible for all activities—costs, revenues and investments—that occur within their department, regardless of their authority over decisions that affect these matters.

3. Intrafirm transfer price is

   a. The price for which a product is sold from one firm to another.
   b. The price for which a product is sold from one division of a firm to another division within the same firm.
   c. The price at which inventory is carried within the firm.
   d. The price at which transfers are made within a division of a firm, for example, when transferred from work-in-process inventory to finished goods inventory.

4. Cost-based transfer price is computed as

   a. Historical, full cost.
   b. Cost according to the standard cost system.
   c. Budgeted cost.
   d. Variable costs only.
   e. May be any of the above.

5. Market-based transfer prices are related to

    a.   Full cost of the selling division plus a fair profit.

    b.   What the buying division could purchase the product for from an outside source.

    c.   An agreed upon price negotiated between buyer and seller.

    d.   Standard cost plus an agreed upon markup for profit.

6. Which of the following items does *not* constitute a hindrance to market-based transfer prices?

    a.   Such market prices may not be readily available since the intermediate product may not have a well-defined market.

    b.   Reliable market prices would be difficult or time-consuming to obtain.

    c.   Comparisons of market prices are difficult because of differences in quality and other factors not easily measured or perceived.

    d.   Market prices are not a fair measure of a product's worth and should not be used to make internal pricing decisions.

7. Segment income is defined as:

    a.   Revenue less variable costs.

    b.   Contribution margin minus all fixed costs.

    c.   Controllable income minus uncontrollable fixed costs for the division.

    d.   Net income before taxes plus interest.

    e.   The same as controllable income.

8. Return on investment (ROI) is equal to

    a.   Revenue divided by investment.

    b.   Asset turnover times revenue earned.

    c.   Contribution margin divided by sales.

    d.   Margin earned times turnover of assets.

    e.   Controllable income divided by investment.

9. Residual income analysis is a means of determining

    a.   The amount by which income exceeds the income required to meet the minimum ROI.

    b.   The amount of income required to meet minimum ROI.

    c.   The amount of income required to equal two times minimum ROI.

    d.   The amount of income from a proposed new investment to maintain the minimum ROI.

    e.   The amount of investment required to equal the minimum ROI.

ILLUSTRATIVE PROBLEMS

1. Below is the most recent segmented income statement for Hilltop Sound Systems:

Hilltop Sound Systems
Segmented Income Statement—Contribution Margin Approach
Year Ended December 31, 199a

	Division 1	Division 2	Total
Sales	$ 2,160,000	$ 1,440,000	$ 3,600,000
Variable costs:			
Manufacturing			799,200
Selling			504,000
Total			1,303,200
Contribution margin			2,296,800
Controllable fixed costs:			
Manufacturing salaries			99,000
Sales salaries			105,000
Sales promotion			28,000
Total			232,000
Controllable income			2,064,800
Uncontrollable fixed costs:			
Depreciation			110,000
Property taxes			30,000
Insurance			22,000
Total			162,000
Segment income			1,902,800
Common fixed costs:			
Building occupancy			350,000
Administration			375,000
Advertising			250,000
Interest on indebtedness			300,000
Total			1,275,000
Net income before taxes			$ 627,800

Requested:

Complete the segmented income statement for Hilltop Sound Systems using the following additional information.

	Division 1	Division 2
Variable costs (as % of sales):		
Manufacturing	25%	18%
Selling	12%	17%
Controllable fixed costs (fraction of total company):		
Manufacturing salaries	2/3	1/3
Sales salaries	11/15	4/15
Sales promotion	4/7	3/7
Uncontrollable fixed costs (ratio of total company):		
All costs in this category	60	40

2. Referring to Hilltop Sound Systems above, compute ROI for divisions 1 and 2:

	Division 1	Division 2
Investment in assets	$4,418,400	$3,991,000
ROI (return on investment)	_____	_____

3. The manager of Division 1 of Hilltop Sound Systems has proposed that the company invest $875,000 in new equipment, inventory and other assets to produce a new keyboard instrument that would earn an estimated $201,250 segment margin per year.

  a. What is ROI for this investment? _____

  b. If the company requires a minimum ROI of 20%, what is the residual income computation for the new proposal?

     Residual income =

  c. If this proposal is approved and if the proposed asset costs and income earned occur as indicated, what will the new ROI for the entire Division 1 become? _____

4. Referring again to Hilltop Sound Systems, the manager of Division 2 reports that a fire destroyed an older portion of the plant, including equipment, where one product line was produced. As a result, it is anticipated that segment margin will be reduced by $118,700 and the asset value of the division will diminish by $971,000. Compute the new ROI.

5. The Jarnagin Farm Machinery Company has several divisions that produce components of the company's farm equipment. Each division is semiautonomous, in that it can make decisions to buy from outside suppliers if a company division does not have a competitive price. The board of directors is reviewing company policy on internal transfers and would like an accountant's point of view on the matter. What should be the guideline to limit the purchase of components from outside suppliers with respect to price, compared to that of the company's own division suppliers?

Requested:

Write a brief memo to management giving your view on internal transfers and what kind of guidelines should be established to limit purchases from outside the company when these same items are also available from inside sources.

VOCABULARY

ACCOUNTABILITY. The measure of how successfully assigned operating results are accomplished in a decentralized organization.

AUTHORITY. The right to make the decisions necessary to perform assigned tasks in a decentralized organization.

BUSINESS SEGMENTATION. The division of an organization's work into specialized units.

CONTROLLABLE INCOME. Segment revenues less all variable and fixed costs controllable by the segment manager.

COST-BASED TRANSFER PRICING. A transfer price that is based on some form of the selling segment's costs.

COST CENTER. A responsibility center in which only controllable costs are considered with no concern for revenues or invested assets.

DECENTRALIZATION. The structuring of an organization into well-defined segments with a delegation of decision-making authority downward throughout the organization.

DELEGATION. The downward distribution of job assignments and corresponding decision-making power to managers in an organization.

INVESTMENT CENTER. A responsibility center in which the controllable revenues, costs, and investment in operating assets are considered in evaluating its performance.

MARGIN EARNED. One of the two components of ROI analysis that is computed by dividing some measure of income by sales.

MARKET-BASED TRANSFER PRICING. A transfer price that is based on essentially the same amount the selling segment of a firm would receive from an outside sale.

NEGOTIATED MARKET-BASED TRANSFER PRICING. A transfer price agreed on by both a selling segment and a buying segment of the same firm who act as though they represent the market in their negotiations.

PROFIT CENTER. A responsibility center in which both controllable revenues and costs are considered in the evaluation of the center's performance.

RESIDUAL INCOME (RI) ANALYSIS. An evaluation of the amount of income earned in excess of a certain minimum rate of return on the investment in operating assets.

RESPONSIBILITY. The obligation on the part of managers to whom authority is delegated to attain the desired results.

RESPONSIBILITY ACCOUNTING. A specialized form of accounting used to evaluate the financial performance of responsibility centers.

RESPONSIBILITY CENTER. A business segment organized as a cost center, profit center, or investment center so responsibility accounting can be performed.

RETURN ON INVESTMENT (ROI) ANALYSIS. A technique used to evaluate profitability by multiplying the margin earned times its turnover of assets. Alternatively, income can be divided by the investment in operating assets.

SEGMENTED INCOME STATEMENT. An income statement that shows the contribution margin, controllable income, and segment income for each of an organization's segments as well as the net income for the firm as a whole.

SEGMENT INCOME. The revenues of a business segment less its direct variable and fixed costs.

SUBOPTIMIZATION. A potentially adverse effect of transfer pricing that occurs when the overall profitability of a firm is less than it could have been with a better pricing decision.

TRANSFER PRICE. The price used to transfer products or services between segments of the same firm.

TURNOVER OF ASSETS. One of the two components of ROI analysis that is computed by dividing the sales by the investment in assets required to achieve the sales.

THE ANSWERS

MATCHING ATTRIBUTES

1.	K	5.	I	9.	C	13.	B	17.	N
2.	F	6.	L	10.	O	14.	E	18.	H
3.	Q	7.	J	11.	A	15.	R		
4.	M	8.	G	12.	P	16.	D		

MULTIPLE CHOICE

1.	b	4.	e	7.	c
2.	b	5.	b	8.	d
3.	b	6.	d	9.	a

ILLUSTRATIVE PROBLEMS

1.

Hilltop Sound Systems
Segmented Income Statement—Contribution Margin Approach
Year Ended December 31, 199a

	Division 1	Division 2	Total
Sales	$ 2,160,000	$ 1,440,000	$ 3,600,000
Variable costs:			
Manufacturing	540,000	259,200	799,200
Selling	259,200	244,800	504,000
Total	799,200	504,000	1,303,200
Contribution margin	1,360,800	936,000	2,296,800
Controllable fixed costs:			
Manufacturing salaries	66,000	33,000	99,000
Sales salaries	77,000	28,000	105,000
Sales promotion	16,000	12,000	28,000
Total	159,000	73,000	232,000
Controllable income	1,201,800	863,000	2,064,800
Uncontrollable fixed costs:			
Depreciation	66,000	44,000	110,000
Property taxes	18,000	12,000	30,000
Insurance	13,200	8,800	22,000
Total	97,200	64,800	162,000
Segment income	1,104,600	798,200	1,902,800
Common fixed costs:			
Building occupancy			350,000
Administration			375,000
Advertising			250,000
Interest on indebtedness			300,000
Total			1,275,000
Net income before taxes			$ 627,800

2. Division 1:

$$\text{ROI} = \frac{\text{Income}}{\text{Sales}} \times \frac{\text{Sales}}{\text{Investment}} = \frac{1,104,600}{2,160,000} \times \frac{2,160,000}{4,418,400}$$

$$= .51139 \times .48886 = .25, \text{ or simply} \frac{1,104,600}{4,418,400} = .25$$

Division 2:

$$\text{ROI} = \frac{798,200}{1,440,000} \times \frac{1,440,000}{3,991,000} = .5543 \times .3608 = .20$$

3a.

$$\text{ROI} = \frac{201,250}{875,000} = 0.23, \text{ or } 23\%$$

b.

$$\text{Residual income} = \$201,250 - (.20 \times \$875,000) = \$26,250.$$

c.

$$\frac{\$201,250 + 1,104,600}{\$875,000 + 4,418,400} = \frac{\$1,305,850}{\$5,293,400} = .2467 \text{ or } 24.67\%$$

4.

$$\frac{\$798,200 - 118,700}{\$3,991,000 - 971,000} = .225 \text{ or } 22.5\%$$

5. The company's divisions should buy from other divisions within the Jarnagin Company whenever the products are available from such sources in the required quantities, with a specified quality, at a competitive price. However, the purchase decision should be reviewed by a company official so that the decision is best for the overall company, not just for one specific division. Sometimes a decision benefits one division but not another, and the impact on the overall company must be the final consideration.

CHAPTER 14

COST ALLOCATION: A CLOSER LOOK

Chapter 14 indicates the circumstances in which full costing is necessary to determine product costs. Full costing requires the allocation of overhead costs to the user departments on a logical and predetermined basis. Further, service department costs must be allocated on producing departments in order to include these costs in product costs.

LEARNING OBJECTIVES

1. Describe why cost allocation is necessary when the cost of producing a product, offering a service, or operating a segment of a business must be computed.
2. Explain what cost objectives, cost pools, and cost allocation bases are.
3. Recognize when separate departmental rates should be used to apply manufacturing overhead to products instead of using a single plantwide rate.
4. Distinguish between direct departmental overhead costs, indirect departmental overhead costs, and service department costs.
5. Define three cost allocation bases—usage, activity, and capacity.
6. Discuss the problems associated with inequitable cost allocations.
7. List the basic steps involved with service department cost allocation.
8. Describe how three service department cost allocation methods—direct, step, and reciprocal—are used.
9. Explain why a dual cost allocation base is necessary for certain service department costs.
10. Differentiate between actual and budget performance data in selecting cost allocation bases.
11. Outline the major steps involved with the cost allocations needed to compute departmental overhead rates.
12. Prepare a cost allocation schedule that provides the information needed to calculate predetermined departmental overhead rates.

LEARNING TIPS

When we learn a new subject, sometimes we learn why we shouldn't do something, then learn why we might do that something—under certain circumstances. This is the case in Chapter 14. We learned in Chapter 13 why allocated costs on a decentralized performance report were not useful—in fact, could be harmful. Allocated costs in certain managerial decision-making situations also creates problems. Now, in Chapter 14, we learn why such allocated costs may be necessary.

Of course, the answer to the apparent contradiction is that circumstances vary. In certain circumstances, cost allocation is harmful, and in certain other, rather limited situations, cost allocation is necessary. Chapter 14 makes the distinction clear.

Most topics in our text deal with providing information for persons within the organization. Most of the reports resulting from the cost allocation topics in Chapter 14 go to external users. This is a guideline in knowing when to use cost allocation and when to avoid it. Read on.

REVIEW

1. **Describe why cost allocation is necessary when the full cost of producing a product, offering a service, or operating a segment of a business must be computed.**

   Although we learned in Chapter 13 that cost allocation is foreign to control, and therefore we don't include allocated costs on segment performance reports, there *are* situations in which *full* costing is necessary. Full costing includes the overhead, administrative and other related costs.

   When we go into a restaurant, we know that the cost of the meal we order and eat includes the cost of the raw food and the preparation costs for that food. Preparation costs include the chef's time, utilities for preserving and heating the food, and of course the condiments, utensils and dishes that are a part of serving the food. As we think about it, though, we know the building rent, lights, taxes, insurance and supervision costs all must be included in the food costs. So must the manager's salary, advertising, property taxes and contributions to charity. Full costing includes a lot of invisible costs.

   Many times contracts with the government and other groups require statements that are full-costed. We know that generally accepted accounting principles require full costing for external reporting, but now we realize it is also true for segment reporting in some circumstances.

   A benefit in using full costs in internal reporting is to make managers aware of the costs of support services and central administration, even though they have no control over such costs.

2. **Explain what cost objectives, cost pools, and cost allocation bases are.**

   Cost objective. A cost objective is any activity or output for which cost measurement is performed. Recall that we used the term cost objective earlier when we discussed choosing a base for overhead application in a job or process costing system. A cost objective, then, might be a product, service, project, department or other segment of the business.

   Cost pool. A cost pool is the amount to be allocated. An example is building occupancy costs which might include building taxes, insurance, maintenance, and utilities. These costs may be accumulated in a cost pool as they are incurred. Then, on a periodic basis, e.g. monthly, the entire amount in the cost pool is allocated to the various departments that occupy the building.

   Cost allocation base. The cost allocation base is the basis, sometimes arbitrary, used for allocating the cost pool to the beneficiaries of the service. It is most logical that the allocation base relate to the cause of the cost. For example, labor cost is the basis for computing payroll taxes. Thus, we may say payroll costs cause payroll taxes. The causal basis for allocation is not always clear, however.

   The base for allocating the building occupancy cost pool to the departments that occupy the building usually is square footage of the area occupied by each department. (Logically, we know that departments occupy space—therefore, cubic space occupied would be more correct—but allocating on the basis of square feet of floor area usually gives the same result, and this method saves some time.) Personnel department costs may be allocated on the basis of number of employees in each department. What do you think would be a fair basis for allocating janitorial (custodial) services?

3. **Recognize when separate departmental rates should be used to apply manufacturing overhead to products instead of using a single plantwide rate.**

Departmental rates should be used for applying overhead whenever a plantwide rate would result in unfair charges for some departments or products. This unfairness may occur when some departments are more highly automated than others or when some products require much more time in some departments than others.

Suppose, for example, that Gold Medal Furniture Company spray paints its metal office furniture with robots, so that the paint department requires only one human worker. The upholstery and assembly departments, however, are labor-intensive, so labor cost is quite high. It would not be fair to apply overhead cost to each department using direct labor hours as the base.

4. **Distinguish between direct departmental overhead costs, indirect departmental overhead costs, and service department costs.**

There are three categories of manufacturing overhead identified in Chapter 14:

Directly traceable. These costs can be directly traced to a department. An example would be the utilities of a department that has its own meter to measure exactly how much was used with that department. This is a direct cost of the department, but indirect with respect to the products produced within that department.

Common benefit. These costs are incurred for the common benefit of several departments. Building occupancy costs such as building depreciation, property taxes and insurance are examples. Several departments may occupy the building, so these common costs must be allocated.

Service department. These overhead costs develop from the departments that provide service to producing departments. For example, many departments may use the computer services that are provided by the information systems department. Personnel services, purchasing, and maintenance are other such service departments.

5. **Define three cost allocation bases—usage, activity, and capacity.**

One of three bases of cost allocation are most frequently used. They are usage, activity, and capacity. These are defined below:

Usage. Many overhead costs are charged to the departments on the basis of measured use of some service. One such cost would be computer usage charged at so much per hour of computer time or lines of printed output.

Activity. Another acceptable basis for allocating overhead cost is the volume of activity. For example, maintenance cost could be allocated to departments on the basis of number of service calls each department requested for maintenance service.

Capacity. This basis for allocating overhead costs looks at service facilities as fixed costs designed to handle a given level of service. Whether it is used or not, service will be charged to the departments on a level of service created for use. In this way, departments may pay for stand-by capacity. This may be true of building occupancy, in which each department that occupies a particular building is charged for a pro rata share of rent, taxes, heat and light expense, possibly as so much per square foot of area occupied or assigned, regardless of whether full utilization is made of such space.

6. **Discuss the problems associated with inequitable cost allocations.**

Sometimes overhead costs are assigned to departments on the basis of ability to pay. That is, the richest get soaked the most. This approach penalizes the successful and hard-working, and gives relief to the slothful. For example, O. W. Holmes food store has the following sales records:

	1990			1991	
	Amount	%		Amount	%
Groceries	$ 3,000	66.7	$	3,000	57.1
Produce	750	16.7		750	14.3
Meats	750	16.7		1,500	28.6
Total	$ 4,500		$	5,250	

If some expenses, such as administrative expenses, are allocated on the basis of sales, Meats would be penalized for their success in increasing their percentage of total sales while the other two departments were static. Most managers would consider this unfair.

7. **List the basic steps involved with service department cost allocation.**

There are four steps involved in allocating service department costs:

a.   Prepare a flexible budget of manufacturing overhead for each service department.
b.   Select an appropriate basis for cost allocation for each service department.
c.   Choose a cost allocation method by which the service department costs are to be distributed to the other departments.
d.   Allocate the service department costs according to steps b and c above.

8. **Describe how three service department cost allocation methods—direct, step, and reciprocal—are used.**

a.   *Direct method.* The first method, the direct method, is the simplest and least sophisticated. The direct method does not allocate any service department costs to other service departments, but only to the producing departments. This is done on some predetermined basis such as square feet of area occupied, sales, number of employees in each department, and so forth.

This method is illustrated using the Graceland Park segmented income statement data from Chapter 13. Graceland has two service departments with the following costs:

Administration	$ 69,300
Advertising	55,000

Advertising will be allocated to the producing departments on the basis of sales, while administration will be allocated on the basis of salary and wage expense of each department. These data are recapped below:

	Sales	Salaries and Wages
Rides	$ 850,000	$ 255,000
Gifts	320,000	64,000
Food	480,000	211,500
Administration	-	48,000
Advertising	-	20,000
Total	$ 1,650,000	$ 598,500

Allocations of the total service department costs, using the direct method, follow. (In each case, decimals are carried out five places and allocated amounts are rounded to the nearest whole dollar.)

Advertising costs of $55,000 are allocated on the basis of sales:

Departments and allocation base	Amounts Allocated
Rides (850,000/1,650,000 x $55,000)	$ 28,333
Gifts (320,000/1,650,000 x $55,000)	10,667
Food (480,000/1,650,000 x $55,000)	16,000
Total allocated	$ 55,000

Administrative costs of $48,000 are allocated on the basis of *producing department* salaries and wages costs only:

Departments and allocation base	Amounts Allocated
Rides (255,000/530,500 x $48,000)	$ 23,073
Gifts (64,000/530,500 x $48,000)	5,791
Food (211,500/530,500 x $48,000)	19,136
Total allocated	$ 48,000

b.   *Step method.* Using the second method of allocation, the step method, one must first choose which of the service departments will be allocated first, thus determining which will not be allocated to other service departments. In this case, the choice is relatively easy since advertising is allocated on the basis of sales and neither service department has sales. Therefore, we will allocate administration first, then advertising.

Administrative costs of $48,000 are allocated on the basis of salary and wage costs. Note that salary costs for the administration department are excluded from the total.

Departments and allocation base	Amounts Allocated
Rides (255,000/550,500 x $48,000)	$ 22,234
Gifts (64,000/550,500 x $48,000)	5,580
Food (211,500/550,500 x $48,000)	18,442
Advertising (20,000/550,500 x $48,000)	1,744
Total allocated	$ 48,000

Advertising costs of $56,744 (the original $55,000 plus the $1,744 allocated from administration) are allocated to the producing departments on the basis of sales, as before.

Departments and allocation basis		Amounts Allocated
Rides (850,000/1,650,000 x $56,744)	$	29,232
Gifts (320,000/1,650,000 x $56,744)		11,005
Food (480,000/1,650,000 x $56,744)		16,507
Total allocated	$	56,744

c. *Reciprocal method.* The third method of service department cost allocation, the reciprocal method, involves the use of a series of reciprocal equations in order to allocate each service department costs to each other service department and each producing department. This method is substantially more complex than the step method above, and frequently little is gained from the additional refinement. It will not be further discussed here.

9. **Explain why a dual cost allocation base is necessary for certain service department costs.**

Often service department costs consist of both variable and fixed costs. Fixed costs are usually related to the department's capacity to render service. Suppose, for example, that a vehicle maintenance department is established to maintain company vehicles in top condition. $350,000 of equipment is purchased, a maintenance supervisor is hired, company warehouse space is converted into garage use and various supplies are purchased and mechanics are hired. All of this is done in anticipation of performing substantial service to company vehicles.

Most of these costs are fixed and will continue even if the facilities are idle. Among the fixed costs are equipment depreciation, garage space costs (including heating and lighting), and supervisory and mechanics' wages. Only supplies and hourly wage employees, and possibly very small amounts of utility costs, are variable. Once the commitment is made to acquire and equip these facilities, substantial costs are committed for the future. If some departments do not use these services—but perhaps send their vehicles to outside shops for maintenance—the fixed costs go on. Therefore, it is reasonable that potential users of these services be billed for fixed costs, *regardless of whether they use the services*, and be billed for variable costs on the basis of service usage.

10. **Differentiate between actual and budget performance data in selecting cost allocation bases.**

When allocating service department costs to other departments, budgeted costs are generally preferable to actual costs. The reason for this is that actual costs are not known until the end of the accounting year, thus cannot be allocated as the accounting period progresses. Further, allocation of actual costs include variances from budget, which should not be the responsibility of the user department, but should be the responsibility of the service department manager. This gives the service department manager greater incentive to strive for efficient performance.

11. **Outline the major steps involved with the cost allocations needed to compute departmental overhead rates.**

The major steps required to allocate costs and compute departmental overhead rates are:

a. Prepare flexible budgets for producing and service departments.

b. Indentify those indirect costs of the department that are incurred for benefit of other departments.

c. Select a basis for allocating costs for each indirect departmental cost and each service department cost to be allocated.

d. Choose a method for allocation of service department costs.

e. Prepare a schedule showing calculations of cost allocation.

f. Upon completion of the allocation schedule, compute predetermined departmental overhead rates for all production departments.

12. **Prepare a cost allocation schedule that provides the information needed to calculate predetermined departmental overhead rates.**

Greene Manufacturing Company has the following budget data applicable to 1991:

Manufacturing Overhead	Budgeted Amount	Cost Allocation Base
Factory office	$154,000	Number of employees
Building occupancy	300,000	Square footage
Maintenance Department:		
Variable overhead	84,000	Budgeted maintenance
Fixed overhead	75,000	Capacity commitment
Cutting Department:		
Variable overhead	47,900	
Fixed overhead	210,000	
Finishing Department:		
Variable overhead	51,980	
Fixed overhead	196,000	

Allocation Base	Factory Office	Maintenance	Cutting Department	Finishing Department
Square footage	3,000	3,000	30,000	24,000
Number of employees	5	9	72	99
Maintenance hrs.	0	0	5,000	10,000
Maintenance capacity commitment			40%	60%

The allocation priority using the step method is:

1. Building occupancy
2. Factory administration
3. Maintenance Department

Based on the above data, the following cost allocation schedule was prepared.

Greene Manufacturing Company
Cost Allocation Schedule
Year Ending December 31, 1991

			Service		Production	
			Factory Office	Maintenance	Cutting	Finishing
Direct overhead costs:						
Variable			-0-	$84,000	$47,900	$51,980
Fixed			$154,000	75,000	210,000	196,000
Allocate building occupancy costs:						
$300,000	x	.05	15,000			
	x	.05		15,000		
	x	.50			150,000	
	x	.40				120,000
			169,000			
Allocate factory office costs:			(169,000)			
			=======			
$169,000	x	.05		8,450		
	x	.40			67,600	
	x	.55				92,950
				182,450		
Allocate maintenance costs:						
Variable costs				(84,000)		
5,000 hrs.	x	$5.60			28,000	
10,000 hrs.	x	$5.60				56,000
Fixed costs				(98,450)		
				======		
$98,450	x	.40			39,380	
	x	.60				59,070
Total budgeted production department overhead costs (a)					$542,880	$576,000
					======	======
Budgeted direct labor hours (b)					144,000	192,000
					======	======
Predetermined departmental overhead rate per direct labor hour (a/b)					$3.77	$3.00
					====	====

MATCHING ATTRIBUTES

Below in Group A are listed attributes that may be identified with the cost allocation terms from Chapter 14 listed in Group B. Indicate, by use of the identifying letter of the appropriate Group B item, which description in Group A best matches which Group B term.

Group A

B   1.   Basis for assigning the cost pool to beneficiaries of the service for which the cost is compiled.

C   2.   An activity, product, service or department for which cost measurement is performed.

D   3.   An amount to be allocated; may be a single cost item or an accumulation of several costs.

H   4.   All costs directly traceable to a product or service plus a fair share of the indirect costs.

K   5.   Source of overhead costs related to services rendered to other departments.

F   6.   Overhead of departments, such as manager's salary.

A   7.   Overhead costs that benefit multiple cost objectives.

I   8.   Single overhead rate for entire company, or factory.

E   9.   Service department costs are not allocated to other service departments.

J   10. Each service department's costs are allocated to all other departments that it services.

L   11. Each service department's costs are allocated to all other departments not already closed out.

G   12. Assign service department fixed and variable costs separately.

Group B

A.	Common benefit	G.	Dual cost allocation base
B.	Cost allocation base	H.	Full cost
C.	Cost objective	I.	Plantwide rate
D.	Cost pool	J.	Reciprocal method
E.	Direct method	K.	Service departments
F.	Directly traceable	L.	Step method

MULTIPLE CHOICE

For each of the following items choose the most appropriate completion phrase.

1.   Cost allocation is

   a.   Useful for performance evaluation of a cost center.

   b.   Necessary for full costing for financial reporting purposes.

   c.   Not allowed by the government for most contracts, because only variable costs are permitted.

   d.   Part of responsibility accounting reports; managers must be responsible for allocated costs.

2.   Cost allocation consists of three cost considerations:

   a.   Cost accounting, sunk cost, opportunity cost.

   b.   Cost objective, cost pool, fixed cost.

   c.   Cost objective, cost pool, cost allocation base.

   d.   Fixed cost, variable cost, mixed cost.

   e.   Labor costs, material cost, overhead cost.

3. The use of plantwide overhead rates has an advantage when

    a.   Some departments are labor intensive, some highly automated.

    b.   Different departments have completely different processes.

    c.   Specialized departments do not exist, as in some small firms.

    d.   A sophisticated cost accounting system accurately pinpoints costs for each operation and department.

    e.   A job order costing system is used.

4. Three types of manufacturing overhead costs are described in this chapter. Which of the following is *not* one of these overhead costs?

    a.   Costs that can be traced directly to the individual departments.

    b.   Indirect costs incurred for the benefit of more than one cost objective, e.g., depreciation or rent of the building.

    c.   Service department costs that provide support for producing departments.

    d.   Administrative costs that are incurred for the benefit of all departments.

5. Usage is one basis for allocating manufacturing overhead costs to departments. Which of the following is *not* an advantage of usage for this purpose?

    a.   Usage relates well to the causal relationship we wish to obtain when allocating costs.

    b.   Usage involves measuring both quantity of service used and rate charged for that service.

    c.   Usage is easily understood by managers who are charged the cost.

    d.   Calculations for usage are usually straightforward and easy to follow.

6. Another basis for cost allocation is activity. An example of using activity for this purpose is:

    a.   Charging computer cost on the basis of actual hours and minutes taken by the computer to do each department's reports.

    b.   Charging company automobile expense on the basis of miles driven by each department's personnel.

    c.   Charging personnel department costs one-fourth to each of four departments that benefit from the service.

    d.   Charging maintenance department costs on the basis of number of machines to be maintained in each department.

7. A third basis for allocating overhead costs is capacity. Which of the following is true for this basis?

    a.   The assumption for this basis of cost allocation is that the amount of cost pool costs are mostly fixed.

    b.   Capacity costs are primarily variable.

    c.   This is allocated evenly to each department.

    d.   Capacity concept relates to the physical size (e.g., square feet) of each department.

8. The ability-to-pay approach to cost allocation

   a. Is fairest since those departments least able to pay receive the smallest cost allocation.
   b. Bases allocation on sales revenues, which is easy to measure and fairest.
   c. Is not logical since there is usually no cause-and-effect relationship.
   d. Is a good idea because each department's results are independent of each other department for determining the amount allocated.

9. There are three methods for allocating service department costs to producing departments. Included among them are:

   a. Direct, indirect, and mixed methods.
   b. Step, side-step, and step-up methods.
   c. Reciprocal, inverse, and remainder methods.
   d. Direct, step, and reciprocal methods.
   e. Indirect, step-down, and inverse methods.

10. Allocating service department costs to producing departments involves four steps. Which of the following is *not* one such step?

   a. Prepare manufacturing overhead flexible budget for each service department.
   b. Select appropriate cost allocation bases for the various service departments.
   c. Choose an ordering sequence for distributing service department costs to other departments.
   d. Allocate service department costs according to management prerogative.

ILLUSTRATIVE PROBLEMS

1. Stillwater Manufacturing Company has two producing departments, Mixing and Forming, and two service departments, Building Services and Administrative Services. Overhead costs are allocated to all departments on the following bases:

Cost Category	Allocation Basis	Budgeted Cost
Building occupancy	Square footage	$99,000
Employee benefits and payroll taxes	Payroll cost	243,000

Pertinent department data for cost allocation are:

Department	Area		Budgeted Payroll Cost
Administrative Services	4,500	sq. ft.	$135,000
Building Services	900	sq. ft.	45,000
Forming	5,400	sq. ft.	270,000
Mixing	7,200	sq. ft.	450,000
	18,000	sq. ft.	$900,000

Requested:

Allocate the Building Occupancy and Employee Benefits and Payroll Taxes to each department by completing the following schedule.

Cost Allocation	Administrative Services	Building Services	Forming	Mixing	Total
Building occupancy					
Employee benefits and payroll taxes					

2. Referring to problem 1 above, assume the same department structure and the following departmental costs *before* the overhead allocations that you prepared above.

Department	Previous Budget Costs	Total Allocations From Above	Total Costs After Allocations
Administrative Services	$208,800		
Building Services	136,800		
Forming	162,400		
Mixing	292,400		

Requested:

   a.   Complete the above schedule with the costs allocated in item 1 and then add the row data across.

   b.   Complete the following schedule by allocating the total service departments to producing departments. Allocate Building Services costs on the basis of square feet and Administrative Services on the basis of payroll costs. Note: Do not allocate one service department's costs to another service department.

Service Department Costs	Forming	Mixing	Total

3. Repeat 2b above, except this time allocate Building Services costs to both producing departments *and* the other service department on the same basis as above. Then allocate the Administrative Services Department costs to the two producing departments. Complete the following schedule and compare your final department costs with those above.

Service Department Costs	Forming	Mixing	Total

VOCABULARY

ABILITY-TO-PAY COST ALLOCATION BASE. A cost allocation approach based on the assumption that the most successful segments of a business should be charged with the largest amounts of indirect costs.

ACTIVITY COST ALLOCATION BASE. A cost allocation base involving some measure of a cost objective's activity that requires a certain level of support from a cost pool.

CAPACITY COST ALLOCATION BASE. A cost allocation base that considers the operating capacity of a cost pool available to a cost objective.

COST ALLOCATION BASE. The means chosen to link a cost pool to a cost objective.

COST ALLOCATION METHOD. The sequencing process used to determine how service department costs are allocated to other departments.

COST OBJECTIVE. Any activity for which separate cost measurement is performed.

COST POOL. A group of homogeneous costs that are to be allocated to more than one cost objective.

DEPARTMENTAL OVERHEAD RATE. A predetermined overhead rate established for each department.

DIRECT METHOD. The cost allocation method that does not recognize any interrelationships between the service departments since their costs are charged directly to the production departments.

DUAL COST ALLOCATION BASE. The allocation of a service department's costs on the basis of a separation between the variable costs and fixed costs involved.

EQUALITY COST ALLOCATION BASE. The distribution of costs equally among cost objectives regardless of how the costs are utilized.

FULL COST. The direct costs traceable to a cost objective plus a fair share of all indirect costs required to support the cost objective.

PLANTWIDE OVERHEAD RATE. A single predetermined overhead rate used to apply manufacturing overhead throughout the production operation.

RECIPROCAL METHOD. The cost allocation method that recognizes all interrelationships between service departments.

STEP METHOD. The cost allocation method that recognizes some of the relationships between service departments but does so on a one-way basis only.

USAGE COST ALLOCATION BASE. A cost allocation base that is a measure of the amount of a cost pool utilized by a cost objective.

THE ANSWERS

MATCHING ATTRIBUTES

1.	B	5.	K	9.	E
2.	C	6.	F	10.	J
3.	D	7.	A	11.	L
4.	H	8.	I	12.	G

MULTIPLE CHOICE

1.	b	4.	d	7.	a	9.	d
2.	c	5.	b	8.	c	10.	d
3.	c	6.	b				

ILLUSTRATIVE PROBLEMS

1.

Cost Allocation	Administrative Services	Building Services	Forming	Mixing	Total
Building occupancy					$99,000
4,500/18,000 x $99,000	$24,750				
900/18,000 x $99,000		$4,950			
5,400/18,000 x $99,000			$29,700		
7,200/18,000 x $99,000				$39,600	
Employee benefits and payroll taxes					243,000
135,000/900,000 x $243,000	36,450				
45,000/900,000 x $243,000		12,150			
270,000/900,000 x $243,000			72,900		
450,000/900,000 x $243,000				121,500	
Total	$61,200	$17,100	$102,600	$161,100	$342,000

2a.

Department	Previous Budget Costs	Total Allocations From Above	Total Costs After Allocations
Administrative Services	$208,800	$61,200	$270,000
Building Services	136,800	17,100	153,900
Forming	162,400	102,600	265,000
Mixing	292,400	161,100	453,500
Total	$800,400	$342,000	$1,142,400

b.

Service Department Costs	Forming	Mixing	Total
Administrative Services			$270,000
270,000/720,000 x $270,000 =	$101,250		(101,250)
450,000/720,000 x $270,000 =		$168,750	(168,750)
Building Services			$153,900
5,400/12,600 x $153,900 =	66,023		(66,023)
7,200/12,600 x $153,900 =		87,877	(87,877)
Total	$167,273	$256,627	$-0-

3.

Service Department Costs

	Building Services	Administrative Services	Forming	Mixing	Total
Before Allocation	$153,900	$270,000	$265,000	$453,500	$1,142,400
Allocate Bldg. Serv.	(153,900)				(153,900)
$153,900 x .263		40,476			40,476
$153,900 x .316			48,632		48,632
$153,900 x .421				64,792	64,792
Allocate Admin. Serv.		(310,476)			(310,476)
$310,476 x .375			116,429		116,429
$310,476 x .625				194,047	194,047
Total costs			$430,061	$712,339	$1,142,400

CHAPTER 15

QUANTITATIVE METHODS AND MANAGERIAL ACCOUNTING

Because of time limitations, you may not cover all chapters in this book. I hope you do not miss this important chapter. It provides a glimpse at some quantitative models that may be helpful in decision making. Accountants provide much of the data for management decisions, and this chapter offers a new format for some of that data.

LEARNING OBJECTIVES

1. Recognize why quantitative methods are important in managerial accounting.
2. Explain why decision making under uncertainty is inevitable and how risk analysis is used.
3. Calculate and use the expected value of the outcomes of a decision as well as the related standard deviation.
4. Realize how a payoff table is utilized in decision making and how to determine the value of perfect information.
5. Develop a statistical cost control chart using sampling techniques.
6. Explain how a fixed order quantity model is used to manage inventory in some businesses.
7. Identify the main considerations of the order quantity decision in inventory management and the impact of a just in time inventory system.
8. Discuss the major issues associated with the reorder point decision in inventory management.
9. Recognize why the ABC method is an important part of inventory planning and control.
10. List the basic features and application of linear programming.
11. Construct a graphic linear programming model.
12. Realize how shadow prices are used to evaluate the profitability of capacity expansion.
13. Describe the main features and benefits of the Program Evaluation and Review Technique (PERT).
14. Develop a PERT network.
15. Formulate a linear programming problem with the simplex method and interpret the optimal solution. (Appendix to the chapter.)

Learning Tips

There is a little math in this chapter, but it is not very complex. If you enjoy algebra and a little bit of calculus you will find the math a breeze, while those who don't will have to struggle a little. If you are in the latter category, I suggest you join the group and see how these tools are useful. You may also find them interesting and even fun to work.

Review

1. **Recognize why quantitative methods are important in managerial accounting.**

   Some information needs of management require more complex analysis than is possible by simple arithmetic or low-level algebra. Some of the tools of operations research are required to look into the possible future outcome of certain managerial problem situations. This chapter provides an introduction to such techniques.

2. **Explain why decision making under uncertainty is inevitable and how risk analysis is used.**

   It is seldom possible to make decisions about the future in an environment of certainty. This is true because decisions are future-oriented, and the future always contains elements of uncertainty. It has been said that nothing is certain except death and taxes. But even about these certainties, one might ask "when" and "how much"?

   Risk analysis is a commonly used approach to the solution of business problems. Risk analysis involves the assigning of probabilities (chances) to future events. In attempting to budget next year's wage rate for a particular labor group (if this rate has not yet been settled between management and labor), a manager might assign the following probabilities:

Probable Wage Rate	Probability
$7.50/DLH	.30
7.80/DLH	.40
8.25/DLH	.30
All three levels	1.00

   If we are covering all possible conditions, the probabilities in our analysis must sum to 1.00 (100%).

3. **Calculate and use the expected value of the outcomes of a decision as well as the related standard deviation.**

   Referring to the above uncertainty about the wage rate for the budget period, the manager can calculate the *expected value* of that wage rate in the following way:

Probable Wage Rate	Probability	Expected Value
$7.50/DLH	.30	$2.25
7.80/DLH	.40	3.12
8.25/DLH	.30	2.475
All three levels	1.00	$7.845

The expected value of the wage rate for the budget period is the sum of the products of the individual wage values and their respective probabilities, or $7.845. This value can then be used to prepare the budgeted labor cost. Assume the budgeted direct labor hours for the period is 21,000. Then, the budgeted direct labor cost for this budget category is 21,000 x $7.845 = $164,745.

To calculate the standard deviation, we must add two columns to the above table, sum the second column that is added, then take the square root of the sum. The following table shows the computation of the square root of $0.29 from the data above.

1 Probable Wage Rate	2 Probability	3 Expected Value	4 Column 1 - $7.845 Squared	5 Column 2 x Column 4
$7.50/DLH	.30	$2.25	$0.119025	$0.03570
7.80/DLH	.40	3.12	.002025	.00081
8.25/DLH	.30	2.475	.164025	.04921
Totals	1.00	$7.845		$0.08572

Thus, the standard deviation is the square root of $0.08572, or approximately $0.29. This standard deviation indicates the risk of relying on the mean value (expected value) of $7.845 for projection purposes is rather small.

4. **Realize how a payoff table is utilized in decision making and how to determine the values of perfect information.**

The King Company is considering entering a new product line. However, after considerable market research, the company decides it will only be profitable if Congress passes favorable trade legislation (to limit imports from foreign countries). After discussing this matter with the district's Congressional representative, the company president, K. K. King, decides there is a 60% chance such legislation will be passed.

King's controller and marketing executive determine that if the company enters the new product line $1,500,000 profit will result if the trade bill is passed, only $100,000 if it is not. If the company does not enter the new line, it will earn $800,000 in profit if the trade bill passes, $400,000 if it does not. This is illustrated with the following payoff table:

	Trade Bill	
	Passed	**Not Passed**
Probabilities - - - - - - - ->	.60	.40
Enter new product line	$1,500,000	$ 100,000
Do not enter new line	800,000	400,000

Based upon this table:

$\bar{x}$ (new product line) = .6($1,500,000) + .4($100,000)   = $940,000;

$\bar{x}$ (no new product)   = .6($800,000) + .4($400,000)   = $640,000.

Thus, there is a $300,000 difference in profit between having favorable trade legislation passed and not having such legislation passed.

From the preceding analysis, it is clear that the company should enter the new product line if the trade legislation is passed, and if the trade bill is not passed, the company should not enter the new product line. The value of perfect information is the difference between the best result with perfect information and the best result with current information.

With perfect information:

$\bar{x}$ =   .6($1,500,000) + .4($400,000)   = $1,060,000

With current information:

$\bar{x}$ =   .6($1,500,000) + .4($100,000)   =   940,000
                                                      ──────────

$\bar{x}$ (perfect information)   = $ 120,000
                                                   ========

5. **Develop a statistical quality control chart using sampling techniques.**

A statistical quality control chart is a chart that shows the results of samples of product compared to mean (average) performance. The purpose of such a control chart is to show if (or when) a production process is out of control. Out of control refers to unacceptable nonrandom variances from the mean or standard performance.

The Buris Company makes probes in large quantities. The controller Dan Bower decides to establish a quality control chart to represent the time of producing probes. Individual samples of four are taken to show the time to produce each batch of probes. He prepares the following schedule of sample data.

Sample Data Results of
Direct Labor Hours Per Batch

Sample	1	2	3	4	Sample Mean	Sample Range
1	3.1	3.2	3.4	3.0	3.175	.4
2	3.3	3.5	3.6	3.0	3.35	.6
3	2.8	2.7	3.0	2.9	2.85	.3
4	2.7	2.8	2.9	3.3	2.925	.6
Overall sample mean, $\bar{\bar{x}}$					3.075	
Average range, $\bar{r}$						.475

In constructing the control chart, the limits are calculated as follows:

Upper control limit   =   3.075 + .73(.475)   =   3.42

Lower control limit   =   3.075 - .73(.475)   =   2.73

The coefficient of .73 comes from Professor Helmkamp's table of coefficients related to sample size.

Sample Size	Coefficient
4	.73
5	.58
6	.48
7	.42

A standard statistics textbook that has a quality control chapter will give a larger table of coefficients. The control chart follows:

Upper limit of 3.42 hours ————————————————————————

$\bar{x}$

$\bar{x}$

Mean of 3.075 hours ————————————————————————

$\bar{x}$

$\bar{x}$

Lower limit of 2.73 hours ————————————————————————

6. **Explain how a fixed order quantity model is used to manage inventory in some businesses.**

A fixed order quantity model is a quantitative model that establishes the most economical number of items to order each time an order is placed so that total inventory costs are at a minimum. Total inventory costs consist of order costs plus carrying costs. This value is called EOQ, for economic order quantity. It is important to know the best time to place the order, as well as the quantity to order. A model can also be developed to establish this point, which is called RP, for reorder point.

7. **Identify the main features of the order quantity decision in inventory management and the impact of a just in time inventory system.**

The two relevant costs included in the EOQ model are carrying costs and ordering costs. *Carrying costs* are the costs of keeping inventory items in stock, and they include insurance, taxes, warehouse rent, utilities, interest on the investment, and obsolescence. *Ordering costs* are the costs of purchasing inventory items, and they include receiving and inspection costs, handling costs, and clerical and managerial costs of placing and verifying purchase orders and bids.

The total cost function for EOQ is:

$$TC = D/Q(A) + Q/2(I)$$

where:

TC	=	total annual costs of ordering and carrying inventory
D	=	annual demand, in units
Q	=	order quantity, in units
A	=	cost of placing one order
I	=	annual cost of carrying one unit in inventory

The EOQ formula is:

$$EOQ = \sqrt{\frac{2DA}{I}}$$

For the Stillwell Company the following facts apply to model 626 engines.

D	=	1,000 units
A	=	$14.40, per order
I	=	$8.00, per unit, per year

Then,

$$EOQ = \sqrt{\frac{2(1,000)(\$14.40)}{\$8.00}} = 60 \text{ units}$$

If the carrying costs, I, were $2.00, the EOQ would be 120 units. If, instead, the ordering costs were $3.60, the EOQ would be 30 units. To generalize, if ordering costs are relatively low, it is desirable to order more often and carry larger inventories, but if carrying costs are relatively low, it is better to order less often and carry larger inventories.

Just in time inventory systems have a goal of zero inventories. The systems seek to minimize ordering costs as well. With ordering costs in the numerator of the EOQ model, a zero ordering cost would result in a zero inventory. The EOQ and JIT systems are congruent.

8. **Discuss the major issues associated with the reorder point decision in inventory management.**

The inventory reorder decision is concerned with having enough stock on hand during the reorder (lead) time to satisfy customer demand. Since the firm is in business to sell stock to customers, being out of stock represents lost sales, and therefore, lost profits. To carry excess stock costs money, as shown above. It is important, then, to determine the appropriate reorder point, so that there is enough stock on hand to satisfy customer demand during the waiting time for reorder and delivery, but not too much.

Customer demand is usually somewhat erratic, so the firm is never sure just how great demand will be. Therefore, in addition to the expected demand, an additional safety stock is maintained to serve as a buffer against uneven demand. The expected customer demand during reorder (lead) time plus the safety stock equals reorder point. If expected demand is 45 units and safety stock is 8 units, the firm will reorder when the inventory level drops down to 53 units on hand.

It is common for management to calculate this reorder point from historical records of inventory usage, using simple probability analysis.

9. **Recognize why the ABC method is an important part of inventory planning and control.**

Many business firms stock thousands, or tens of thousands, of different inventory items. It would be impractical to calculate EOQ for each of these items, although, with modern computer methods, it would be possible. More practical is the ABC method of inventory management, which classifies all inventory items into one of three possible categories:

a. Group A is for perhaps the 10% to 15% of the inventory items with the highest dollar value. Because of their high cost, group A items must be tightly controlled, such as through EOQ models.

b. Group B items are more in number but lower in dollar cost than group A items. Hence, the control method may be less sophisticated, and therefore, less costly to operate.

c. Group C is for the largest number of inventory items, but the lowest dollar cost, in total. The controls and record keeping for this group are far less stringent than for either group A or group B items.

10. **List the basic features and applications of linear programming.**

Linear programming is a mathematical technique for allocating scarce resources. Four characteristics common to all linear programming situations are:

a. An objective function, which is a mathematical statement of the goals to be obtained. This function is often to maximize profit or minimize cost.

b. Several alternatives, such as products, must exist.

c. Constraints, or limitations, must be expressed and considered.

d. All relationships must be expressed in linear equations.

11. **Construct a graphic linear programming model.**

When linear programming models have only two variables, it is possible, and often simpler, to set the model up graphically. Each variable, or alternative, requires one axis on the graph. The following example illustrates the use of the graphic method.

Belle City Pottery produces clay flower pots and earthen pet caskets on a time-available basis, with certain monthly limitations. Animal caskets are all similar, while clay pots are all classified together. The two categories are called caskets (K) and pots (P). Lot size of pots is a set, while caskets are counted as units.

Both caskets and pots pass through two processes, molding and kiln. Time requirements for each are:

	Minutes Per Unit	
	Molding	Kiln
Caskets	15	10
Pots	12	15

Contributions to fixed costs and overhead are:

Caskets	$2.50
Pots	2.20

Maximum quantities of each per week are:

Caskets	36
Pots	65

In preparing the week's schedule there are ten hours available in molding and nine hours in kiln. What is the best allocation of these products to maximize profit contribution? The following formulations are developed.

The restraints are:

I	15K + 12P	<=	600
II	10K + 15P	<=	540

Formula I says it takes 15 minutes for each casket and 12 minutes for each set of pots processed in Process I (Molding). Ten hours or 600 minutes are available in that process. Formula II indicates that 10 minutes are required to produce each casket in Process II (Kiln), while fifteen minutes are required for a set of pots. Total time available is nine hours, or 540 minutes.

The objective function is expressed as:

III	Z	=	2.50K + 2.20P

This equation indicates that $2.50 is contributed for each casket produced and $2.20 for each set of pots.

The following inequalities indicate that the values for both K (caskets) and P (pots) must be greater than or equal to zero.

IV	K	>=	0
V	P	>=	0

With the above five formulations, it is possible to develop the graphic linear programming model. Formula I is graphed by setting first K, then P equal to zero. This creates the following inequalities:

0K + 12P	<=	600, and
P	<=	50

Also,

15K + 0P	<=	600, and
K	<=	40

Following the same technique for Formula II, we get the following results:

$$0K + 15P \qquad <= \qquad 540, \text{ and}$$
$$P \qquad <= \qquad 36$$

Also,

$$10K + 0P \qquad <= \qquad 540, \text{ and}$$
$$K \qquad <= \qquad 54$$

Figure 15-1 shows the final result of graphing each of the five formulations described above. Note the broken line that indicates the objective function.

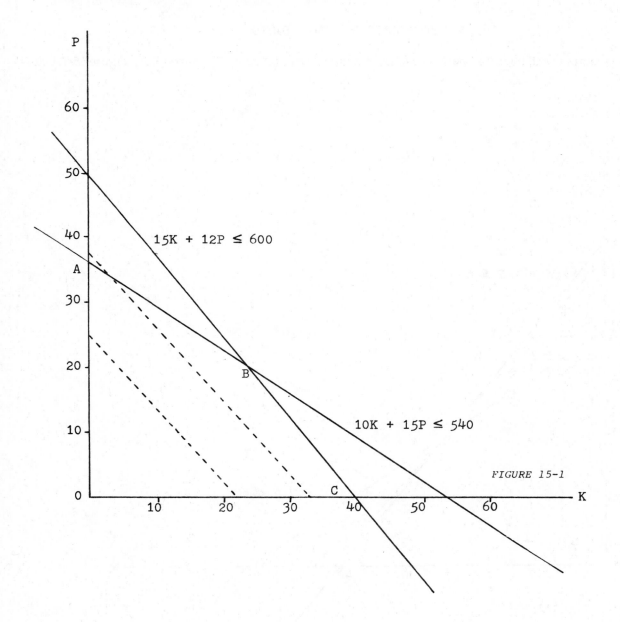

$$15K + 12P \leq 600$$

$$10K + 15P \leq 540$$

FIGURE 15-1

Analysis of the objective function at the exterior points of A, B anc C determines the maximum profit contribution point.

At point A, 36 P's are produced, and no K's. Thus,

$$Z = \$2.50\,(0) + \$2.20(36) \quad = \quad \$79.20$$

At point B, 24 K's and 20 P's are produced. Thus,

$$Z = \$2.50(24) + \$2.20(20) \quad = \quad \$104.00$$

At point C, 40 K's are produced, and no P's. Thus,

$$Z = \$2.50(40) + \$2.20(0) \quad = \quad \$100.00$$

It is apparent, then, that point B is where the objective function is maximized, as in Figure 15-2, below.

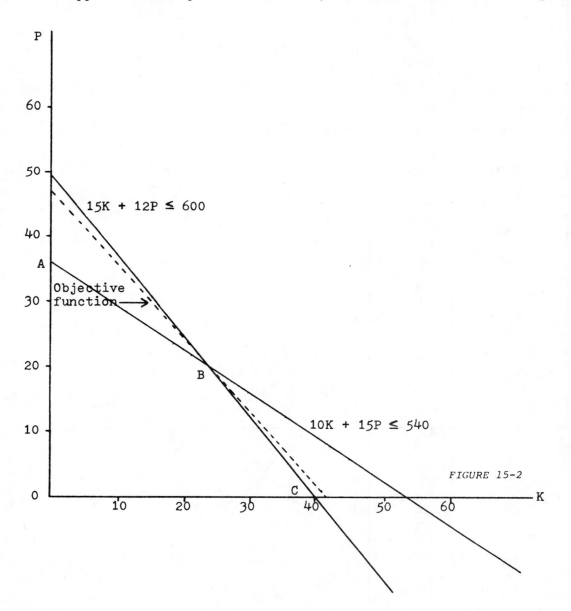

FIGURE 15-2

Two final inequalities might be added to the problem:

$$
\begin{array}{llll}
\text{VI} & K & <= & 36 \\
\text{VII} & P & <= & 65
\end{array}
$$

These final constraints indicate that for marketing or other reasons, the maximum quantities of each product are as indicated in these inequalities. They would be added into the graph in the appropriate places, with inequality VI modifying the solution as shown in Figure 15-3.

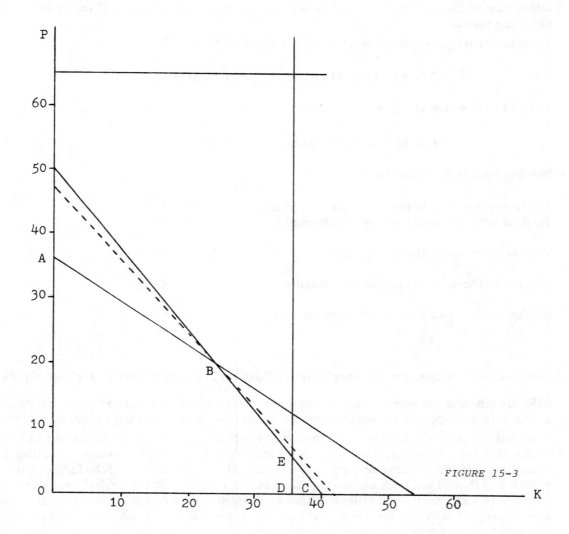

FIGURE 15-3

12. **Realize how shadow prices are used to evaluate the profitability of capacity expansion.**

    A shadow price is the opportunity cost of not expanding capacity. That is, it is the profit that would have been earned had the production capacity been expanded. If this shadow price is greater than the cost of expansion, it would be profitable to make the expansion.

    A common way to calculate shadow prices is by adding capacity to a limiting constraint and measuring the incremental income (or contribution) that results from the change. Then, this incremental income is divided by the incremental capacity to determine the shadow price.

    Molding capacity of 600 minutes is expanded by 10% to 660 minutes. This permits the production of 44 rather than 40 caskets. Optimizing of the objective function occurs at point B' rather than B, with the following results.

    There is no change in point A. At point B', P = 14.286 and K = 32.571. Thus,

    $$Z = \$2.50(32.571) + \$2.20(14.286) = \$112.86$$

    At point C' there are 44 K's and no P's. Thus,

    $$Z = \$2.50(44) + \$2.20(0) = \$110.00$$

    Shadow price is determined as follows:

Total contribution with the additional 60 minutes	$112.86
Total contribution with the original 600 minutes	111.00
Shadow price for additional capacity	1.86
Divided by the number of additional minutes	60
Shadow price per additional minute of capacity	$ 0.031

13. **Describe the main features and benefits of the Program Evaluation and Review Technique (PERT).**

    PERT is a time and cost management system that in many ways operates like a budget. It is used for one-time activities, as opposed to assembly-line production—or any repetitive production, for that matter.

    PERT is a network of activities that comprise an entire project, such as construction of a building, a bridge or a dam. However, it has also been successfully used to help manage consulting projects, financial audits and political campaigns. The essence of the program is the scheduling of interrelated activities so that all activities are accomplished in order and on time. A critical path is computed to determine which group of activities is critical to completion on schedule, then that path is monitored meticulously. If activities on the critical path fall behind schedule, additional resources must be allocated to those activities to get back on schedule.

    The benefits are similar to the benefits of a standard cost system or a budgetary control system.

14. **Develop a PERT network.**

    Two Land o' Lakes students, Hansen and Olson, decided to manufacture a special "Wood 'n' Wheels" cart for small children to be marketed in Creative Toys retail stores throughout the Midwest. They agreed to make a prototype cart out of the same materials they would use to manufacture the unit, white pine and purchased aluminum wheels and hardware.

    Hans and Ols thought it would be wise to use PERT, a technique they learned in management accounting at the Big U, to schedule the prototype construction. The following diagram and table of activity times resulted.

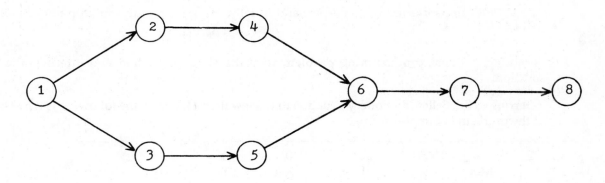

PERT Activity Table

Estimated Hours Activity	Acty. #	O	M	P	T	Path
Purchase wheels and hardware	1 - 2	1.00	2.25	5.00	2.50	A
Buy lumber, nails, paint	1 - 3	.75	1.25	3.25	1.50	B
Assemble wheels	2 - 4	1.00	1.30	1.30	1.25	A
Cut, assemble lumber	3 - 5	1.50	2.50	3.50	2.50	B
Lubricate and test	4 - 6	0.25	0.50	0.75	0.50	A
Sand, paint and dry	5 - 6	0.50	1.50	2.50	1.50	B
Final assembly	6 - 7	0.50	1.40	1.40	1.25	A & B
Test and adjust	7 - 8	0.10	0.40	1.30	0.50	A & B

In the above table,

$$O \quad = \quad \text{optimistic time,}$$
$$M \quad = \quad \text{most likely time,}$$
$$P \quad = \quad \text{pessimistic time, and}$$
$$T \quad = \quad \text{estimated time, calculated as} \quad \frac{O + 4M + P}{6}$$

The critical path is the longest path, in terms of total activity time. By adding the A times and B times in the above table, the following results occur:

$$A = 6.00 \text{ hours} \qquad B = 7.25 \text{ hours}$$

Hence, B is the critical path. The longest time for completing the project is 7.25 hours. This is also the shortest time, since the project cannot be completed until both activity paths are completed.

Slack time is the longest time on a particular path minus the shortest time. On path A there exists slack time of 1.25 hours (7.25 - 6.00). After the project begins actual time for each activity is recorded and compared with estimated times. If actual time for any activity on the critical path exceeds the estimated time, the critical path is lengthened. If actual time for any activity not on the critical path exceeds the estimated time, there is no effect on the critical path unless the excess time exceeds the slack time on that path.

Actual PERT networks are very complex and usually require computers to keep track of all activity times.

15. **Formulate a linear programming problem with the simplex method and interpret the optimal solution.**

Referring to the Belle City Pottery situation in Review item 11. above, the following is the restatement of the problem in Simplex format:

Z		2.50	2.20	0	0	
	Mix	K	P	X	Y	Capacity
0	X	15	12	1	0	600
0	Y	10	15	0	1	540
	C	0	0	0	0	
	Z-C	16	12	0	0	

This tableau shows the objective function, Z = $2.50K + $2.20P + $0X + $0Y. This function indicates that $2.50 will be earned for each unit of product K sold; $2.20 will be earned for each unit of product P sold; and $0 will be earned for each unit of X and Y. X and Y are called slack variables to indicate the amount of time available in each production facility. The final solution, after two iterations, is shown below for this problem:

Z		2.50	2.20	0	0	
	Mix	K	P	X	Y	Capacity
2.50	K	1	0	-.076	-.1143	24
2.20	P	0	1	-.095	1/7	20
	C	2.50	2.20	.019	.60	104
	Z - C	0	0	-.019	-.60	

Because there are no positive values in the Z - C row, the optimum solution has been reached. The Z row indicates the profit (or contribution) that will be earned from each unit of product immediately below the Z value. The C row indicates the opportunity cost for removing each unit of the product indicated in the Mix row.

Thus, in the optimum solution, for each unit of K removed, $2.50 reduction in profit will occur. For each unit of P removed, $2.20 reduction in profit will occur.

MATCHING ATTRIBUTES

Below, in Group A are listed attributes that may be identified with the quantitative methods terms listed in Group B. Indicate, by use of the identifying letter of the appropriate Group B item, which description in Group A best matches which Group B term.

Group A

____M____ 1. Diagram and schedule of activities of large one-time projects to plan and control time and cost.

_____ 2. Diagram of method to optimize a profit or loss function within the constraints of limited facilities.

_____ 3. Set of activities that requires the longest elapsed time for completion.

_____ 4. Available time for completion of a set of activities that will not delay the total project.

_____ 5. Graphical limits of where the answer could lie.

_____ 6. The mathematical formula (inequality) that the model seeks to maximize or minimize.

____L____ 7. The mathematical likelihood (chance) that an event will occur.

_____ 8. The time an activity will take to complete if there are more than the usual number of delays and difficulties.

____D____ 9. The product of the value of an event and the mathematical chance the event will occur added to the product of the values of other events times their chances of occurrence.

_____ 10. The time an activity will take to complete if there are no delays or mishaps.

_____ 11. The computed time it will take to complete an activity based on a formula of optimistic, pessimistic and most likely times.

____P____ 12. The computed dispersion around an expected value of actual values.

_____ 13. A schedule of outcomes and probabilities for the occurrence or nonoccurrence of events.

____B____ 14. The number of units or amount to be purchased each time a purchase order is placed.

_____ 15. The period from when an order is placed until the materials arrive from the vendor.

_____ 16. A measure of unused capacity (linear programming).

Group B

A.	Critical path	I.	Optimistic time
B.	Economic order quantity	J.	Payoff table
C.	Estimated time	K.	Pessimistic time
D.	Expected value	L.	Probability
E.	Feasible solution area	M.	Program Evaluation and Review Technique
F.	Graphic linear programming	N.	Slack time
G.	Lead time	O.	Slack variable
H.	Objective function	P.	Standard deviation

MULTIPLE CHOICE

For each of the following items choose the most appropriate completion phrase. Use the following PERT network to answer questions 1 through 4 below:

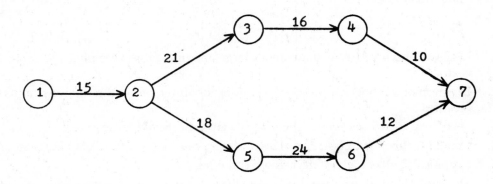

1. What is the critical path time to complete the network above?

   a.   69
   b.   62
   c.   131
   d.   15
   e.   None of the above.

2. The optimistic time for activity 2 - 3 is 15 and the most likely time is 20. What is the pessimistic time?

   a.   20
   b.   15
   c.   21
   d.   18
   e.   None of the above.

3. What is the amount of slack time in this network?

   a.   0
   b.   69
   c.   62
   d.   7
   e.   None of the above.

4. Program Evaluation and Review Technique is a special case of

   a.   Budgeting
   b.   Probability analysis
   c.   Project scheduling
   d.   Time and cost control
   e.   All of the above.

The graphic linear programming model below is to be referred to in answering questions 5 through 7.

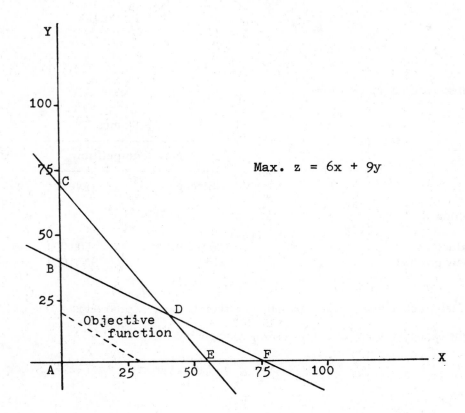

5. The feasible solution area in the above graph is:

   a.   ABDE
   b.   ACE
   c.   ABF
   d.   BCD
   e.   DEF

6. If product Y had a maximum value of 30 because of a marketing constraint,

   a.   The feasible solution area would be increased in size.
   b.   The feasible solution area would be reduced in size.
   c.   The objective function would be doubled.
   d.   The objective function would be reduced.
   e.   The objective function would be eliminated.

7. Regardless of your answers above, profit is maximized at point

    a.   A
    b.   B
    c.   C
    d.   D
    e.   E

8. Payoff table of Swanson Marketing Company

	Outcomes	
	New Competition	
	Strong	Weak
Probabilities of outcomes	.4	.6
Courses of action:		
Market new product	($200,000)	$500,000
Do not market new product	$150,000	$200,000

Based on the payoff table above, the expected payoff of marketing the new product is:

    a.   Greater than the expected payoff of not marketing the new product.
    b. $500,000
    c. $300,000
    d. $180,000
    e.   ($200,000)

9. Inventory management models are designed to minimize total inventory costs. These costs consist of:

    a.   Ordering costs and storage costs.
    b.   Carrying costs and interest costs.
    c.   Ordering costs and carrying costs.
    d.   Interest, storage, purchase and obsolescence costs.
    e.   Out-of-stock costs and safety stock costs.

10. In linear programming, the concept of shadow pricing is helpful for management decision making. A shadow price is:

    a.   An opportunity cost of not expanding capacity.
    b.   The extra revenue created from plant expansion.
    c.   The price paid for expanding capacity.
    d.   The price charged for additional products created by expansion.
    e.   The net income from a capacity decision.

11. The simplex tableau for the Brenner Co. production situation is:

Brenner Co.

Z 0	Mix	20 A	12 B	0 X	0 Y	Capacity
0	X	10	12	1	0	1,200
0	Y	8	6	0	1	840
	C	0	0	0	0	
	Z-C	20	12	0	0	

Based on this tableau, which of the variables represents the slack variable(s)?

a. A
b. B
c. X
d. Y
e. X and Y

12. Referring again to the Brenner Co. Simplex tableau in item 11 above, the maximum number of units of product A that could be produced by the company is:

a. 10
b. 12
c. 8
d. 105
e. 120

ILLUSTRATIVE PROBLEMS

1. The Union Grove Plastics Company manufactures plastic kitchen and other household products, but has excess capacity. A discount house has offered to buy quantities of plastic toys called "Pharra" and "Stevo" that could be produced with existing facilities and equipment.

   The Mixing Department requires .3 hour for each unit of P (Pharra) and .4 hour for each unit of S (Stevo). Extruding Department requires .5 hour for each unit of P and .2 hour for each unit of S. There are 120 hours available in Mixing and 90 hours in Extruding. The objective is to maximize contributions to profit, with S contributing $1.50 per unit and P contributing $2.00 per unit.

Requested

    a.   Draw the graphic linear programming solution for Union Grove Plastics.

    b.   Label the feasible solution area.

    c.   Compute and label the optimum solution.

2. Referring to the Union Grove Plastics Company situation above, determine the shadow price effect of expanding mixing capacity by 24 hours. Show your work on the above graph with computations below.

3. Southroads Construction Co. is planning the construction of a small project and has developed the following PERT network.

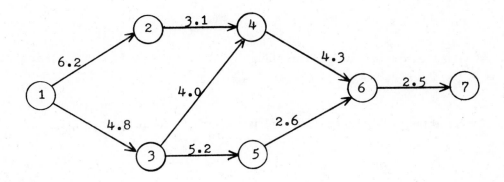

Requested

a. With a dark or colored line, draw the critical path on the above network.

b. Compute the latest time for reaching event 7.

c. What is the existing slack time in activity 4 - 6?

d. If the optimistic time for activity 3 - 5 is 3.8, and the pessimistic time is 7.4, what is the most likely time?

4. The Alma-Helene Company is planning a sale. The manager, Alma Neil, had developed the following payoff table to represent the effects of weather on whether to go outdoors with the sale.

**Alma-Helene Company
Payoff Table**

	Outcomes	
	Good Weather	Bad Weather
Probabilities of occurrence	.7	.3
Courses of action:		
Have outdoor sale	$35,000	$5,000
Cancel outdoor sale	20,000	$10,000

Requested

    a.   Based upon the above payoff table for Alma-Helene Company, what is the expected value of having the outdoor sale?

    b.   What is the expected value of cancelling the outdoor sale (and having an indoor sale)?

    c.   In this situation, what is the value of having perfect information?

VOCABULARY

ABC METHOD. A technique used to classify inventory items on the basis of their relative investment.

AREA OF A FEASIBLE SOLUTION. The area of a graphic linear programming model within which the optimal solution is found.

CARRYING COSTS. Such incremental costs as the opportunity cost of funds invested in inventory, interest charges, storage space, insurance, and taxes incurred because a firm maintains inventory balances.

COEFFICIENT OF VARIATION. An indicator of risk that is calculated by dividing the expected value into the related standard deviation.

CONSTRAINT INEQUALITIES. Linear inequalities formalizing the constraints within which an optimal linear programming solution must be found.

CRITICAL PATH. The sequence of activities from the beginning of a PERT network to its end with the longest completion time and minimal amount of spare time.

ECONOMIC ORDER QUANTITY (EOQ). The best amount of inventory to order because it optimizes the trade-off between the related ordering costs and carrying costs.

EXPECTED VALUE. The arithmetic mean using a weighted-average approach with probabilities applied as the weights.

GRAPHIC LINEAR PROGRAMMING. The visual display of the equations and inequalities involved in a linear programming problem that can be described with two-dimensional space.

LEAD TIME. The time period between placing an inventory order and receiving it.

LINEAR PROGRAMMING (L.P.). A mathematical technique used to determine the best allocation of scarce resources.

MOST LIKELY TIME. The amount of time that should be required for a given activity in a PERT network more frequently than any other estimate.

OBJECTIVE FUNCTION. An equation that describes what is to be maximized or minimized in a linear programming application.

OPTIMISTIC TIME. The least amount of time a given activity in a PERT network could require.

ORDERING COSTS. Incremental costs incurred to prepare, process, and record an inventory order.

PESSIMISTIC TIME. The greatest amount of time a given activity in a PERT network could require.

PROBABILITY. The relative likelihood of a given outcome occurring.

PROGRAM EVALUATION AND REVIEW TECHNIQUE (PERT). A quantitative method used to plan and control projects with numerous interrelated steps.

QUANTITATIVE METHOD. A model developed with mathematics and/or statistics to assist management in making effective decisions.

REORDER POINT (RP). The measure of when an inventory order should be placed.

RISK ANALYSIS. A probabilistic assessment of the outcomes possible in a particular decision.

SAFETY STOCK. The amount of inventory maintained in excess of the expected demand during lead time when an inventory order is placed.

SAMPLE MEAN. The average of the values chosen for a given sample.

SAMPLE RANGE. The difference between the highest and lowest values of a sample.

SHADOW PRICE. The opportunity cost of not adding to capacity that is determined with linear programming.

SIMPLEX METHOD. A form of linear programming based on matrix algebra that optimizes an objective function subject to a series of constraints.

STANDARD DEVIATION. A measure of the dispersion or spread around the expected value of several numbers.

UNCERTAINTY. The possibility that the actual outcomes from a decision may be different from the expected outcomes.

THE ANSWERS

Matching Attributes

1. M	5. E	9. D	13. J
2. F	6. H	10. I	14. B
3. A	7. L	11. C	15. G
4. N	8. K	12. P	16. O

Multiple Choice

1. a	4. e	7. d	10. a
2. e	5. a	8. a	11. e
3. d	6. b	9. c	12. d

Illustrative Problems

1a.

Maximize Z   = $2.00 P + $1.50 S
Subject to:

.3 P + .4 S	<=	120	Mixing
.5 P + .2 S	<=	90	Extruding
P	>=	0	
S	>=	0	

b.

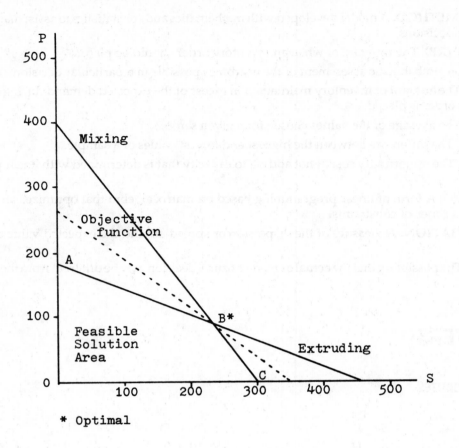

P

500 —

400 —

Mixing

300 —

Objective
function

200 —

A

100 —

B*

Feasible
Solution
Area

Extruding

C

0 —

100   200   300   400   500   S

* Optimal

c.

Point A: $2.00 (180)	=	$360			
Point C: $1.50 (300)	=	$450			
Point B: .3 P + .4 P	=	120	.3 P + .4 S =		120
(.5 P + .2 S = 90) x -2	=		-1.0 P - .4 S =		-180

-.7 P				=	- 60
P				=	85.71
.3(85.71) + .4		S		=	120
		S		=	235.72
Point B: $2.00 (85.71) + $1.50 (235.72)				=	$525 (Optimal)

2.

Point A: $2.00(180)	=	$360			
Point C: $1.50(300)	=	$450			
Point B: .3 P + .4 S	=	144	.3 P + .4 S	=	144
(.5 P + .2 S = 90) x -2	=	-	1.0 P - .4 S	=	-180

	- .7 P	=	-36
	P	=	51.43
.3(51.43) +	.4 S	=	144
	S	=	321.43

2.   Point A: $2.00(180) = $360
    Point C: $1.50(300) = $450
    Point B: $.3P + .4S = 144$ $.3P + .4S = 144$
             $(.5P + .2S = 90) \times -2 =$ $\underline{-1.0P - .4S = -180}$
                                              $-.7P \qquad = -36$
                                              $P \qquad = 51.43$

             $.3(51.43) + .4S = 144$
                        $S = 321.43$

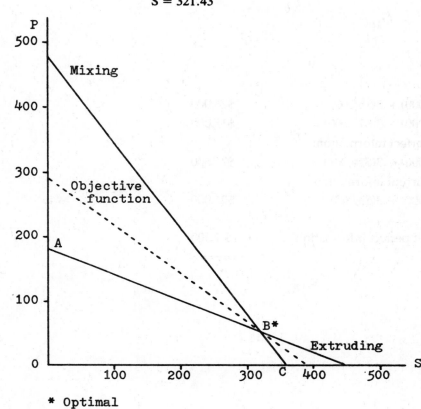

* Optimal

3a.

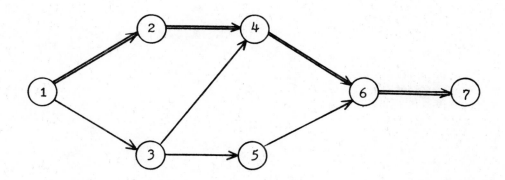

Critical path $= 1 - 2 - 4 - 6 - 7$

b. $6.2 + 3.1 + 4.3 + 2.5 = 16.1$

Critical path = 1 - 2 - 4 - 6 - 7

b. 6.2 + 3.1 + 4.3 + 2.5 = 16.1
c. Slack time = 0
d. Most likely time = 5

$$5.2 = \frac{3.8 + 4m + 7.4}{6}$$

$$4m = 20$$
$$m = 5$$

4.

a.	.7($35,000) + .3($5,000) =	$26,000
b.	.7($20,000) + .3($10,000) =	$17,000
c.	With perfect information:	
	.7($35,000) + .3($10,000) =	$27,500
	With current information:	
	.7($35,000) + .3($5,000) =	$26,000
	Value of perfect information	$ 1,500

CHAPTER 16

ANALYSIS OF FINANCIAL STATEMENTS

This chapter and the following one are more related to financial accounting than to managerial accounting. Analysis of financial statements certainly has many implications for management decision making, as does accounting for changing prices. However, the majority of this work is done for creditors and investors rather than for managers.

Management, however, is very interested in the creditor and investor implications of financial statements. Also, management is very motivated to have a high level of receptiveness of these financial statements by outsiders. Some top executives are said to do whatever it takes to create investor appeal in the statements.

LEARNING OBJECTIVES

1. Explain the objectives of financial statement analysis.
2. Perform horizontal analysis, trend analysis and vertical analysis.
3. Compute and use ratios to analyze a firm's profitability.
4. Compute and use ratios to analyze a firm's liquidity.
5. Compute and use ratios to analyze a firm's solvency.
6. Recognize the limitations of financial statement analysis.

LEARNING TIPS

For this chapter, try to put yourself in the seat of the firm's top executives. You are concerned about the ability of the firm to pay debts as they come due and of having adequate liquidity to take advantage of investment opportunities. Also, you want the investing public to see the firm as a strong candidate for their investment. You want the firm to have a very good credit rating and for the stock price to continue to rise.

This chapter will teach you many of the analysis techniques you will need to determine how the firm stands in these crucial areas. Be an analyst for your firm!

REVIEW

1. **Explain the objectives of financial statement analysis.**

    Financial statement analysis is designed to determine the financial strength of the firm. Specifically, this relates to the firm's debt-paying ability and its liquidity standing. This is accomplished by identifying certain traditional relationships among financial statement items and categories, and by looking at trends in specific statement classifications.

2. **Perform horizontal analysis, trend analysis, and vertical analysis.**

We divide our financial statement analysis into the broad categories of: horizontal, trend, and vertical. Basically, horizontal refers to comparing similar amounts among years, while vertical refers to comparing various data on the same financial statement to one number, such as sales, all within the same time frame.

Trend analysis is similar to horizontal analysis, except that it is performed when comparing three or more years' data. One year, usually the first year, is chosen as the base year, then other years are stated as a percentage of their base year value.

3. **Compute and use ratios to analyze a firm's profitability.**

Profitability ratios are those ratios that measure a firm's earning performance for a period or periods. Based on the Calvin Corporation financial statements in Figure 16-1, the following profitability ratios will each be illustrated for 1992.

FIGURE 16-1a

CALVIN CORPORATION
Comparative Income Statements
For the Years Ended December 31, 1989 and 1988
(000's omitted)

	Year Ended December 31		Change From 1991 to 1992		Common Size Statements	
	1992	1991	Dollar Amount	Percent	1992	1991
Sales	30,960	27,350	3,610	13.2%	100.0%	100.0%
Less: Cost of Goods Sold	23,120	19,878	3,242	16.3%	74.7%	72.7%
Gross profit on sales	7,840	7,472	368	4.9%	25.3%	27.3%
Expenses:						
Selling expense	2,990	2,266	724	32.0%	9.7%	8.3%
Administrative expense	1,790	1,772	18	1.0%	5.8%	6.5%
Interest expense	830	700	130	18.6%	2.7%	2.6%
Income tax expense	500	760	(260)	-34.2%	1.6%	2.8%
Total expenses	6,110	5,498	612	11.1%	19.7%	20.1%
Net income	1,730	1,974	(244)	-12.4%	5.6%	7.2%
Preferred stock cash dividends	90	90	0	0.0%	0.3%	0.3%
Net income available to common stockholders	1,640	1,884	(244)	-13.0%	5.3%	6.9%

FIGURE 16-1b

CALVIN CORPORATION
Comparative Balance Sheets
December 31, 1989 and 1988
(000's omitted)

| | December 31 | | Change From 1991 to 1992 | | Common Size Statements | |
	1992	1991	Dollar Amount	Percent	1992	1991
Assets						
Current Assets:						
Cash	1,180	720	460	63.9%	5.2%	3.7%
Marketable securities	1,140	1,056	84	8.0%	5.1%	5.4%
Accounts receiv. (net)	4,380	3,136	1,244	39.7%	19.4%	16.0%
Inventory	6,080	5,788	292	5.0%	27.0%	29.5%
Prepaid expenses	400	320	80	25.0%	1.8%	1.6%
Total Current Assets	13,180	11,020	2,160	19.6%	58.5%	56.3%
Long-term investments	1,200	1,350	(150)	-11.1%	5.3%	6.9%
Plant and equip (net)	7,740	6,860	880	12.8%	34.4%	35.0%
Other assets	400	360	40	11.1%	1.8%	1.8%
Total Assets	22,520	19,590	2,930	15.0%	100.0%	100.0%
Liabilities						
Current Liabilities:						
Notes payable	1,840	1,472	368	25.0%	8.2%	7.5%
Accounts payable	3,140	3,285	(145)	-4.4%	13.9%	16.8%
Accrued expenses	320	288	32	11.1%	1.4%	1.5%
Total Current Liab.	5,300	5,045	255	5.1%	23.5%	25.8%
Long-term liabilities	6,800	5,590	1,210	21.6%	30.2%	28.5%
Total Liabilities	12,100	10,635	1,465	13.8%	53.7%	54.3%
Stockholders' Equity						
Preferred stock, 10%	900	900	0	0.0%	4.0%	4.6%
Common stock ($10 par)	4,500	4,500	0	0.0%	20.0%	23.0%
Additional paid-in cap.	600	550	50	9.1%	2.7%	2.8%
Retained earnings	4,420	3,005	1,415	47.1%	19.6%	15.3%
Total Equity	10,420	8,955	1,465	16.4%	46.3%	45.7%
Total Liabilities and Stockholders' Equity	22,520	19,590	2,930		100.0%	100.0%

Return on total assets. This ratio measures the percentage return on the firm's total assets. The formula is:

$$\frac{\text{Net income} + \text{interest expense (net of tax)}}{\text{Average total assets}}$$

For Calvin Corporation this is:

$$\frac{1,730 + 830\,(1.0 - .23)}{.5 \times (22,520 + 19,590)} = \frac{2,369}{21,055} = 11.25\%$$

Return on total assets. This ratio measures the percentage return on the firm's total assets. The formula is:

$$\frac{\text{Net income} + \text{interest expense (net of tax)}}{\text{Average total assets}}$$

For Calvin Corporation this is:

$$\frac{1{,}730 + 830\ (1.0 - .23)}{.5 \times (22{,}520 + 19{,}590)} = \frac{2{,}369}{21{,}055} = 11.25\%$$

In order to compute the interest expense net of tax, the interest rate is multiplied by the tax rate, which for 1992 is approximately 23%.

Return on common stockholders' equity. This ratio measures the rate of return of owners' equity, or assets provided by the common stockholders. The formula is:

$$\frac{\text{Net income} - \text{preferred stock cash dividend requirement}}{\text{Average common stockholders' equity}}$$

For Calvin Corporation this is:

$$\frac{1{,}730 - 90}{(9{,}520 + 8{,}055) \times .5} = \frac{1{,}640}{8{,}788} = 18.66\%$$

Common stockholders' equity is equal to total stockholders' equity minus preferred stock.

Return on sales. This ratio measures the rate of net income to sales. Its formula is:

$$\frac{\text{Net income}}{\text{Sales}}$$

For Calvin Corporation this is:

$$\frac{1{,}730}{30{,}960} = 5.59\%$$

Earnings per share. This important ratio measures the return per share of common stock. The formula is:

$$\frac{\text{Net income} - \text{preferred stock cash dividend requirement}}{\text{Weighted-average number of common shares outstanding}}$$

For Calvin Corporation this is:

$$\frac{1,730 - 90}{450} = \frac{1,640}{450} = \$3.64$$

Price-earnings ratio. This ratio measures the current amount investors are paying for each dollar of earnings. The formula is:

$$\frac{\text{Market price per share of common stock}}{\text{Earnings per share}}$$

For Calvin Corporation this is:

$$\frac{47.50}{3.64} = 13.04 \text{ times}$$

This means that investors are currently paying $13.04 for each dollar of earnings, based on a current stock market price of $47.50 per share.

Dividend yield. This ratio measures the net return to the stockholders according to the current stock market price. The formula is:

$$\frac{\text{Annual dividend per share of common stock}}{\text{Market price per share of common stock}}$$

For Calvin Corporation this is:

$$\frac{.50}{32.50} = 1.54\%$$

This is quite a low rate of yield. The $0.50 dividend per share can be verified by:

Retained earnings, December 31, 1991		$ 3,005
Add: net income, 1992		1,730
Less: cash dividends:		
Preferred stock	$ 90	
Common stock		
($0.50 x 450 shares)	225	(315)
Retained earnings, December 31, 1992		$ 4,420

Dividend payout ratio. This ratio measures the portion of the common stock earnings that are paid out in the form of dividends. This formula is:

$$\frac{\text{Total dividends paid to common stockholders}}{\text{Net income - preferred stock cash dividend requirement}}$$

For Calvin Corporation this is:

$$\frac{225}{1,730 - 90} = 13.72\%$$

4. **Compute and use ratios to analyze a firm's liquidity.**

Liquidity ratios are those ratios that measure the firm's ability to pay its short-term obligations as they come due. These ratios will also be illustrated with the use of data from the Calvin Corporation financial statements in Figure 16-1.

Current ratio. This very commonly used ratio shows the relation between current assets and current liabilities. This formula is:

$$\frac{\text{Current assets}}{\text{Current liabilities}}$$

For Calvin Corporation this is:

$$\frac{13,180}{5,300} = 2.49$$

The current ratio measures the creditors' margin of safety. Usually a ratio of 2:1 is used as a rule of thumb, but should not be relied upon blindly.

Quick ratio. Sometimes called the acid test ratio, the quick ratio measures liquidity to a tougher standard than does the current ratio. Current assets are reduced by the amount of inventory and prepaid expenses. The formula is:

$$\frac{\text{Cash + marketable securities + net receivables}}{\text{Current liabilities}}$$

For Calvin Corporation this is:

$$\frac{1,180 + 1,140 + 4,380}{5,300} = \frac{6,700}{5,300} = 1.26$$

Receivables turnover. This ratio measures the average number of times the accounts receivable are converted into cash in a year. This formula is:

$$\frac{\text{Net sales}}{\text{Average receivable balance}}$$

For Calvin Corporation this is:

$$\frac{30,960}{.5 \times (4,380 + 3,136)} = 8.24$$

By dividing this turnover rate into 365 days, the average number of days it takes to collect accounts receivable is calculated.

$$\frac{365}{8.24} = 44.30 \text{ days}$$

This should be compared with the credit terms of the company.

Inventory turnover. This ratio measures the adequacy of inventory and the efficiency with which inventory is managed. This formula is:

$$\frac{\text{Cost of goods sold}}{\text{Average inventory balance}}$$

For Calvin Corporation this is:

$$\frac{23,120}{.5 \times (6,080 + 5,788)} = 3.90$$

The average number of days for a complete inventory turnover is the above value divided into 365 days.

$$\frac{365}{3.90} = 93.59 \text{ days}$$

5. **Compute and use ratios to analyze a firm's solvency.**

Solvency ratios are used to measures a firm's ability to meet long-term obligations as they come due and still have enough cash for normal operations. These ratios will also be illustrated by use of the data in Figure 16-1.

Debt to total assets. This ratio, sometimes called the debt ratio, measures the relationship between total liabilities and total assets. This formula is:

$$\frac{\text{Total liabilities}}{\text{Total assets}}$$

For Calvin Corporation this is:

$$\frac{12,100}{22,520} = 53.73\%$$

This means that approximately 54% of the firm's assets in 1992 are provided by creditors.

Times interest earned. This ratio is a measure of the firm's ability to meet interest payments on the debt from current earnings. This formula is:

$$\frac{\text{Net income} + \text{interest expense} + \text{income tax expense}}{\text{Interest expense}}$$

For Calvin Corporation this is:

$$\frac{1,730 + 830 + 500}{830} = 3.69$$

Thus, Calvin Corporation earns enough to pay the annual interest on debt nearly four times.

6. **Recognize the limitations of financial statement analysis.**

There are four basic limitations to financial statement analysis. They are:

a. The relationships determined to exist for the period(s) involved in the analysis may not remain in effect for the future. Thus the primary reason for the analysis—forecasting the future—may not be served because of the impact future changes may bring.

b. The analysis is based on the financial statements, which consist of a mixture of historical (original) costs for assets and current dollar values (for such accounts as sales and many operating expenses). Unless these historical costs are adjusted for price changes, such comparisons and ratios may be meaningless or misleading.

c. Much of the analysis is based on year-end financial statement data. Such data may not be typical of balances during the year. Thus, misleading conclusions may be drawn.

d. When using financial statement analysis for comparing different companies, one might be comparing apples and oranges. Sometimes companies just aren't comparable because of the diverse nature of the separate businesses, and such incomparability is often not apparent from the figures that result from the analysis.

MATCHING ATTRIBUTES

Below in Group A are listed attributes that may be identified with the terms in Group B. Indicate by use of the identifying letter of the appropriate Group B item which attribute best matches which Group B term.

Group A

_____ 1. A firm's ability to satisfy its long-term commitments with enough left over to keep operating successfully.

_____ 2. Statement that presents all items as a percentage of some common base amount.

_____ 3. Compares the proportional changes in a specific item from one period to the next.

_____ 4. Compares changes in an account or item over a series of years.

_____ 5. Annual Securities and Exchange report to be filed by publicly traded companies.

_____ 6. Financial advisory services firm.

_____ 7. Interpretation of relationship between two items on financial statements.

_____   8. $100 \times \dfrac{120,000}{150,000} = 80.0\%$

_____   9. $\dfrac{\text{Current assets}}{\text{Current liabilities}}$

_____   10. $\dfrac{\text{Cost of goods sold}}{\text{Average inventory balance}}$

Group B

A.	Common size statement	F.	Moody's
B.	Current ratio	G.	Percentage change
C.	Form 10-K	H.	Ratio analysis
D.	Horizontal analysis	I.	Solvency
E.	Inventory turnover	J.	Trend analysis

MULTIPLE CHOICE

For each of the following items choose the most appropriate completion phrase.

1. The use of five to 10 years of comparative financial statements in identifying trends and changes is called what kind of analysis?

   a.   Vertical

   b.   Parallel

   c.   Diagonal

   d.   Horizontal

   e.   Trend

2. The current ratio indicates:

   a.   Whether a company has been paying its debts on a timely basis.

   b.   How profitable a company has been.

   c.   The dollar amount of funds available to meet short-term obligations.

   d.   A company's ability to pay off short-term obligations as they mature.

3. The reason for subtracting inventory from current assets when calculating the quick ratio (acid test ratio) is:

   a.   To eliminate the problem of FIFO versus LIFO.

   b.   To eliminate one of the least liquid of current assets.

   c.   To better measure the possibility of stock-outs.

   d.   To provide a better estimate of the current ratio.

   e.   None of the above.

4. Determine the cost of goods sold for a firm with the following data:

Current ratio	3.1
Acid test ratio	2.4
Current liabilities	$800,000
Inventory turnover	6 times

    a. $3,360,000

    b. $1,960,000

    c. $2,160,000

    d. $2,840,000

    e. $1,640,000

5. A company has a current ratio of 2 to 1. This ratio will decrease if the company:

    a.   Receives a 5% stock dividend on one of its marketable securities.

    b.   Pays a large account payable that had been a current liability.

    c.   Borrows cash on a six-month note.

    d.   Sells merchandise for more than cost and records the sale using the perpetual-inventory method.

Use the following data to answer the next three questions.

Below is incomplete financial information for KAN Company (a Junior Achievement company), whose books have not been closed for the period:

Expenses	$ 40	Current Liabilities	$200
Current Assets	500	Long-term Liabilities	100
Revenues	60	Noncurrent Assets	-0-
		Preferred Stock	-0-

6. If there were five shares of common stock outstanding, the earnings per share would be:

    a. $4

    b. $8

    c. $12

    d. $100

7. Return on common stockholders' equity is:

    a.   6.66%

    b.   10%

    c.   12%

    d.   20%

    e.   Cannot be determined from given information.

8. Working capital is:

   a. $200
   b. $300
   c. $400
   d. $500
   e. $320

The following data refer to LaJolla Produce Company:

Market price of common stock of the company	$36
Net earnings	$6,000
Preferred dividends declared during year	$3,000
Common dividends declared during year	$2,000
Weighted-average number of shares of common stock outstanding during the year	1,000

9. What are LaJolla Produce Company's earnings per common share?

   a. $3.00
   b. $3.60
   c. $6.00
   d. $10.00

10. The price-earnings ratio for LaJolla Produce Company is:

   a.   3.6
   b.   6
   c.   10
   d.   12

11. The financial ratio that measures the percentage of assets provided by creditors and the extent to which leverage is being used is:

   a.   Return to total assets.
   b.   Price earnings ratio.
   c.   Times interest earned.
   d.   Quick ratio.
   e.   Debt to total assets.

ILLUSTRATIVE PROBLEMS

Given below are comparative financial statements of the Graber Company.

Graber Company
Comparative Financial Statements

Balance Sheets	12/31/X5	12/31/X6
Assets:		
Cash	$ 3,000	$ 4,000
Accounts Receivable	2,000	2,000
Inventory	1,800	2,000
Prepaid Rent	700	500
Land	6,000	6,000
Total Assets	$ 13,500	$ 14,500
	=====	======
Liabilities and Equity:		
Accounts Payable	$ 2,000	$ 3,000
Wages Payable	1,400	700
Note Payable (due 10/1/X7)	3,000	3,000
Bonds Payable (due in 10 years)	2,000	2,000
Preferred Stock, $100 par, 12%	1,000	1,000
Common Stock, no-par,		
100 shares outstanding	2,800	2,800
Retained Earnings	1,300	2,000
Total Liabilities and Equity	$ 13,500	$ 14,500
	=====	=====

Income Statements	12/31/X5	12/31/X6
Sales	$ 10,000	$ 12,000
Cost of Goods Sold	6,000	7,000
Gross Profit Margin	4,000	5,000
Selling Expenses	1,500	2,000
Interest Expense	1,000	1,000
Income Tax Expense	500	700
Total Expenses	3,000	3,700
Net Income	$ 1,000	$ 1,300
	=====	=====

Additional Information:

    a.   Total dividends paid in 19X5 were $500, and in 19X6 were $600.

    b.   Market price of the preferred stock was $98 and $99.50 at the ends of 19X5 and 19X6, respectively. Common stock market prices were $60 and $65, respectively, for those two years.

    c.   All shares of stock were sold in 19X2; none have ever been reacquired.

Requested

Based on the Graber Company statements above, compute each of the profitability, liquidity, and solvency ratios presented in this chapter, for the year 19X6.

Profitability Ratios

Return on total assets =

Return on common
stockholders' equity =

Return on sales =

Earnings per share =

Price-earnings ratio =

Dividend yield =

Dividend payout =

Liquidity Ratios

Current ratio =

Quick ratio =

Receivable turnover =

Average days outstanding =

Inventory turnover =

Average days to turn inventory =

Solvency Ratios

Debt to total assets =

Times interest earned =

VOCABULARY

COMMON SIZE STATEMENT. A financial statement in which the amount of each item reported in the statement is presented as a percentage of some specific base amount also reported in the statement.

COMPARATIVE STATEMENTS. Financial statements for the current year and prior years presented together to facilitate the analysis of changes in account balances.

HORIZONTAL ANALYSIS. That part of an analysis based on the comparison of amounts reported for the same item in two or more comparative statements with an emphasis on the change from year to year.

RATIO. Division of the amount reported for one financial statement item by the amount reported for another financial statement item. Ratio analysis is the evaluation of the relationship indicated by this division.

TREND ANALYSIS. That part of financial statement analysis involved with comparing the changes in a particular item over a series of years. In trend analysis, a base year is selected. Statement items in subsequent statements are expressed as a percentage of their value in the base year.

VERTICAL ANALYSIS. That part of financial statement analysis in which the focus of the study is on the proportion of individual items expressed as a percentage of some specific item reported in the same statement. (See Common Size Statement.)

THE ANSWERS

MATCHING ATTRIBUTES

1.	I	5.	C	9.	B
2.	A	6.	F	10.	E
3.	D	7.	H		
4.	J	8.	G		

MULTIPLE CHOICE

1.	d	5.	c	9.	a
2.	d	6.	a	10.	d
3.	b	7.	b	11.	e
4.	a	8.	b		

ILLUSTRATIVE PROBLEMS

The following ratios are computed for 19X6.

Profitability Ratios

Return on total assets $= \dfrac{\$1,300 + 1,000(1 - .35)}{\$14,000} = \dfrac{\$1,950}{\$14,000} = 13.93\%$

Return on common
stockholders' equity $= \dfrac{\$1,300 - 120}{.5(\$4,800 + 4,100)} = 26.52\%$

Return on sales $= \dfrac{\$1,300}{\$12,000} = 10.83\%$

Earnings per share $= \dfrac{\$1,300 - 120}{100} = \$11.80$

Price-earnings ratio $= \dfrac{\$65}{\$11.80} = 5.51 \text{ times}$

Dividend yield $= \dfrac{\$4.80}{\$65} = 7.38\%$

Dividend payout $= \dfrac{\$600 - 120}{\$1,300 - 120} = 40.68\%$

Liquidity Ratios

Current ratio $= \dfrac{\$8,500}{\$6,700} = 1.27$

Quick ratio $= \dfrac{\$4,000 + 2,000}{\$6,700} = .90$

Receivable turnover $= \dfrac{\$12,000}{\$2,000} = 6$

Average days outstanding $= \dfrac{365}{6} = 60.83 \text{ days}$

Inventory turnover $= \dfrac{\$7,000}{\$1,900} = 3.68$

Average days to turn inventory $= \dfrac{365}{3.68} = 99.18 \text{ days}$

Solvency Ratios

Debt to total assets $= \dfrac{\$8,700}{\$14,500} = 60\%$

Times interest earned $= \dfrac{\$1,300 + 1,000 + 700}{\$1,000} = 3$

CHAPTER 17

STATEMENT OF CASH FLOWS

George Washington, one of the richest persons in North America in colonial days, was usually cash-poor. One condition may help to explain the other. Washington's investments in land (the bulk of his wealth) tied up his cash. Cash is vital to any business for paying obligations and taking advantage of investment opportunities. Investors and managers alike keep a close eye on the cash inflows (receipts) and disbursements (outflows) of the enterprise as one measure of the firm's health.

LEARNING OBJECTIVES

1. Explain the purpose and use of cash flow information.
2. Classify cash receipts and cash payments by operating, investing, and financing activities.
3. Identify the content and form of the statement of cash flows.
4. Describe the difference between the direct and indirect approach to reporting net cash flow from operating activities.
5. Report the effects of exchanges of noncash items.
6. Prepare a formal statement of cash flows.

LEARNING TIPS

Throughout your study of financial accounting you were taught accrual accounting, and cash receipts and disbursements were seldom mentioned. This is true also in most of this text in managerial accounting. However, in capital budgeting and cash budgeting, you were taught the importance of cash flows. In this chapter, the distinction between accrual accounting and cash flows must again be emphasized. Cash is one of a firm's most vital assets, and it will enhance your learning if you can keep your mind trained on its importance and how the accountant makes the conversion from accrual accounting to cash accounting.

Review

1. **Explain the purpose and use of cash flow information.**

   The primary purpose of the statement of cash flows is to provide information about the cash inflows and cash outflows of a business.

   The statement of cash flows (SCF) can assess:

   a.   A firm's ability to generate cash flows in the future;
   b.   A firm's ability to meet obligations and pay dividends;
   c.   A firm's needs for external financing;
   d.   The reasons for the differences between financial accounting net income and the related cash flows; and
   e.   The cash and noncash aspects of the firm's transactions during the period.

2. **Classify cash receipts and cash payments by operating, investing, and financing activities.**

   a.   *Operating activities* are those that involve the production or delivery of goods or the providing of services to customers. Cash flows from operating activities generally result from cash payments to suppliers, to employees, to governments for taxes and to lenders for interest. In addition, cash receipts from operating activities include the sale of goods or services for cash and the collection of accounts receivable and interest for loans made. It is important to note that operating activities are those that are normal to the day-to-day activities of the business.
   b.   *Investing activities* are those that involve lending money, acquiring securities that are not cash equivalents and buying or selling productive assets that are to be used in the operating activities of the business.
   c.   *Financing activities* are those that involve obtaining resources from owners and creditors. Most borrowing and repayments are financing activities. However, the settlement of accrued expenses and accounts payable is considered an operating activity.

3. **Identify the content and form of the statement of cash flows.**

   The content and form of the statement of cash flows is illustrated in detail in the next section of this review. Therefore, it will not be provided here.

4. **Describe the difference between the direct and indirect approach to reporting net cash flow from operating activities.**

   The cash flow from operating activities may be reported directly or indirectly. The direct method would show cash collections from customers and cash received from interest and dividends. Cash payments for expenses are reported by major class such as to suppliers for goods and services, to employees for wages, and to governments for taxes. The indirect method would indicate the same amount of cash flows but the information would be shown by adjusting net income for those transactions that did not require cash outflows and for those transactions that required cash outflows but were indicated in net income.

   Direct Method. The direct method will show the major classes of cash inflows and outflows from operations. To illustrate, the following income statement and selected balance sheet accounts are shown. The normal procedure is to convert the accrual basis amounts to cash basis amounts.

N and H Corporation
Income Statement
For Year Ended December 31, 1992

Sales		$		120,000
Cost of Goods Sold				54,000
Gross Profit on Sales		$		66,000
Operating Expenses:				
Salary Expense	$		27,000	
Insurance Expense			4,200	
Advertising Expense			5,500	
Depreciation Expense			10,000	
Total Operating Expenses				46,700
Income Before Taxes				19,300
Tax Expense				7,700
Net Income		$		11,600

Selected Comparative Balance Sheet Data

		December 31		
		1991		**1992**
Accounts Receivable	$	10,000	$	12,000
Accounts Payable		8,000		7,000
Inventory		15,000		13,000
Prepaid Insurance		8,000		6,500
Salaries Payable		3,000		6,000
Taxes Payable		5,700		7,700

In a like manner, any decrease in a balance sheet asset account that relates to operations would result in an increase in cash flows from operations.

Indirect Method. If we look at the N and H income statement and partial balance sheet presented above, we will demonstrate the use of the indirect method.

N and H Corporation
Statement of Cash Flows
For Year Ended December 31, 1992

Net Income		$ 11,600
Adjustments to Net Income		
Increase in Accounts Receivable	$ (2,000)	
Decrease in Prepaid Insurance	1,500	
Decrease in Inventory	2,000	
Decrease in Accounts Payable	(1,000)	
Increase in Salaries Payable	3,000	
Increase in Taxes Payable	2,000	
Depreciation Expense	10,000	15,500
Cash Flows from Operations		$ 27,100
		=======

Two observations are important. First, the *net* cash flow from operations is the same regardless of method used. Second, since depreciation, or other similar cost allocation, represents no cash outflow in the current year, we must add to net income the amount of the depreciation, amortization or depletion expense for the year.

To convert from accrual accounting to cash basis accounting the following procedure is used.

Cash received from customers = accrual sales revenue + beginning balance of accounts receivable - ending balance of accounts receivable. We add the beginning balance to adjust net income for collections made this year for sales recognized as revenues last year. Similarly, we deduct the ending balance of accounts receivable to adjust the current revenue for cash not collected from this year's sales.

In our example, the cash received from customers this year would be:

$$\$120,000 + \$10,000 - \$12,000 = \$118,000$$

Cash paid to suppliers for purchases = accrual cost of goods sold - beginning inventory + ending inventory + beginning accounts payable - ending accounts payable. The adjustment for the inventories can be viewed as using the beginning inventory which could consist of merchandise purchased last year thereby not requiring cash outflows this year. The ending inventory adjustment could be viewed as current year purchases that might have required cash outflows this year. The adjustments for the beginning and ending payables can be visualized as increasing current year cash outflows for the beginning payables with just the opposite effect for the ending payables. In our example, the cash paid to suppliers for purchases would be:

$$\$54,000 - \$15,000 + \$13,000 + \$8,000 - \$7,000 = \$53,000$$

Accrual cost of goods sold - beginning investment + ending inventory + beginning payables - ending payable = cash paid out.

Cash paid for expenses = accrual expenses - beginning prepaid expenses + ending prepaid expenses or accrual expenses + beginning accrued expenses - ending accrued expenses. The adjustments of course depend on the nature of the expense account and the related balance sheet account. In our example, the salary expense related balance sheet account is salaries payable, therefore the adjustment from accrual expense to cash outflow is determined as follows:

Accrual salary expense + beginning salary payable - ending salary payable. In this example, 27,000 + 3,000 - 6,000 = 24,000 cash paid out for salaries in the current year. The reasoning is that the conversion of accrual salary expense must be accomplished by the addition of wages owed at the end of the previous accounting period and decreased by the ending amount that was not paid during the current period.

Alternately, the conversion of accrual advertising expense would be determined as follows:

Accrual advertising expense - beginning prepaid advertising
+ ending prepaid advertising would be 5,500 - 8,000 + 6,500 =
4,000 cash paid out.

Similarly the cash paid out for taxes would be calculated as: Accrual tax expense + beginning taxes payable - ending taxes payable, or 7,700 + 5,700 - 7,700 = 5,700 cash paid out. The insurance expense needs no adjustment as there is no related balance sheet account. The summary of the statement of cash flows using the direct approach would be:

N and H Incorporated
Statement of Cash Flows
For Year Ended December 31, 1992

Cash flow from customers		$ 118,000
Cash outflow		
To suppliers for purchases	$ 53,000	
To employees for salaries	24,000	
For insurance and advertising	8,200	
For income taxes	5,700	90,900
Net Cash Flows From Operations		$ 27,100

Indirect Method. This method will present the same *net* cash flow from operations as does the direct method. Rather than showing the major classes of operating cash receipts and payments the indirect method will present the net cash flow from operations by adjusting net income for the effects of accounting accruals and deferrals. Stated differently, items that were added in the determination of net income but did not result in cash inflows are deducted from net income to convert to cash flows. Examples would include year-end interest accruals where interest has been earned but not yet received. Similarly, items that were deducted in the determination of net income but cash was not paid out would be added to convert to cash flows.

The procedure used for the indirect method is to analyze changes in the balance sheet accounts that relate to operations. For example, an increase in accounts receivable from the beginning of the period would indicate that customers owe us more money at year-end than at the beginning. Therefore the sales revenue that was reported on the income statement as a result of credit sales would not equal the cash inflows from sales because more money was owed at the end of the year than at the beginning. To adjust to cash inflows we would deduct from net income the increase in accounts receivable. In fact, a general rule to follow on the indirect method is that any increase in a balance sheet asset account that relates to operations would result in a reduction in cash flows from operations.

Cash flows from investing and financing activities can be determined by either the direct or indirect method. The investing activities include lending and collecting money, acquiring and selling noncash equivalent securities, and buying and selling productive assets. The cash flows should be shown individually by activity at their gross amounts. The financing activities generally include receiving resources from owners and borrowing resources and their repayment to creditors. The financing activities should also be shown individually at their gross amounts. An example of the cash flows from investing and financing activities is shown:

Cash flows from investing activities	
Purchase of equipment	($XXXX)
Proceeds from sale of equipment	XXXX
Purchase of investment securities	(XXXX)
Loans made	(XXXX)
Collections on loans	XXXX
	———
Net cash from investing activities	$XXXX
	======
Cash flows from financing activities	
Proceeds from long-term debt	$ XXXX
Payments to reduce short-term debt	(XXXX)
Proceeds from issuing capital stock	XXXX
	———
Net cash from financing activities	$XXXX
	======

5. Explain how to report the effects of exchanges of noncash items.

Direct exchange transactions that do not involve the use of cash must also be presented either in the body of the SCF or disclosed in a separate schedule. See the statements above for the techniques and results involved.

6. Prepare a formal statement of cash flows.

See the statements in response to objective 4 above for cash flow statements using both the direct and indirect methods.

MATCHING ATTRIBUTES

Below in Group A are listed attributes that may be identified with the terms in Group B. Indicate, by use of the identifying letter of the appropriate Group B item, which attribute best matches which Group B term.

Group A

_____ 1. Include the acquisition of resources from owners and from creditors.

_____ 2. Provides information concerning cash receipts and disbursements.

_____ 3. Represent significant investing and financing activities that may be reported either in the body of the SCF or in a separate schedule.

_____ 4. Shows major classes of operating revenues as cash inflows from operations.

_____ 5. This adjusts accrual basis net income to cash from operations by adding or subtracting revenues, noncash expenses, gains and losses.

_____ 6. Examples include money market funds and commercial paper.

_____ 7. Cash outflows from these activities include loans made by the firm and payments to acquire assets.

_____ 8. Reports cash flow from operations by presenting the cash from the major class of operating activity.

Group B

A.	Cash equivalents	E.	Investing activities
B.	Direct method	F.	Noncash transactions
C.	Financing activities	G.	Operating activities
D.	Indirect method	H.	Statement of cash flows

MULTIPLE CHOICE

1. The purpose of a statement of cash flow is:

   a. To provide detailed information about changes in individual working capital accounts.

   b. To help readers of annual reports to understand a company's financial policies for generating and using new resources.

   c. To replace a detailed income statement by reporting funds provided from operations.

   d. None of the above.

2. Which of the following would be added to net income from operations when preparing a statement of cash flow?

   a. An increase in inventory.

   b. An increase in accounts receivable.

   c. A decrease in prepaid expenses.

   d. A decrease in accounts payable.

3. When a statement of cash flow is prepared, an increase in ending accounts receivable over beginning accounts receivable will result in an adjustment to recorded net income because:

   a. All changes in noncash accounts must be reported under the all-financial-resources concept.

   b. An increase in accounts receivable is an increase in funds greater than reported income.

   c. Accounts receivable are not cash, and therefore net income must be reduced by the ending accounts receivable balance.

   d. Sales on account reported on the income statement are greater than the amount of cash collected from accounts receivable.

4. In computing cash provided by operations, net income is reduced by:

   a. Cash dividends declared and paid.

   b. Bad debts written off.

   c. A decrease in accounts receivable.

   d. A decrease in accounts payable.

5. The statement of cash flow is a connecting link between two:

   a. Income statements.

   b. Statements of retained earnings.

   c. Balance sheets.

   d. Statements of changes in owner's equity.

Use the following information to answer the next three questions.

Ballard Company
Balance sheets as of December 31, 1991 and 1992

Assets		1991		1992
Cash	$	30,000	$	40,000
Other current assets		30,000		50,000
Machinery and equipment (net)		100,000		150,000
Land		600,000		823,000
Patents		24,000		21,000
Total Assets	$	784,000	$	1,084,000

Liabilities & Stockholders Equity				
Current liabilities	$	44,000	$	49,000
Bonds payable		100,000		120,000
Preferred stock		110,000		115,000
Common stock		120,000		140,000
Retained earnings		410,000		660,000
Total Liabilities and Stockholders' Equity	$	784,000	$	1,084,000

Additional information in 1992:

A building with an original cost of $40,000 and accumulated depreciation of $18,000 was sold for $21,000. No other buildings were bought or sold during the year. Amortization of patents for the year was $3,000, and depreciation of machinery was $10,000. No patents were bought or sold during the year. Dividends declared and paid during the year were $30,000. Retained earnings was affected only by net income and dividends.

6. Given the above information, total cash provided by operations in 1992 was:

   a. $298,000
   b. $260,000
   c. $278,000
   d. $293,000

7. Given the above information, machinery purchased during the year cost:

   a. $0
   b. $82,000
   c. $60,000
   d.   The answer cannot be determined.

8. Given the above information, what is the effect of the common stock of $20,000 and preferred stock of $5,000 being issued to obtain some land?

   a.   It is not reported on the statement of cash flow.

   b.   It is a $25,000 source of cash for the company.

   c.   It is a $25,000 significant financing activity that is reported on the statement of cash flow.

   d.   The $20,000 financing and investing activity for the common stock is reported on the statement of cash flow, but the issuance of $5,000 preferred stock is not reported on the statement.

Use the following information concerning DOE Corporation to answer the next three questions.

Account	Beginning Balance	Ending Balance
Cost of goods sold	$ -0-	$ 600
All other expenses	-0-	250
Inventory	80	50
Net sales	-0-	1,000
Accounts receivable	100	200
Accounts payable	50	90
Prepaid rent	30	40
Accrued payables	-0-	-0-

9. The amount of cash that DOE received from customers during the period was:

    a. $800
    b. $900
    c. $1,000
    d. $1,100
    e. $1,200

10. Total purchases for the period were:

    a. $600
    b. $630
    c. $650
    d. $550
    e. $570

11. For this question assume that Tolliver's purchases for the year were $570. If so, total cash expenditures for purchases during the period would be:

    a. $530
    b. $620
    c. $660
    d. $520
    e. $480

ILLUSTRATIVE PROBLEMS

Nantz Company, Inc. prepared the following balance sheets data at the end of 1991 and 1992.

	12/31/1991	12/31/1992
Cash	$ 1,000	$ 4,000
Accounts receivable	9,000	11,000
Inventory	12,000	13,000
Total current assets	$ 22,000	$ 28,000
Equipment	50,000	60,000
Accumulated depreciation, equipment	(10,000)	(14,000)
Total assets	$ 62,000	$ 74,000
Accounts payable	$ 4,000	$ 7,000
Taxes payable	2,000	1,000
Total current liabilities	$ 6,000	$ 8,000
Bonds payable	18,000	10,000
Common stock	30,000	45,000
Retained earnings	8,000	11,000
Total liabilities and equities	$ 62,000	$ 74,000

You have been asked to prepare a statement of cash flow for Nantz Company, Inc. for the year ended December 31, 1992. The following additional information was determined from an examination of the books and records of Nantz Company:

1. Net income for 1992 was $7,000.
2. Dividends for 1992 were $4,000.
3. During 1992 equipment purchases were $15,000.
4. Equipment with a cost of $5,000 and accumulated depreciation of $2,000 was sold for $3,000 cash during 1992.
5. Bonds in the amount of $8,000 were redeemed during 1992.
6. Common stock was sold during 1992 for $15,000.

Prepare the statement of cash flow in the space provided on the following page.

Vocabulary

CASH EQUIVALENTS. Short-term, highly liquid investments such as treasury bills.

DIRECT EXCHANGE (NONCASH) TRANSACTIONS. Transactions that represent joint investing and financing activities with no direct effect on cash, such as the exchange of common stock for a plant asset.

DIRECT METHOD. A method of reporting cash flows from operating activities by which major classes of operating revenues and expenses are shown as cash inflows and cash outflows from operations.

FINANCING ACTIVITIES. Activities involving the acquisition of resources from (1) owners and providing them with a return on and a return of their investments, and (2) creditors and repaying the amounts owed or otherwise settling the obligation.

INDIRECT METHOD. A method of reporting cash flow from operating activities by which accrual basis net income is adjusted to cash basis net income by adding or subtracting noncash expenses, revenues, losses, and gains.

INVESTING ACTIVITIES. Activities involving (1) lending money and collecting on the loans, and (2) acquiring and selling (a) securities that are not cash equivalents, and (b) productive assets that are expected to produce revenues over several periods.

OPERATING ACTIVITIES. Activities involving the production or delivery of goods for sale and the providing of services.

STATEMENT OF CASH FLOWS (SCF). A financial statement that reports cash receipts and cash payments for a firm for a specific time period.

THE ANSWERS

MATCHING ATTRIBUTES

1.	C	4.	G	7.	E
2.	H	5.	D	8.	B
3.	F	6.	A		

MULTIPLE CHOICE

1.	b	4.	d	7.	b	10.	e
2.	c	5.	c	8.	c	11.	a
3.	d	6.	c	9.	d		

ILLUSTRATIVE PROBLEM

Nantz, Incorporated
Statement of Cash Flows
For the Year Ended December 31, 1992

Sources of cash:		
Operations:		
Net income	$ 7,000	
Deductions not requiring		
cash outlays: Depreciation	6,000	
Changes in current accounts to		
account for accruals and deferrals:		
Increase in accounts receivable	(2,000)	
Increase in inventory	(1,000)	
Increase in accounts payable	3,000	
Decrease in taxes payable	(1,000)	
Cash from operations	$ 12,000	
Investing activities:		
Sale of equipment	3,000	
Financing activities:		
Sale of common stock	15,000	
Total sources of cash	$ 30,000	
Uses of cash:		
Investing activities:		
Purchase of equipment	15,000	
Financing activities:		
Payment of dividends	$ 4,000	
Retirement of bonds	8,000	12,000
Total uses of cash		27,000
Increase in cash		$ 3,000